WORK CLEAN

THE LIFE-CHANGING POWER OF
MISE-EN-PLACE TO ORGANIZE YOUR
LIFE, WORK, AND MIND

DAN CHARNAS

RODALE.

RODALE *wellness*

Live happy. Be healthy. Get inspired.

Sign up today to get exclusive access to our authors, exclusive bonuses, and the most authoritative, useful, and cutting-edge information on health, wellness, fitness, and living your life to the fullest.

Visit us online at RodaleWellness.com

Join us at RodaleWellness.com/Join

Rodale books may be purchased for business or promotional use or for special sales. For information, please write to:
Special Markets Department, Rodale Inc., 733 Third Avenue, New York, NY 10017

Printed in the United States of America

Rodale Inc. makes every effort to use acid-free ♾, recycled paper ♻.

Illustrations by Christina Gaugler

Book design by Christina Gaugler

Library of Congress Cataloging-in-Publication Data is on file with the publisher.

ISBN 978–1–62336–592–9 hardcover
ISBN 978–1–62336–814–2 paperback

Distributed to the trade by Macmillan

2 4 6 8 10 9 7 5 3 1 hardcover
2 4 6 8 10 9 7 5 3 1 paperback

We inspire and enable people to improve their lives and the world around them.

rodalewellness.com

For Wendy & Isaac.
My right place is where you are.

My sincerest desire is that you exhaust

all the strength and the effort of your lives . . .

and every moment of every day

into your practice.

—DOGEN

CONTENTS

A NOTE FROM THE AUTHOR

IMAGINE IF, early in our schooling or career, we learned a system to organize ourselves and manage our work. We could carry this system with us no matter where we worked or what we did for a living—be we contractor or teacher, salesperson or doctor. And with this system we would have a code to guide our conduct; techniques to help us channel our energies, thoughts, and emotions productively; and the means to get through a tough workload and deliver with excellence.

Bits of that philosophy live in many professions and corporate cultures. Pieces of that system exist in any number of organizational methods.

But only one profession has developed a refined philosophy and comprehensive system of *how* to work. That profession is the culinary arts, and that philosophy and system is called *mise-en-place*.

It's a French phrase translating as "put in place." In the kitchen mise-en-place means to gather and arrange the ingredients and tools needed for cooking. But for many culinary professionals, the phrase connotes something deeper. Mise-en-place is a tradition of focus and discipline, a method of working and being. Many cooks call it a way of life.

What makes the professional kitchen's system so special? Over the past 2 centuries, chefs and cooks all over the world developed an informal regimen of values and behaviors in response to the unique demands and constraints of those kitchens. Because of those singular circumstances, chefs and cooks created an approach to work that has no equivalent.

What makes that approach applicable outside the kitchen? What wisdom could a chef impart, for example, to a lawyer, when those two jobs are so different? The simple answer is that lawyers weren't forced to create that system. Chefs were. And the values and behaviors that spring from that chefly system aren't about *cooking*, but about achieving *excellence*. So many of us have convinced ourselves that because we are busy, we are working to the fullest extent of our abilities. But chefs know that there is a big difference between working hard and working *clean*.

That mise-en-place might be useful outside the kitchen, and that the chef's philosophy of working might be as nourishing to our minds as the chef's food is to our bodies—those ideas are why this book exists.

———————————

This book teaches the lessons of mise-en-place in three courses. The first section, *The Power of Working Clean,* takes us straight to an exceptional kitchen where we'll spend a day discovering how mise-en-place works and how it helps its practitioners focus amid chaos. Then we'll spend a very different kind of day in an office, showing how we work without mise-en-place and how we often suffer for it. We'll see that mise-en-place applies to the office despite its differences from the kitchen. And we'll learn the three universal values of working clean: preparation, process, and presence.

The second course, *The Ingredients of Working Clean,* breaks mise-en-place into 10 distinct behaviors, each its own chapter. Each of the 10 chapters begins with a story, taking us into the life of a chef and how he or she learned that behavior. We then look at what chefs do and know that we might not. Then we suggest exercises and habits to integrate that behavior into our work lives outside the kitchen.

The third course, *Working Clean as a Way of Life,* converts those ingredients into a recipe for regular use. First, we reshape the values and behaviors of mise-en-place to fit our lives outside the kitchen and lay out the Work Clean system for organizing our workflow. Then we'll walk together through an ideal day of working clean, which weaves all the values and behaviors we've learned into an average workday and includes the book's most important recommendation: *developing a regular practice of planning, a 30-minute Daily Meeze.*

Working clean can transform your life, and this book gives you many useful ways to do just that.

As the global economy changes, our personal career trajectories become more like those of culinarians—nonlinear, itinerant, with plenty of false starts and surprises, successes and failures. Restaurants open and restaurants close, but because of mise-en-place, chefs and cooks bend where we might tend to break. A personal mise-en-place imparts a kind of learned resiliency that, if you practice it, can travel with you from workplace to workplace, from opportunity to opportunity. Mise-en-place can provide comfort as we move through those spaces because we understand that the responsibility for our success lies in our self-direction. Any door we walk through, we carry our own mise-en-place with us.

Some additional notes about the writing of *Work Clean:*

- I am a journalist, not a chef. I have never worked in a professional kitchen. I became intrigued by mise-en-place not because I was interested in cooking, but because, as an outsider, I saw in that system something beautiful and elegant that transcended kitchen work. Thus I approached this project in three ways. First, as a reporter, I have used the tools of my profession, interviewing more than 100 people from the culinary world, including chefs, line cooks, students, instructors, and restaurateurs, spending many months observing the kitchens in which they work. Second, as an executive and manager, I bring a career of experiences working in corporate, academic, and start-up environments; and I carry a professional history of both successes and instructive failures. Third, as a college professor and as a 2-decade-long teacher of a spiritual discipline, yoga, I recognize in the chef a kindred mission to educate, and I see many commonalities between the chef's philosophy, mise-en-place, and other spiritual traditions.

■ I worked to represent my sources accurately and to honor them, their aspirations, experience, and expertise. The stories, thoughts, feelings, or words of chefs and cooks come from reporting, not invention. For dialogue I use quotation marks to denote replication and italics to signify approximation.

■ I refer to mise-en-place above as a *philosophy* (what chefs believe) and a *system* (what chefs do). Later in this book I refer to it as an ethical *code*. Mise-en-place is all those things. Chefs themselves use the term to denote the array of ingredients at their station, their *setup* (e.g., "That idiot dropped sauce all over my mise-en-place!"), but also *the practice of preparing that setup* for themselves or other cooks (e.g., "If you can come in on time and get your mise-en-place done every day, then I'll let you cook."), and *the mind state* of someone who knows exactly how to think, plan, and move (e.g., "She has good mise-en-place."). Mise-en-place is all those things, too.

■ I do not use the words *chef* and *cook* interchangeably, even though some people do—and even though some chefs humbly call themselves "cooks" and some cooks proudly call themselves "chefs." In this book a "chef" leads a staff of cooks, and "cooks" work for a chef. For simplicity, "chef" and "cook" include "baker."

■ I wrote this book for the layman, but I hope that it will also be useful for current and future culinarians. My suggestions are mostly for the workplace, but they can also be used at home. And though I aim those suggestions at people who work in offices, mise-en-place applies to classrooms, hospitals, and other work settings.

■ To deconstruct mise-en-place, I drew from sources in the world of fine dining—not because mise-en-place doesn't exist in diners and chain restaurants, but because the philosophy is more exacting, evolved, explicit, and articulated in fine-dining kitchens.

■ I have interviewed chefs all over North America, but most of the chefs I've selected to profile are based in New York. I've done this in part to weave together the narratives of chefs who share the same teachers. In particular, the students of Jean-

Georges Vongerichten, Alfred Portale, and Charlie Palmer figure prominently in this book.

■ Lastly, I wrote this book on mise-en-place because I couldn't find one to read. But I would be remiss if I did not credit two people, Michael Ruhlman and Anthony Bourdain, for introducing the concept into public consciousness. *The Making of a Chef,* Ruhlman's magnificent account of his journey to learn about becoming a chef by embedding himself as a student at the Culinary Institute of America, was published in 1997 and has to be one of the first contemporary accounts of mise-en-place as a personal and professional culture. Reading Anthony Bourdain's notions about mise-en-place in the midst of his rollicking memoir *Kitchen Confidential*, published in 2000, was like reaching an eye of reverence in a hurricane of irreverence. Bourdain has at times called mise-en-place his religion. When you deconstruct the principles and regard the faithfulness with which chefs practice them, mise-en-place approaches that. Bourdain is observing the world's mise-en-place now: As a chef he's a better journalist than many journalists are; as a journalist, more influential on a generation of young cooks than he ever could have been as a chef. I've only spoken to Ruhlman by phone and only shaken Bourdain's hand once, long ago as a customer at his restaurant, but I don't think this book would have been possible without them, and I have endeavored to honor their work.

It may seem odd to advance mise-en-place as a spiritual practice, with spirituality's implications of balance, especially when so many chefs and cooks do not live balanced lives at all. But mise-en-place is a philosophy of how to start things and how to complete things, how to speed up and how to slow down, how to say "yes" to things and "no" to others, and as such, when practiced consciously, mise-en-place can be helpful in creating balance.

I cannot promise you, nor would I want to, that working clean is easy. It is not. Chefs and cooks spend their entire careers perfecting these principles. But I do promise that whenever you work clean, you will be the best that you can be.

THE POWER OF WORKING CLEAN

FOCUS

How mise-en-place works

CHEF DWAYNE LIPUMA'S entire kitchen staff just quit. He's looking at reservations for 40 people for lunch, then another 140 for a banquet tomorrow. To make all those meals, LiPuma's bosses have provided him with 19 recruits, some of whom have never cooked in a fine-dining restaurant. Aside from LiPuma's assistant and a pastry chef, not one of the staff has ever seen the menu, much less prepared the items on it, all gourmet dishes with elaborate presentations.

But by the end of the day, the diners will leave satisfied. In fact, the customers—some of whom have waited months for a reservation at LiPuma's restaurant, American Bounty—will scarcely notice that their entire meal was made by neophyte cooks.

A miracle perhaps? Nope. It's a regular day for Chef LiPuma. In 3 weeks, when LiPuma has his crew trained and confident, they will leave and a new group of inexperienced cooks will replace them. He will repeat this process every 3 weeks, thus providing the penultimate course for students who will soon graduate from the Culinary Institute of America.

What makes this impossible rhythm possible is not a miracle. It's a system called *mise-en-place*.

LEARNING TO COOK, LEARNING TO WORK

The Culinary Institute of America, called the CIA without irony by people who think more about the epicurean than they do espionage, sits like a citadel on the banks of the Hudson River almost 100 miles north of New York City. Its grand campus in Hyde Park, New York, centered around a former seminary—housing an average of 2,400 students, 140 full-time faculty, 49 kitchens, and four student-staffed restaurants—the CIA is among the world's most renowned culinary schools, with branches in Texas, northern California, and Singapore.

From the first day of classes to the last, CIA students will hear the term *mise-en-place,* pronounced like "me's on plahhs." It's on the lips of Tim Ryan, the president of the college, as he greets new enrollees. A few of the students may have heard the term before they arrived, perhaps in a kitchen for which they worked during high school or thereafter. Some will refer to their textbook, *The Professional Chef,* which provides the English translation of the term, "put in place," and a definition: "the preparation and assembly of ingredients, pans, utensils, and plates or serving pieces needed for a particular dish or service period." At first, mise-en-place blends into the dozens of French words and phrases they must remember as they make their way through their introductory class, Culinary Fundamentals, like *mirepoix, brunoise, tourner, arroser, fond de veau, roux, consommé.* But as students learn the basic techniques they'll need to succeed in all the courses that follow—knife cuts, making stock, making sauce, cooking vegetables and meat—they learn that mise-en-place encompasses an entirely different set of vital skills, and that putting their ingredients and tools in place is just the first level of a deceptively simple concept that keeps unfolding.

Instructors invoke mise-en-place when they tell students to keep their cutting boards and workstations clean and when they tell them to arrange their tools in a certain order and return them to that order after they use them; when they move too slow and also when they move too fast; when they move too much and when they move too little; when they start tasks too early and when they finish them too late; when they talk too much and when they don't say enough; when they don't use their five senses: taste, touch, smell, sight, sound; and when they fail to use their sixth sense: common. As the days go by, the chef-instructors begin to talk about a deeper notion: *mental* mise-en-place, the idea that students can't master physical organization without first organizing their minds. It starts with the CIA timeline, a paper form that chefs expect students to use every day and master. In preparation for each class, students must list their needed tools, ingredients, and tasks for the day. They must arrange those tasks in time, plotting precisely when each thing is supposed to happen. When students find themselves running behind in class or skipping steps, the chefs refer to the student's timeline; usually the chefs can point to the error in thinking that resulted in the error in behavior. Students commit these timelines to memory. Then they begin to tackle planning on-the-fly, the mental work that allows them to move smoothly from one task to the next. Over time, mise-en-place begins to reveal itself as a set of values: Apprenticing oneself. Getting to class early, not just on time. Working with intensity. Cultivating a sense of urgency. Remaining alert. Aiming for perfection.

This idea of mise-en-place, a curriculum unto itself, begins to migrate outside the kitchen. Students load their backpacks and lay their clothes out at night before bed, iron their chef's whites and shine their shoes. They use timelines and prep lists to study for their academic courses, not just their cooking classes. They organize their desks, their closets, their rooms. They even begin "mise-en-placing" their social activities to maximize their time off.

Then the students go home for their first holiday and wonder how the rest of the world changed so much since they were last in it.

Maybe, like Alexandra Tibbats, they watch their parents scurry around the house for car keys that should, of course, have been put back where they belonged, or wait hours for high school friends who can't seem to show up on time. Or maybe they're like Kaitlin Ngo, whose mother watches in stunned silence as Kaitlin—for whom the opening of a suitcase had always been comparable to the uncorking of a geyser—now demurs on a quick shopping excursion to stay home and methodically unpack.

The students return to the CIA and learn to cook *à la carte* breakfasts, lunches, and dinners for their classmates. At the end of their first year, they go on their "externship"—18 weeks working in a restaurant in the real world. Some will cook; others will do the kinds of jobs that kitchen trainees are expected to do: working in the prep kitchen, cutting vegetables and cleaning. They will marvel at how fast and smooth everyone around them seems to move, confirming how much they still don't know. As their second year draws to a close, they will be assigned to one of the CIA's four first-class restaurants, and the training wheels come off. Some of them will enter the kitchen of American Bounty and be greeted by a smiling Chef Dwayne LiPuma.

But LiPuma is not here to assess their cooking skills because they've learned and been evaluated on all their techniques already. What LiPuma will be teaching and testing here is their physical, mental, and ethical mise-en-place, without which they will never be able to use any of those techniques in a professional setting.

WELCOME TO AMERICAN BOUNTY

Nineteen students dressed in clean chef whites gather in a wood-paneled private dining room next to the lobby-bar of American Bounty. It's 7:45 a.m. when Chef Dwayne LiPuma walks in for the first day of class. For the next 75 minutes he'll lecture them on the daily work schedule and the rules of the kitchen, review the menu dish-by-dish, and describe how he'll grade them. LiPuma is 5 feet 6 inches of compacted power, with spiky brown hair and metal-rimmed glasses. He talks fast, *very* fast, Martin Scorsese-on-a-double-espresso fast.

"Welcome to American Bounty," he says. "We are going into the whirlwind. Your anxiety level is off the chart. Everybody's except for mine."

LiPuma is calm because he has his own mise-en-place. He's done everything he can to ensure the success of his new charges. He ordered the previous class to prepare a few days' worth of ingredients so the new class won't have to do any physical mise-en-place except for arranging those ingredients. LiPuma tells them they can ease their fears by getting the lay of the land—a "plan" in the literal sense of the term, the French word for "map." *Make a mental diagram of where everything is and should be. Know the recipes. And come to class every day with your timeline.* "No timeline means 20 percent off your daily grade," he warns. He knows that when they get into the professional world, these students won't write timelines. Instead they'll internalize them.

"I'm not going to teach you how to cut a carrot," he tells them. "I'm going to teach you how to organize yourself."

It's one thing to apply cooking techniques to a recipe and construct a plate. It is quite another thing to do that a dozen times with speed and consistency. LiPuma argues that organization is going to deliver the speed they'll need. Speed will come from their brain's basal ganglia memorizing repeated muscle movements, which—if they are to be quick—should be as small as possible. They will gain some of that speed by *selecting their tools* with care. "What kind of ladle do you need for the soup?" LiPuma asks. "An 8-ounce ladle. Why? Because that's the portion size." If students have a 2-ounce ladle, they will have to ladle four times instead of one. They will win additional speed by *arranging their tools.* "I should be able to blindfold you," the chef says, "and when I say, 'Pick up your tongs,' you know that they're always right there, that your ladle is right there, that your oil is right here." They will accrue even more speed by properly *arranging their ingredients.* LiPuma wants all their ingredients "zoned out": all the ingredients for one dish in one area. "The less your hand moves, the more efficient you are."

"You'll see," he continues. "By being organized, you will be more efficient. By being more efficient, you will have more time in your day. By having more time in your day, you will be more relaxed in your day; you will be able to accomplish the task at hand in a clear, concise, fluid motion." LiPuma promises them that by the time they leave his kitchen, they'll be smooth and calm, like him.

"Like oil on glass," he says.

DAY ONE

The students enter the kitchen at 9:00 a.m. They have 1 hour to produce "demo plates"—one sample dish of every menu item on their station. Each student is responsible for two or three menu items. On tougher stations students work in pairs. The demo plates give them a chance to practice before service and give LiPuma a peek at their skills: Can they actually do the cooking?

At 10:00 a.m., once their demos are done, they take a break for "family meal," prepared by a team of three students. Chef LiPuma kicks everyone out of the kitchen and doesn't let them back in until 11:00 a.m. "They need to decompress," LiPuma says. "They get so stressed out. And sometimes when you leave the scenario that's stressing you out—*Oh, God! I've got all this work!*—and you step back, eat something, rethink it, and revisit it, it's not so stressful. Plus, they *need* to eat, *period*. Because they'll skip eating, leave here, and they'll have nowhere to eat until dinner."

But while his students decompress in the dining room, LiPuma *compresses* their time in the kitchen. He doesn't want them to work through lunch and thus encourage a lazy pace. With cuisine as it is with culinary students, no transformation happens without heat. LiPuma needs to cook his class, too.

While they're eating, LiPuma and his sous-chefs-in-training straighten students' mise-en-place, writing reminders on the stainless steel tables with a black-ink Sharpie: "Your chervil is brown," "Paper towel under parsley," "Brush with olive oil." At 11:00 a.m. the students return. They have 45 minutes before the first lunch orders start coming in.

All morning, as the students work, Chef LiPuma prowls the "line"—the row of ovens, burners, and grills where most of his cooks stand and most of the kitchen's food gets prepared.

Some students use the wrong tools for the job: Zoe tries to cook potato pancakes in pans that are too big and use too much oil. Alex puts the butternut squash soup in a pot that's too small. "It's gonna burn," LiPuma says. Later Alex blots extra-virgin olive oil onto bruschetta with a paper towel. "Don't do that!" LiPuma moans. "Get a *brush.*" Caitlyn discovers that the smashed potatoes left for her by the previous class have been put in a narrow, plastic quart container and have thus disintegrated under their own weight. "Why don't you make a necklace out of them?" LiPuma says. Caitlyn cooks replacement potatoes and puts them back in the same container, repeating the failure.

Other students don't check the ingredients prepared for them by the previous class: Rahmie places his own bruschetta in the oven to toast without noticing that there's no olive oil on them at all. "It doesn't matter that this is what they left you," Chef says. "*You* gotta make it right!"

With first day jitters, many students move too fast. "Juan!" Chef LiPuma says, seeing four cuts of steak on the grill. "What are you cooking *all* that beef for? When are you supposed to mark off that meat?"—meaning sear it so it acquires a nice crust and grill marks on the exterior before cooking to a finish in the oven. "When I come back from family meal," Juan replies. LiPuma nods: "So finish marking *one.* Easy there, Slick." When Juan and the others return from family meal, they continue to rush and confuse the proper order of things. They begin cooking side dishes well before the proteins are ready. "This is à la carte cooking, guys," LiPuma booms over the class PA system. "You cook your vegetables and starches on pickup," not when food is ordered. In other words, proteins get the heat when the order comes in, and when the chefs *later* call for pickup, *that's* when they heat the starches and vegetables, as they take less time. They remove meat from the oven when it's still raw. "Don't take anything out of the oven until you clear it with me first," LiPuma orders. The students bring warm plates down from the heat lamps well before their dishes are ready, letting them get cold. "If somebody plates on a cold plate again, zero for the day!" LiPuma bellows. "Are we clear?" "Yes, Chef!" the crew shouts.

Other students move too slow. Because meat takes a certain amount of time to cook—as much as 20 minutes from raw to medium-well—many line cooks "pre-cook" their protein to rare, reducing the time it takes to heat it to the final temperature, or "doneness," once an order comes in. The goal is to always stay one item ahead of the incoming orders. But almost all the students are having a hard time understanding how this process works. Once service starts, LiPuma must constantly remind the line cooks to move on orders as soon as they come in. "Drop a pan!" he yells as an order comes in for lamb. Ronald takes some lamb out and begins seasoning it. Here comes LiPuma, straight for him: *If you don't drop that pan before you season, then you'll be twiddling your thumbs waiting for that pan to get hot.* "Are you helping time or hurting time?" LiPuma asks. "Hurting time," Ronald replies, slapping a pan down on the range.

A pork order has come in for Zoe. Here comes LiPuma:

"That pork's in the oven?" he asks her.

"Yes, chef," she replies.

"Now you want to replace that one, right? You already seared off another one?"

"I'm gonna sear off another one when that one's done."

LiPuma scrunches his face: "Say what?!"

Zoe stammers. She doesn't understand that she can't wait to get the next one started.

"No, what you're *going* to do right now is drop a pan and start getting it hot. And by the time you're done seasoning it, the pan will be hot."

It's not that Zoe isn't prepared. She arrived in class with a perfect, color-coded timeline with every ingredient and tool, with every task she needs to do and when she needs to do it. She has a plan for the day. But each of those tasks has an internal order, too, and she just doesn't know the correct order. This is what LiPuma is teaching everyone: order in space, order in time.

Some students move too much. Rahmie takes handfuls of garlic, onions, chorizo, and potatoes, brings them over to the stove, and drops them into a hot pan with oil and stock to make a broth for steamed mussels. "Do you think it might be easier to bring the pan to the mise-en-place than your mise-en-place to the pan? Maybe less moves?" LiPuma asks him. "Yes, Chef," Rahmie replies. LiPuma will continue to bust the ever-smiling Rahmie's chops about the dish. Now Rahmie jiggles the pan. "Don't worry about *shaking* it," LiPuma says. "Just get the rest of the ingredients in there and *then* you can do the little shaky-shaky thing that you guys like to do."

Other students don't move enough. The family meal crew stands around a pot of rice, stirring occasionally. "How long are you going to mother that rice?" LiPuma calls to them. "Put a lid on it and go away, do something else." *They don't understand,* LiPuma says. *Every time they stir it, they're cooling it, and it's taking longer to cook. They do it because they're nervous, and it's a comfort zone. But they're wasting valuable time that they could be using to prep for the next few days of service.* "What are you doing, man?" LiPuma asks Ronald. "Cooking the mushrooms," Ronald replies. "They're in the oven! You can't even *see* them! Get outta here! Go do sumthin'! Go bag up the chilis!" LiPuma walks past Zoe. "Are you leaning, Zoe? Don't *lean.* There's a bunch of other stuff you can do!"

Some students don't communicate enough. An order comes in for lamb, and LiPuma yells to Ronald, "Take the lamb and put it in the oven." He hears nothing. He yells again, with a bite: "Take the lamb and put it in the oven!" "Yes, Chef!" Ronald replies. "That's a good answer," LiPuma says. But LiPuma is having a problem with all the "Yes, Chef!" he's getting. When he calls out a quantity of something, he wants them to tell him what they heard: *Two fish! One pork!*

Other students communicate too much. The pastry chef calls twice for a food runner while the waiters talk among themselves. "Hey! Hey! Pickup pastry!" LiPuma screams. "Shut up now and pay attention!" The back waiters ought to know better; they were the last class of cooks in this kitchen before this one.

Students put things on their cutting boards—hot pans that will scorch them and clean plates that will pick up liquid and scraps from them. They don't know their meat temperatures, nor how to measure them. And nobody keeps a clean station. The whole service, LiPuma pushes pans aside, carries them to the dishwasher. In the middle of service, LiPuma gets on the microphone: "What we're working on today is *organization*. Take a look: The fryer has leeks all over it. The stations are all dirty, things are greasy." But LiPuma expects these issues, all attributable to nerves and inexperience.

At 1:30 p.m. service is done. "I'm gonna show you how to break everything down," LiPuma says. "Take all your proteins and bring them to the butchers. Take all your sauces, put them in the correct size container. Go put them in an ice bath, label it. Everything that's dirty—pots, pans, everything—bring them to the dishwasher ever so nicely." Within 15 minutes the spotless hot line gleams like no cooking happened at all.

At 2:00 p.m. they gather to recap the day. "The barking is over, it's all about the love now," LiPuma says. "How was your day? Just okay, right? And that's *okay*. Five days from now, it's gonna be all automatic because you're gonna be organized, you're gonna know systems, you're gonna have station management, you're gonna be able to elevate your cuisine. As you become more organized, you'll see that you'll save time. It's all about ergonomics, finding the right way of cooking, the sequence and order of cooking—pork in the oven, potato down, apples in, spinach going." This is what LiPuma calls *flow*. "Once you find a system that works best for that dish, you just keep that wheel running. You do the same routine over and over again to get muscle memory and get faster and faster." LiPuma points his students toward tomorrow, when they'll work on communication and their "callbacks" to the chef.

They'll need these skills. Tomorrow they'll triple their workload. By the end of this 3-week course, they'll not only have mastered their own physical and mental mise-en-place, they'll be giving the following class their first few days' worth of prepared ingredients as well.

MISE-EN-PLACE FOR LIFE

Students spend 2 to 4 years at the CIA learning how to cook. But that's only half of their education. Just as important is the CIA's shadow curriculum in which students learn how to *work*. Without learning how to work, and work *clean*—meaning to do that work with economy of time, space, motion, and thought—they can't cook professionally. Mise-en-place, by graduation day, becomes a motto for all. Valedictorian Eli Miranda compares it to the philosophy he learned while serving in the US Navy. "To succeed, you must set yourself up for success and be ready for anything that comes your way." Some of Miranda's fellow students have chosen to express their ardor for mise-en-place in a more personal way, beneath their dress whites, having inked those words permanently into their skin. And they will remember their days at the CIA when their alumni magazine, *Mise-en-Place*, finds them as they move around the culinary world.

Wherever they go in that world, in whatever kitchens they work, mise-en-place will be the common language. Even in the places where the term itself isn't spoken, the behaviors and mindset of mise-en-place are expected. In Japanese kitchens, they may not say "mise-en-place," but Japanese chefs talk about concepts like *jun-bi* (to set up, prepare) and *sei-ri* (sorting, arranging) as part of the fundamental duties of the cook and cook's apprentice, the *oi-mawashi*. Chef Masa Takayama, who runs the revered Japanese restaurant in New York City that bears his first name, begins his planning on paper—not by writing a list, but by drawing a plate and the food that will appear on it. Then Chef Masa literally makes that plate (he's a potter as well as a chef) before he prepares the food, mise-en-place at its most esoteric. At small restaurants, mom-and-pop operations, food carts, and humble diners, practical mise-en-place enables one or two employees to feed dozens and sometimes hundreds of people per day. At national restaurant chains and huge catering operations, mise-en-place governs the movement of hundreds of men and women and millions of dollars' worth of material and ingredients to serve diners by the thousands. Chef Ralph Scamardella oversees the top-grossing restaurant in America, TAO Las Vegas, as part of his job supervising the TAO Group's nearly two dozen restaurant kitchens across the country; at TAO New York, he runs a 24-hour operation from two vast kitchens providing room service to two hotels and à la carte dining in two different restaurants—TAO and Bodega Negra. At TAO alone, he employs a brigade of specialized sushi chefs, barbecue masters, and dumpling makers, feeding 1,200 people in four shifts, or "table turns." Michael Guerriero has a different challenge. A graduate of the CIA, he runs the massive kitchen at the United States Military Academy at West Point. At lunch the chef must feed 4,000 cadets in 15 minutes.

Our culinarians will also encounter more than a few disorganized, dirty, inefficient kitchens in their careers. But most of them will strive to reach the top of the proverbial food chain. What they will encounter at the summit is the most refined version of what they learned in school. Cooks who have the opportunity to *stage* (pronounced "staahj" with French inflection, meaning a limited or trial job) in Yountville, California, at Chef Thomas Keller's French Laundry—lauded by many critics as the best restaurant in the world—find a calm, clean kitchen whose atmosphere is, at the same time, one of the most intense of any workplace anywhere. Chef Keller posts a plaque beneath a clock in his kitchen that reads "Sense of Urgency." He teaches his cooks how to tie and untie plastic bags and how to open and close refrigerator doors. He works toward a perfect method for everything. That level of control—one that workers in another industry might resent and deride as micromanagement—is welcomed by the cooks at The French Laundry because they want to learn from Keller. The atmosphere of mutual striving delivers what they want: not only the ultimate manifestation of cuisine, their chosen vocation, but the ultimate manifestation of themselves as professionals and as people.

KITCHEN GUIDES

Long ago the chef and the priest were one.

In Japanese Zen Buddhism, the head of the kitchen, or *tenzo*, held one of six high offices in the monastery. A Buddhist monk in Japan named Eihei Dogen in the year 1237 wrote about the sanctity of the cook in a treatise called *Tenzo Kyokun*. "Instructions to the Tenzo," as the title translates, described the tasks of this priest/ chef—a post to which Dogen believed only the most masterful monks should be appointed—and the importance of order and cleanliness in the tenzo's work. On a deeper level, Dogen displays how the work of the cook can instruct anyone outside the kitchen on how to approach all kinds of worldly work with reverence. Dogen writes of preparation—that tomorrow starts today, at noon, when the ingredients for the next day's meals should be assembled—and of cleanliness ("Clean the chopsticks, ladles, and all other utensils . . . conscientiously wash the rice bowl and soup pot"). Dogen also details a process for everything: He decrees the careful conservation of space ("Put those things that naturally go on a high place onto a high place, and those that would be most stable on a low place onto a low place"), of movement ("Do not throw things around carelessly. . . . Handle ingredients as if they were your own eyes"), of ingredients ("Do not allow even one grain of rice to be lost"), and of time ("All day and all night, the tenzo has to make arrangements and prepare meals without wasting a moment").

The profound counsel infusing these instructions boils down to presence. "The tenzo must be present," Dogen writes, "paying careful attention to the rice and soup while they are cooking. This is true whether the tenzo does the work by himself or has assistants helping him." Dogen urges a presence as much mental as physical, a presence manifested through awareness ("Keep your eyes open"); in communication, as when he advises the tenzo to seek input from the five other high-office holders about meals; and by acceptance: Dogen writes at length about the tenzo's responsibility to work humbly with the ingredients at hand.

Presence manifests for the tenzo as focus and commitment, turning work into a form of meditation. *When sitting, just sit. When cooking, just cook. Care for nothing but the work when you work.* "My sincerest desire," Dogen writes, "is that you exhaust all the strength and the effort of your lives . . . and every moment of every day into your practice." Dogen saw this form of complete immersion as a connection with the Divine: "To view all things with this attitude is called Joyful mind"—a curious juxtaposition of exhaustion with joy that resonates with modern chefs and cooks. In the end, Dogen saw the tireless work of the tenzo as a gateway to personal growth. *In serving others with magnanimity, joy, and with the care of a parent,* he counseled, *you are working to better your self.* To Dogen, service wasn't soft or self-effacing. On the contrary, Dogen advised his tenzo to compete with his masters. "If great teachers in the past were able to make a plain soup from greens for only a pittance, we must try to make a fine soup for the same amount. There is no reason why we cannot [surpass] the ancient masters. We must aspire to the highest of ideals without becoming arrogant in our manner." Dogen's kitchen was a laboratory of self-improvement, and the tenzo a dogged pursuer of both worldly and spiritual excellence.

Halfway around the world, in the royal courts of Europe, the cook was more slave than servant. He didn't sit at the right hand of his king, but toiled in obscurity in a sooty cellar. When cooks created a dish or a sauce that found favor and fame—like sauce Béarnaise or sauce Béchamel or soufflé Rothschild—often their invention took the name or title of the cook's patron, not the cook himself.

Then two events transformed the life of the European cook.

The first, around the time of the French Revolution, was the emergence of the restaurant—a business serving an emerging middle class where cooks served on-demand fare (or *à la carte,* meaning "from a menu") determined by the conversation between cook and customer, not the whims of monarchs or aristocrats.

The second began in 1859 when a 13-year-old boy named Georges Auguste Escoffier started working in his uncle's restaurant in Nice. By the time he died at age 88 in 1935, Escoffier had secured the global dominance of French cuisine and elevated the work of the cook to something honorable, if not quite holy.

The young Escoffier wanted to be a sculptor. Dragooned into the kitchen, suffering alongside his fellow cooks under his uncle's physical and verbal abuse, Escoffier kept a positive attitude. "Even though I wouldn't have chosen it," he wrote, "since I am here, let me do my best to improve the standing of my profession."

Escoffier moved to Paris in 1865 and found employ at Le Petit Moulin Rouge, a supper club that catered to the rich and the royal of Europe, whose obsession with French cuisine mounted even as the French empire waned. He worked his way through the various jobs, or "stations," while keeping the soul of an artist. He found joy in creating new dishes and custom menus at the behest of his celebrity clientele.

When German soldiers invaded France in July 1870, Escoffier became the head cook for the second division of the French Rhine Army, which by the end of summer was encircled by German troops in the border city of Metz. Escoffier's kitchen-bred penchant for planning sustained him, as he had stockpiled ingredients and animals to feed the officers and troops. For almost 2 months the French army and civilians were besieged and cut off from supplies. Things got bad when the cavalry started eating their horses. On October 25 Escoffier ran out of food. Three days later the French surrendered Metz, and he was taken prisoner.

After France's defeat, Escoffier was released, but his time in the military seemed to have organized his thinking. When Escoffier began to run kitchens on his own, he transformed the structure of his stations and his crew into a more rigid hierarchy. Escoffier's *brigade de cuisine* now gives modern kitchens around the world a common workflow: The chief of the kitchen, or *chef de cuisine*, at the top; the underbosses, or *sous-chefs*, beneath him; the *chefs de partie* who run the various stations of the kitchen, regimented into distinct areas of responsibility including *garde-manger* (pantry or cold food), *sauté* (cooking on the range), *saucier* (sauces), *patissier* (dessert), *rôtisseur* or *grillardin* (roast or grill), *poissonnier* (fish), and *friturier* (fryer). The brigade is assisted by the *aboyeur* (expediter) and the *plongeur* (dishwasher), and a myriad of other positions. At the climax of the industrial age, the brigade system became a replicable culinary assembly line.

In 1903, Escoffier published *Le Guide Culinaire,* an exhaustive 900-page masterwork that simplified, modernized, and codified the grand tradition handed down from predecessors like Marie-Antoine Carême, establishing common language and procedures that solidified French cuisine as a global standard. These culinary and organizational standards took hold in the British Empire and America in part because Escoffier brought *à la carte*-style dining to the first generation of modern cosmopolitan hotels—the Savoy and the Carlton in London, the Ritz in Paris, then the Pierre in New York City—and on luxury ocean liners that linked America and Europe. Meanwhile, he kept a tenzo-like disposition of service to both the rich and poor alike, supporting London's Little Sisters of the Poor, an early version of contemporary food donation programs, reducing waste for his enterprise in the process.

As a result of these two Western, largely French, innovations— the restaurant and Escoffier's guidelines and systems—the work of a chef became regimented across borders and language gaps. Fine kitchens in New York and Paris worked in much the same way as those in Moscow or Mumbai. These particular planning and organizational behaviors became common knowledge for culinarians, a set of principles that chefs taught their cooks, principles that those cooks would in turn teach to their apprentices. The chef became a contemporary Dogen, a unique if imperfect teacher of not only cooking skills but *life* skills.

A MASTER AT WORK

Thursday nights are hectic at Esca, a restaurant just a few blocks from Times Square in Manhattan. From 5:30 p.m. to 7:30 p.m., patrons pack the dining room for a quick meal in an elegant setting before they dash off to make their eight o'clock curtain times at the Broadway shows nearby. The waiters keep the customers relaxed by demonstrably worrying for them: acknowledging their departure time, advising them against dishes that might take too long to prepare, keeping service snappy, and delivering the check on top of coffee and dessert.

The New York City restaurant business calls this the pre-theater rush. But the chef, Dave Pasternack, moves slowly.

Everything about Pasternack runs counter to what you'd expect.

Balding and burly, he's built like a bodyguard and talks like a cabbie; yet he is one of the most esteemed chefs in the city, regarded as a seafood expert on a par with the likes of Eric Ripert of the four-star Le Bernardin. Pasternack rolls between Esca, the restaurant he co-owns with Mario Batali, and his soon-to-open second restaurant in Chelsea, dressed like a fishmonger in sweatshirt and jeans.

After he changes into his chef's whites and scrubs his hands, Pasternack stands at his workstation in the kitchen, artfully arranging with his pudgy fingers small slices of *crudo*—tender, fresh, raw fish—on frosted plates to be carried to diners who are paying $10 for each tiny mouthful. After plating, he seals the containers of fish and returns them to the "lowboy" refrigerators beneath his station. He takes a white towel and wipes his cutting board clean.

The small printer on the shelf above Pasternack's workstation clacks and spits out curls of white paper. With each order that comes in, the chef repeats a process. First he calls for bruschetta: a tiny *amuse-bouche* (a "pre-appetizer," so to speak) of toasted bread, tomato, olive oil, and herbs to be sent to customers immediately. Actually, he doesn't call for bruschetta. He just says "Ordering!" followed by a number ("Two!" or "Four!"), and the crew at the appetizer station replies "Yes, Chef!" and produces exactly that number of bruschetta plates to be ferried into the dining room by the restaurant's food "runners." Then he shouts to his cooks over the whir of the air vents as he reads the printed ticket: "Order linguine! Order chicken! Order *rombo*!" The cooks at the pasta and grill and sauté stations call back in turn, "Yes, Chef!"

An order comes for *crudo*—the first of many, as *crudo* is the specialty of the house and Pasternack was the first person in America to serve what's basically an Italian version of sashimi. The chef reaches with his right hand into the refrigerator beneath him to bring up plates. If the plates aren't cold enough, he kvetches in Long Island–accented French to the Spanish-speaking dishwashers: "C'est chaud! Il faut froid!" *They're hot. They're supposed to be freezing.* He opens the door of another "lowboy," reaches in, and grabs clear plastic bins of presliced fish. He plates the slices so they all face the same way. Pasternack reaches with his left hand into one of a dozen small containers of garnish. He pinches out pistachios, or crushed almonds, or one of an array of gourmet salts—salt with seaweed, red salt from Hawaii, gaspé salt, sel gris, fleur de sel. Chef has a similar number of options for gourmet olive oil, any one of which he drizzles on the fish before it's whisked out to the diners. Back go the bins into the refrigerator, out comes the chef's white towel. He regards his cutting board as he wipes it clean.

Across from Pasternack, sous-chef Greg Barr works his station. He handles dozens of dishes that will go out to tables across the dining room, and his movements are swift but smooth. "It's a very Zen-like thing for me," Barr says. "You're so in the moment that you don't have stuff from the past. I don't have something from two o'clock here. I don't have something from this morning here. Everything has been cleaned down, all my knives are clean, clean cutting board, clear space to work, clear mind."

Barr and his fellow cooks are quick, clean, and good. But their plates must pass by Pasternack before they get carried to the customers. The chef will sometimes hustle them: "Got my potatoes? C'mon, guys, please." Or he'll make a slight correction: "Don't make your linguine so dry, please! C'mon, *dude*." His eyes scan the order tickets on the rack in front of him, timing them, deciding when to trigger each table's next course. The clock above Pasternack's station runs 15 minutes fast. All the clocks in his kitchen are set 15 minutes fast. Pasternack is never late. At least not in the kitchen, he isn't.

Now Chef Pasternack leaves the kitchen. He walks into the dining room and sits at a table with guests, today some friends and family. He does this often. Pasternack puts hospitality on a par with cooking.

Minutes go by. The printer chatters out a few orders. Then some more. The paper curls and spills out onto Pasternack's empty station. *Click clack click clack . . .*

Tonight two people scrutinize Pasternack's every move. The first is sous-chef Brian Plant, who is "trailing" this evening—meaning he's watching how Pasternack works so he can take over when the chef begins spending more time at his new restaurant. The second is yours truly, mushed against a wall between Plant and a trash can, wondering why Plant is just standing there while the printer spits out its white spool of new orders. In fact, no one steps in to "expedite"; that is, to call out these incoming orders for the cooks at the various stations and set the pace of service. Nothing happens at all while the chef is outside the kitchen. After what seems like an eternity I turn to Plant and ask why.

"It doesn't matter how busy it is, it's *his* space," Plant says. "His place. His space. His pace."

"What about the new orders?" I ask. What about the stuff that needs to be "fired"; that is, finished and collected from the various stations to go out to the diners?

"He knows," Plant says. *He knows what's in here and out there. He'll come back in when he's ready.*

His place. His space. His pace.

What I saw in that moment wasn't so much a *lull* in service as it was a kind of peace, a pause in time and space. This calm— seemingly willed by the mastery of the chef—comes from focus, one of the unsung wages of chefdom. A chef plans, and thus a chef gets to decide what happens and when.

A few minutes later Chef Pasternack returns, without haste, and is soon calling for bruschetta, reading orders, and plating his famous *crudo*. Everyone eats, everyone leaves on time, everyone is happy.

TO TRAIL A CHEF

Chef means "boss."

In French, "chef" is the equivalent of the English word *chief*. A Parisian software engineer is just as likely to utter the words "Oui, Chef"—*Yes, boss!*—as is a Parisian cook. In English, the term *chef* became aligned with the culinary world as a shortened form of the French title *chef de cuisine,* chief of the kitchen. So many of our conceptions and language around food come from the French, including the term *restaurant,* which also has an interesting literal meaning: place of restoration, so named for the restorative soups (*restaurants*) that several of these early establishments sold. The *restaurateur* is someone who restores people, nourishes them. The chef makes that restoration possible. A chef is a boss. A restaurateur restores us. A chef is a boss who helps restore us. There's an English word that approximates that meaning—the boss who helps to restore us. The word is *mentor*.

In almost every profession one can find great mentors. Several professions keep the master-apprentice relationship at their core—medical doctors are supposed to be teachers, as are plumbers. But apprenticeship is baked into the culinary world. The chef-apprentice gives the chef her toil in return for knowledge and experience. Moreover, the tight economy of the kitchen and the complexity of kitchen work mean that good chefs must take the betterment of their charges very seriously. As we've seen, only half of that education is about cooking; the other half is about things like organization, movement, planning, dependability, communication—in other words, mise-en-place.

As a result, no professional in the modern world is more effective or experienced or responsible for teaching organization than a chef.

The chef has been teaching his charges for years; now the chef can teach us. Before the advent of the contemporary culinary school, the only way to get these particular skills was to work in a kitchen, whether that meant starting at the bottom as a dishwasher or, for the more experienced cook, "trailing" a chef—as Brian Plant trailed Chef David Pasternack.

What we are about to do is embark on a different kind of "trail," not to learn how to cook, but to learn how to work, and work *clean*—consciously and efficiently—by exploring the system of mise-en-place and by practicing those behaviors in the world outside the kitchen, a world which sorely needs those values.

CHAOS

How we work without mise-en-place

JEREMY* CHECKED the wall clock as soon as he pushed through the glass office doors. 9:30 a.m. *Right on time!* This was no small victory. Jeremy didn't hear his alarm when it rang at 7:00 a.m. because he had turned his cell phone ringer down the night before. His wife roused him an hour later. Cursing, he showered, grabbed clothes out of the dryer, kissed his wife and 9-year-old son, Adam, and dashed out without breakfast. His wife reminded him that it was his turn to take Adam to his soccer game tonight.

"Yep," Jeremy said. "Be home by six."

Since being recruited 7 months ago to run creative services for the tech division of a big financial firm, Jeremy had neglected his family to focus on his work. This was his first big corporate gig, his first time managing a significant workload, and he didn't want to mess up. The previous night he had worked late going over résumés for a new hire and reviewing his team's marketing ideas in advance of today's big brainstorming meeting.

The list on his "to-do" software had grown so long that consulting it had become more confusing than helpful. And since Jeremy had no time to make a quick task list this morning, on the white-knuckle drive to work he made a mental note of the most important things he needed to accomplish.

---

* *"Jeremy" is an amalgam of anecdotes compiled from real people.*

▪ Finish the slides for his boss Stephen's new client presentation so he'd have it by end of day.

▪ Pick photos for the new Web site and send to the designer.

▪ Hire the Web site copywriter and call her with instructions.

Jeremy had to complete the Web site on a tight turnaround, and he was already behind. So many things had taken longer than he thought they would, because on this job he had so many more things to manage. But the site had to launch next week or they'd lose customers.

Jeremy figured he'd have just enough time before the staff meeting at 10 a.m. to review the slideshow and send it to the printer. After lunch, he'd pounce on the Web site photos, call the new copywriter, and then maybe have some time to *finally* clean his desk. But as he pulled into the parking lot, he remembered: He hadn't done the evaluation forms due to HR today. He'd need an hour or two to complete those forms. Cleaning would have to wait.

His desk had always been a problem in his previous jobs and in college. Now it had become an embarrassment. He was a new employee working in an open office, and everyone could see it. He had people working *for* him whose desks were spotless. Jeremy comforted himself with the conviction that he had less time to be tidy because he had so much more responsibility. As he hustled toward his cubicle, he could see his inbox overflowing with memos, padded envelopes, magazines, and packages.

He pulled out his chair and saw a piece of paper. *Great!* Michelle—the assistant whom he shared with John, his marketing counterpart—had gotten him price quotes for the Web site. He put the paper on his desk atop several other papers, tapped his computer keyboard, and was greeted by a flood of new e-mails—three dozen since last night, many of them résumés from people responding to his job posting. He sorted through them.

"Yo, Jeremy, I need your help!" His designer Robert had computer trouble, and Jeremy prided himself on being able to unstick folks. When he saw that the fix would take longer than expected, he asked Michelle to print out the photos for the Web site. Jeremy returned 20 minutes later to see that Michelle had nicely fanned the photos out on his desk. While he reviewed them, the receptionist came by and tossed his mail on top of the photos. Jeremy was annoyed but let it go. He perched the mail on his teetering inbox, and, seconds later, everything fell out onto his desk. Jeremy began to replace the pile when he heard Stephen's voice.

"Let's go, guys!" 10:00 a.m. Staff meeting time. Jeremy hunted for his notebook. Not finding it, he grabbed a pen and a sheet of blank paper out of the printer and headed into the conference room. Stephen smiled at Jeremy and greeted the staff before starting.

But Jeremy's mind drifted. His pre-meeting efficiency plans dashed, he obsessed about the coming avalanche of Web site work. . . .

" . . . Jeremy, are you good with that?"

Embarrassed, Jeremy nodded instead of admitting that he hadn't heard what his boss said. When it came time for Jeremy to give his update on the Web site, Stephen asked: "What's hosting and data services going to cost us?"

"I have the quotes," Jeremy replied. "Mind if I jump out and get them?"

Jeremy hustled to his desk and . . . *Shoot! Where were the quotes?* He remembered putting them on his desk. Michelle had put the photos for the Web site on top of them. Jeremy realized that he must have moved the sheet into his inbox after it toppled over. No time to find them now.

When Jeremy returned to the meeting, Stephen had another question: "How's it going with the deck?"

The presentation! Jeremy was supposed to have proofed it before the meeting and sent it to the copier.

"On its way," Jeremy lied.

"Great," Stephen replied. "Can you review it with me at four, after the brainstorming meeting?"

Jeremy squirmed until the meeting ended. If he completed that presentation by noon, he could still get it back from the copier by 4:00 p.m.

When the meeting ended, Jeremy darted back to his desk. Now

he resolved to shut everyone and everything out until he finished that presentation. Michelle told him something about the copywriter's contract, and he grunted and kept working. He spent 10 minutes searching and scrolling in his e-mail program to find one piece of data for a slide. Then he saw another e-mail reminding him that expenses were due at 3:00 p.m. He had to get those done; he and his wife needed the money to cover Adam's summer camp. It was noon. He just had to finish proofing first. . . .

"Jeremy, can you come in here?" Stephen beckoned Jeremy into a meeting with Aaron, the business affairs guy, who said: "Before I approve these photo shoot invoices, I need the release forms for the models." The blood in Jeremy's head rushed down to his feet. *He hadn't remembered to bring the release forms to the photo shoot.* A rookie mistake, and he was no rookie. Jeremy could see the surprise and disappointment on Stephen's face when he confessed as much. "How are we going to launch a Web site next week if we haven't gotten these releases?" Aaron asked.

"I'll fix it today," Jeremy replied.

"And remember, three o'clock!" Aaron said.

Yes, Jeremy thought, *expenses due at 3:00 p.m.*

Now he careened through proofing the presentation. At 12:30 p.m., he asked Michelle to take the file to the copier and beg them for a rush.

"I was about to do something for John," she said. John sighed and waved her off. Jeremy thanked him. Jeremy couldn't find his portable drive. Michelle used hers and bolted.

Now the expenses. He picked through his inbox for the envelope with his business trip receipts. It was time to clean this damn inbox. Filing exhausted Jeremy because he had to keep turning around and bending down to the cabinet behind him. Just thinking about it exhausted him. He made a mental note to get one of those desktop files. Jeremy searched for 5 minutes before realizing he must have left the envelope at home. He'd have to submit the receipts he had on hand, which was about half of what he was due.

Jeremy searched for his cell phone to call the modeling agency, but where was his phone? A minute later, Jeremy found it in his jacket and saw that his ringer was still off, and that he had missed two calls from Michelle. He called her back. She said that they could do the printing and binding by 5:00 p.m., but it would cost 50 percent more for the rush. He'd have to tell Stephen about the delay. At 2:00 p.m. Jeremy finished his expenses and clicked "Print." After no breakfast, maybe it was time to go out and grab a quick lunch? But Jeremy wasted another 15 minutes: Walking to the printer, he zagged for the bathroom instead. Walking back to his desk, he forgot about the printer. Walking to the printer, he forgot his stapler.

At 2:35 p.m., in line for food, he felt his phone buzz. His ringer was *still* off. It was Michelle asking if he was coming to the 2:30 p.m. brainstorming meeting. *The meeting!* All this preparation, and he hadn't actually put it *in* his calendar. He raced back to the office. Stephen didn't look up when he entered. Jeremy had read everybody's proposals last night and had told himself he'd make notes in the morning, a half-hour that he had slept through. He sulked and said little during the meeting.

After, he pulled Stephen's coat to tell him that the presentations wouldn't be ready until five. *Could he postpone the run-through until 5:30 p.m. just to be safe?*

"Sure," Stephen said. "I've got a dinner at 6:00 p.m. and a red-eye flight tonight."

What a day. Jeremy rang his new copywriter, Janet, and took 30 minutes to discuss the Web site. At the end of the conversation, Janet asked when she would be receiving her contract. "End of day," said Jeremy, remembering now that Michelle had said something about that contract. *Right!* He had to get a form to Aaron to get him to generate the contract. At 4:00 p.m. he e-mailed it to Aaron. But since he wanted to make sure Aaron didn't miss it, Jeremy walked over to his office. It was dark and empty. His assistant was gone, too.

"I think he's gone for the day," one of the finance people said. "He's flying out with Stephen tonight."

Cherisse, the director of human resources, tapped Jeremy on his shoulder. "Evaluations?"

Back at his desk, Jeremy asked Michelle to fetch the presentations from the copy place.

"I'm doing something for John," she replied.

"Can it wait?" Jeremy asked. "I've got to stay here and do these evaluations. Including yours."

Jeremy felt horrible the moment he said those last two words. But he was panicking.

John stood up. Not happy.

"Dude, are you threatening her?" John asked. Jeremy said no and apologized.

"Find someone else to go," John said.

Jeremy was so mortified he just ran to the copier himself. The evals would have to wait.

At 5:30 p.m., Jeremy walked into Stephen's office with an armful of presentations, 20 in all. Stephen was itching to leave. All business now.

"So are we going to get those releases from the modeling agency tomorrow?" he said.

Damn! He had meant to call the modeling agency and then got distracted by those calls from Michelle.

"I hope to," Jeremy exhaled, sweating. "But listen, do you think you can lean on Aaron to get me the contract for the copywriter as soon as possible? I didn't know Aaron was leaving early today."

Stephen looked up, incredulous. "Are you kidding me?"

"No," Jeremy said, "I went over to his office at four, and he was gone."

"I mean 'Are *you* kidding me?'" Stephen replied. "Aaron told you in the staff meeting that he'd write the contract before he left if you got him the form by three o'clock. I asked you, 'Jeremy, are you good with that?' and you sat there in that meeting and nodded yes. Now you're telling me you don't *remember*?" Stephen sighed, picked up a presentation booklet, and paged through it.

"Where are my changes?" he said, looking at Jeremy. "The changes I asked you to make?"

Jeremy had been in such a rush to complete the presentation that he had forgotten about the e-mail with extra changes that Stephen had sent him yesterday after seeing the draft.

"Shit," Jeremy said, shaking his head.

"Yep, shit. Spelling errors, too."

Stephen dropped the booklet, inhaled sharply, and rose, grabbing his jacket. It was 5:45 p.m. "I've got to go to this dinner. I need you to redo this now. Go to the copy place and stay there until they're done. I wanted to take them on the plane with me, but if you can get them to express mail tonight, I can get them in the hotel by morning."

Stephen looked at the mass of bound presentations on his desk. *About $200 worth of paper and plastic,* Jeremy thought.

"What a waste," Stephen said, as if reading Jeremy's mind. "How much did this cost us?"

Stephen walked out of the door, leaving Jeremy. "Get it done," he heard Stephen say.

Jeremy felt his phone ringing. He pulled it out of his pocket. 6:00 p.m. His wife calling. *Adam's soccer game!* Jeremy was about to have one more difficult conversation in a day that already had more of them than he could remember.

He hoped tomorrow would be a better day.

JEREMY'S PROBLEM

Jeremy's story is familiar to those of us who work in offices. Perhaps we haven't had *one* day go *so* wrong, but most people who make a living with words, images, and numbers struggle with overwhelming workload and communication and make many of the same errors.

Jeremy's problem isn't poor character. His intentions are honorable: to be a good husband and father, to provide for his family, to succeed at his new job, to create an excellent product, to work hard, to please his boss and honor his colleagues. At work, he's generous to a fault: helping his coworkers even when it takes time away from his own tasks and being cordial to the receptionist when he's within his rights to request some different behavior from her.

His problem isn't work ethic. Jeremy works at a furious pace. He doesn't "steal" time from the company by gossiping or playing video games or browsing social media at his desk. If anything, he's stealing time from himself when he shortens his lunch break. Even his distractedness in meetings comes from a desire to be working.

His problem isn't self-discipline. He does have the will and ability to focus.

His problem isn't lack of skill. He knows how to create great Web sites and visual presentations; it's why his boss hired him in the first place.

Jeremy's problem is this: He doesn't have a *philosophy* and a *system* that will help him do all the other things he does. He has the requisite skills to work; he just doesn't know how to handle a *workload*. Jeremy spent tens of thousands of dollars in tuition to understand art, design, and language. He spent years acquiring knowledge of code and the workings of the Internet, and experience in testing his ideas. But his formal education never included instruction on how to organize and conduct his *workflow*; and by the time he was a professional, there were few opportunities or incentives to learn. He has inner discipline to work longer and harder, but he doesn't follow an outer discipline—a body of principles and behaviors—to guide his considerable will and skill. As a result, Jeremy can't execute the work he's trained to do. He gets frustrated and panics, and he's not great at handling those emotions. So he makes mistakes that jeopardize his business and says things that damage his relationships.

Like Jeremy, we may have a personal abundance of talent, energy, and resources. But we remain overwhelmed by the amount of work we have to do, and a big part of our being overwhelmed comes because we have never been taught how to *manage* that work. Even doctors and lawyers confide that they didn't learn many of the essentials of their professions in school. Near the top of that list for them, and for us, is how to prepare, how to create order, and how to prioritize the work at hand.

Almost all modern work requires personal organization. And yet, as in the other half of our lives—personal relationships—little comprehensive training exists. We enter into the chaos of both arenas of our adult lives with minimal counsel and are expected to wing it. At least when we falter in our relationships, psychotherapists are there to help us pick up the pieces. When we get reprimanded on the job or fired, we're pretty much on our own. In the absence of a formal education in organization, we've had to help ourselves.

SURVIVAL SYSTEMS

"I have two kinds of problems: the urgent and the important," President Dwight D. Eisenhower said in 1954, quoting an unnamed college president. In his speech, Eisenhower pointed to what he called a dilemma of modern man: "The urgent are not important, and the important are never urgent."

Eisenhower's wisdom was years ahead of its time at the dawn of the corporate era; the tides of personal organization products and literature wouldn't begin coming in until the 1980s and 1990s. Eisenhower's ideas appeared in the writings of the first big productivity and time-management guru, Stephen R. Covey. Beginning in 1989, millions of people bought Covey's book *The Seven Habits of Highly Effective People*, which outlined a principle-centered approach to order and organization. Covey argued that the pressure of our daily tasks diminishes when we consider the bigger picture of our life and legacy. His 1994 book, *First Things First*, repurposed Eisenhower's ideas as a matrix into which tasks could be sorted and executed, with the "Important" and "Urgent" on two separate, intersecting axes, thus creating four "boxes," or "quadrants." Covey urged his readers to *escape the culture of urgency and do important things first.*

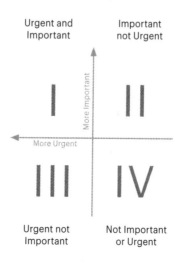

In 2001, David Allen's book *Getting Things Done* offered one of the most comprehensive systems yet for managing daily work and introduced a powerful concept for prioritizing: In all projects, keep a focus on the "next action." By the turn of the millennium, both Covey and Allen had created huge training businesses, salvation systems serving corporations and individuals who couldn't get that kind of education elsewhere.

All told, Americans spend more than $10 billion a year on self-help products, including organization books, tools, seminars, and software. The digital age was supposed to quicken our pace and lighten our load but it has largely done the opposite. The benefits of the tools that allow us to work faster have been overshadowed by the distractions of an Internet-driven information deluge, by the temptation to multitask, and by the increasing workloads brought on by job consolidation. Now we need to be saved from our digital devices as well. Web sites on "lifehacking" abound with the latest ideas and concepts in organization. We are drowning in salvation.

What most of these techniques lack is a holistic approach. One strategy is not a complete *system*. A great method for arranging our space, for example, may not include guidance for organizing our time. And even a comprehensive system may not take into account the person who has to make that system work. Organization doesn't entail only manipulating objects around us—where things go and how tasks should be handled—it needs to deal with our internal environment as well. Organizing is not an intellectual exercise. We must also know how to handle the mental, emotional, and physical challenges and resistance we all encounter. In other words, we don't just need strategies and systems. We also suffer for the lack of guiding principles that account for all our human dimensions.

Such a set of principles exists. It is a body of knowledge that carries the heft of history and the benefits of widespread practice. It is mise-en-place.

KITCHEN VERSUS OFFICE

The Zen-like work habits of so-called blue-collar cooks in the best kitchens stand in stark contrast to the wastefulness of the white-collar world of messy desks, endless meetings, bottomless e-mail chains, and general half-assedness that plagues even the best of companies.

But is it fair to compare the kitchen to the office?

The kitchen and office share some qualities. Workers in both places must contend with a deluge of tasks under tremendous deadline pressure and often inadequate resources. In both environments, workers face a constant stream of inputs and requests, too little time to process them, and many tasks demanding simultaneous attention.

But, as chefs will tell you, the kitchen is a world apart from the office. Kitchens are places of great consistency. Cooks do the same things over and over every day. The menu largely remains the same. The processes that create those menu items don't change. The schedule and setup for that work—when and where things happen—remain constant. Cooks don't have to field e-mails while they sauté, and their prep work isn't interrupted by 2-hour-long staff meetings. Offices can be places of inconsistency. Our jobs—not our titles, but what we actually *do*—change from day to day and sometimes hour by hour. In the morning, we take meetings and roll phone calls; in the afternoon, we write e-mails or learn a new piece of software. Our schedules and setups fluctuate: We might work in the office one day and at a conference or on an airplane the next. As a result, regimenting and streamlining the flow of work is much easier in the kitchen. The kitchen is predictable. The office can be full of surprises.

Kitchen work has a huge physical component. It's manual labor—chopping, frying, plating, grinding, lifting, cleaning. Office work, on the other hand, is almost all mental—talking, writing, reading. Kitchen work is hot, difficult, and dirty. Office work can be only metaphorically so.

Chefs and cooks work with perishable resources, so their decisions, movements, and sense of time are dictated by the ticking clock, and they embody a particular sense of urgency. Office workers' deadlines are usually of a longer range, dictated more by the calendar, so we process time in a more elastic way.

Kitchen work values craft over creativity. Cooks are craftspeople, not creatives. Although chefs and cooks do create new recipes and techniques from time to time, most of the daily work involves careful replication of existing recipes and techniques. And although much of office work can be essentially craft work, office culture is suffused with both the freedom and the burden of creating new things.

Lastly, while cooks work long hours, it's virtually impossible for them to take their work home with them. For those of us who work for corporations or small businesses, academia or professional offices, work never seems to leave us alone.

Given these contrasts it might seem like mise-en-place wouldn't apply to office life, and that chefs and cooks have little to teach us. But these dissimilarities make exploration of mise-en-place in the office compelling. Precisely because the kitchen operates under intense time pressure with perishable resources, it has developed a more refined philosophy of organization. That system abhors waste in all its forms and has evolved distinctive ways of rooting it out. Precisely because the office doesn't have to manage the efficiencies of a kitchen, the people who work in an office aren't obliged to have *any* philosophy or system at all. Even in the best corporate environments, tolerance for waste—waste of time, space, talent, personal energy, and resources—is much higher than in kitchen culture. The way that our Jeremy works, as well-intentioned and overburdened as he is, would be unacceptable in a kitchen. He doesn't plan enough. He doesn't consider his schedule. He's flustered by distractions. He leaves projects lying around half-done. He doesn't arrange or maintain his personal space. He tunes people out. He leaves incoming communication unanswered and outgoing communication unconfirmed. He panics and rushes. He repeats his mistakes. Some people might think of the office as the province of the best and brightest, and the kitchen as the refuge of the less disciplined and less capable. And yet here's the truth: Jeremy might have disappointed and angered his boss and colleagues, but his behaviors are quite common in the best corporations. He might develop a successful career without ever rectifying these shortcomings. In the best kitchens, he'd be fired.

Imagine now if Jeremy had a bit of formal training in mise-en-place. Say he had spent some time in a kitchen, enough time to pick up a few good habits. It wouldn't matter that the nature of his office work was different; the values and habits would be just as transformative for his life. Can Jeremy become, in some way, more like Chef Pasternack or the cooks who work for him? Can he become, even though he is not an owner and entrepreneur, a kind of master—if not of the house, at least of his own space, his own schedule, his own work? What happens when you take mise-en-place out of the kitchen? What would the world be like if everybody had mise-en-place? And can you teach mise-en-place to people who aren't chefs?

HONOR CODE

Journalist and author Michael Ruhlman wished he were a better cook.

Fascinated by the differences between home cooks and their professional counterparts, Ruhlman decided in 1996 to write a book about the process of becoming a chef. He convinced the administration of the Culinary Institute of America to let him enter as a student and follow most of the curriculum for the better part of a year along with a class of degree- and career-seeking candidates.

In the book that resulted, *The Making of a Chef,* Ruhlman's story built to a pivotal moment when a blizzard struck on the night before an important exam. Ruhlman lost control of his car on the snowy, icy drive back from school to the home he shared with his wife, Donna, and baby daughter. The next morning, snow still falling, Ruhlman phoned his chef-instructor Michael Pardus to tell him he thought the drive wasn't worth the risk. He wasn't a student, so he wasn't obliged to take the exam. The chef replied with a civil but patronizing lesson about the difference between professional chefs and the rest of the world. His words answered the question at the core of Ruhlman's quest: *Chefs "get there" no matter what.*

Mortified and indignant, Ruhlman started his car, drove through the storm, took his exam, and *aced* it. In that moment, Ruhlman reflected, he knew that he wanted to be a cook—not to forgo his career as a writer or make his living in a kitchen, but to live his life by the same *code* that cooks live by. In other words, to live by mise-en-place.

After Ruhlman completed his reporting at the CIA and returned with his family to their home in Cleveland, Donna announced that they had only 4 months of cash left before they'd be, as Ruhlman says, "unable-to-pay-the-bills, lose-the-house, flat-out broke." Ruhlman would only see money when he submitted his manuscript.

Ruhlman had written books. Before his time at the CIA, he would have thought it impossible to finish one of this scope in 4 months.

"But I didn't think like that anymore," he says. "I had become a cook."

So Ruhlman began the kind of backwards planning he was trained to do at the CIA. His contract called for 90,000 words. He calculated that if he wrote 1,400 words, 5 days a week, revising on Saturday and resting on Sunday, he would have a book-length manuscript in 4 months.

He stuck to his regimen at his desk as he would have in the kitchen—through holidays and illness and the daily challenges of marriage and childcare. And in the end he delivered the draft on time and secured his advance.

"It turned out to be a pretty good book," Ruhlman says.

Mise-en-place transformed Ruhlman's life outside the kitchen. For a while he *ran* everywhere, trying to maximize every moment. But what Ruhlman retained from the kitchen was its sense of unrelenting honesty about time and space, success and failure. Good chefs and cooks feared and dreaded failure. Ruhlman determined that fear and anger could be healthy motivators, as they were a noble stand against laziness and entropy. Ruhlman worked in kitchens for a time after his stint in culinary school and saw people taking the path of least resistance every day, places where they didn't do things like they did at the CIA; where they boiled their stocks and let them get cloudy; where they put out sloppy plates and kept sloppy stations. If you were willing to give in on one thing, the others would soon follow.

Ruhlman wrote his next book with the man some have called the greatest chef in the world, Thomas Keller. During their time together at The French Laundry in California, Ruhlman saw the concepts of mise-en-place played out to their ultimate manifestation with Keller and his crew. All were there because they wanted to become great chefs themselves (and quite a few of them, like Grant Achatz, have indeed done that).

Ruhlman asked Keller: *What did it take to become great?*

"Make sure that your station is clean," Keller said.

Ruhlman paused, thrown off by the simplicity of the statement. "And?"

"And everything that follows from that," Keller replied.

For Thomas Keller, working clean isn't just about cleanliness, or order, or minimalism. It is about practicing values. *What are your standards? What habits make you successful? How strongly are you willing to hold on to your regimen of good habits in a world that will tempt you to ditch them, often without any immediate consequence? How much are you willing to keep your own focus despite the chaos around you?*

This is what it means to work clean.

And with this understanding we examine the elements of mise-en-place that can apply anywhere: a set of values, and a group of behaviors that flow from them.

THE THREE VALUES OF MISE-EN-PLACE

Mise-en-place comprises three central values: preparation, process, and presence. When practiced by great chefs, these three mundane words become profound. They have formed the core of the conscious chef's work since the time of the tenzo, and they still drive the lives of contemporary chefs. The by-product of these values may indeed be wealth or productivity, but the true goal is excellence.

Preparation

Chefs commit to a life where preparation is central, not an add-on or an afterthought. To become a chef is to accept the fact that you will always have to think ahead, and to be a chef means that thinking and preparation are as integral to the job as cooking. For the chef, cooking comes second. Cooking can't happen without prep coming first.

The fundamental respect of preparation results in a few things: Chefs and cooks expect to do it, and thus, in many cases, they welcome and enjoy it. Their prep will be thorough. They will prep "before" things rather than "during," so it won't be rushed. And that preparation happens all the time, in ways small and large.

Though outside the kitchen we lack many of the imperatives that make preparation and planning crucial—dinner service starts at 6:00 p.m. and you can't "push it back" if you're not ready—we can export the value and gain its benefits: a life where we have availed ourselves of every resource and advantage and have the satisfaction of having done all we can to set ourselves up for success.

Embracing preparation also means jettisoning the notion that prep work is somehow menial, beneath us. No chef is above its rigor. In mise-en-place, preparation is royal—except that, as a chef, it is you who is serving and being served at the same time. Your preparation—and its intellectual cousin, planning—thus becomes a kind of spiritual practice: humble, tireless, and nonnegotiable.

Process

Preparation and planning alone are not enough to create excellence. Chefs must also execute that prepared plan in an excellent way. So they ensure excellent execution by tenacious pursuit of the best process to do just about everything.

Chefs have a certain way of standing, a certain way of moving. They've determined where to place their tools and ingredients to make their work easier and better and faster. They've memorized the best way to execute the dishes they create and determined the best way to handle their equipment. The most successful ones have figured out the best way to handle their people. For the processes that they haven't internalized, they use an outboard memory device called a checklist. Chefs know that success is doing a job right once and then repeating it. The best chefs are always perfecting their processes. Errors become opportunities to do this. "It's okay to make mistakes," Wylie Dufresne, chef-owner of restaurant wd-50, says. "Just don't make the same mistake twice."

A commitment to process doesn't mean following tedious procedures and guidelines for their own sake. It's not about turning humans into hyper-efficient robots. Process is, quite the contrary, about becoming a high-functioning human being and being happier for it. Good process must not only make the work better but also make *you* better. Excellence arises from refining good process—*how can I do this better, or easier, or with less waste?* It's a job, like preparation, that never ends.

Presence

Chefs commit to being present in ways from the mundane to the sublime.

When aspiring chefs sign up for a life in the kitchen, most know that they are agreeing to a life where being early for everything is obligatory. Showing up late is never an option. It's not only about "getting there," it's about "staying there," because a chef also signs up for long hours and, in many cases, no sick days or holidays.

After months and years of repeated prep and process, the cook acquires a deeper kind of presence—becoming one with the work, and the work becoming a kind of meditation. But in the midst of that focus, cooks can't space out. "Kitchen awareness" demands that one not only be "with" the work, but also "with" your comrades and their work at the same time. Awareness must be internal and external at once.

This kind of awareness isn't scatteredness. It is, quite the contrary, something closer to what the Eastern traditions call *mindfulness*.

Many meditation techniques strive to evoke this ability: to focus on an object, or a sound, or a thought, or an action, and yet still be aware of the environment around you. Chefs strive to be focused *and* open.

Finally, committing to be present means that chefs cultivate discreteness, boundaries between their work and their personal lives. To being either *in* or *out*, *on* or *off*. When we work, we put our all into it. When we play, we don't hang on to work. Wherever we are, we're there.

Presence in all its forms—getting there, staying there, being focused, being open, and cultivating boundaries—helps us adjust our preparation and process as the circumstances shift around us, like surfers riding the waves.

These three values—preparation, process, and presence—aren't ideals to admire and applaud. They must be practiced—and can be, by anyone, anywhere.

We can practice these values via 10 distinct behaviors. Let's call these behaviors the *ingredients* of mise-en-place. In the course that follows, we will look at each of them in turn: showing how chefs use them in the kitchen and in their lives, detailing them, and then suggesting several specific and effective ways to apply those behaviors in the world outside the kitchen.

SECOND COURSE
THE INGREDIENTS OF WORKING CLEAN

PLANNING IS PRIME

A chef's story: The lone ranger

WANT EVIDENCE that God laughs at man's plans? Dwayne LiPuma planned to be a forest ranger.

He envisioned himself greeting the day atop a mighty stallion, inhaling the fresh air. In this fantasy he and the horse were in Central Park in the middle of New York City surrounded by adoring young ladies. For an Italian American kid from The Bronx of the 1970s, this was what being a forest ranger was all about.

LiPuma's plan took him all the way to Albuquerque, to the forestry program at the University of New Mexico, where he discovered that the real thing, alas, wasn't like his dream: traipsing through dirt and scrub in the desert, taking soil samples in the mud and looking at them under a laboratory microscope.

LiPuma retreated to New York. He flipped burgers and made sandwiches to bide his time and earn some dough. A few jobs later, LiPuma got serious and enrolled at the Culinary Institute of America. He took his first job after graduation in 1986 in the kitchen of a restaurant called The River Cafe, a small place with a big influence. The River Cafe was built in the late 1970s on the dilapidated Brooklyn waterfront during a time when the owner could scarcely find a bank to loan him money for the venture. But the restaurant became an instant success because of its incomparable view of Manhattan and innovative chefs. LiPuma, fresh from the CIA, worked for the legendary chef Charlie Palmer, impressive considering LiPuma's previous job at an unimpressive suburban restaurant called Orphan Annie's.

LiPuma worked alongside heavyweights and future star chefs like David Burke and Gerry Hayden but couldn't keep up. Every day he'd run out of "prep"—the raw and pre-cooked ingredients he needed for service. Halfway through dinner, his fellow cooks would have to stop what they were doing to help him replenish and finish. Every time LiPuma screeched to a halt, he took the whole line with him. "Why am I recooking my beef because you're not ready with your snapper?" one cook asked. "I'm not getting paid to help you." One day, LiPuma fucked up so bad, a coworker threw him against a refrigerator, denting it. "Do your job or quit," another cook said.

LiPuma decided he wasn't going anywhere. He just had to figure out how to plan better. If he didn't make enough mise-en-place, he'd have to make more. If he didn't have enough time to make more mise, he'd have to make more time. He started coming in earlier than his colleagues did. He just had to be honest about what it took—2 hours, 3 hours, or more—and that's what he'd do. What he didn't want ever again was the feeling of panic. He wanted to come in knowing that he had done everything he could to set himself up for success.

LiPuma spent more time on prep than anyone else in the kitchen. He started making it through service. As his confidence and skill grew, his prep time shrank. He no longer needed to come in 2 hours before work. When he could fend for himself, he became one of Charlie Palmer's crew. When Palmer left The River Cafe to start his own upscale restaurant—Aureole, on Manhattan's Upper East Side—he took LiPuma with him.

Dwayne LiPuma planned to be a forest ranger in Central Park. God, laughing, made him a chef near Central Park to show him how to plan a little better.

Years later, LiPuma found a pithy phrase that encapsulated what he'd learned in the kitchen, courtesy of his brother-in-law, Pierre, a successful executive: *Greet the day.*

On his way to work, LiPuma saw commuters dashing for the subway—flustered, sweating, stumbling—and the next day he'd see those same commuters rushing again. After working in the kitchen, LiPuma couldn't understand what was wrong with these people. Why not get up a half-hour earlier? *Wasn't greeting your day better than fighting it?* Why not make your kid's lunch the night before, lay out your clothes, do anything you need to do so you can get up and not run around like a maniac so you can smile and *enjoy* your day? That was, after all, what LiPuma was beginning to do in the kitchen. Stress and chaos were a normal part of his job. But if he could *control* a little bit of that chaos—preparing for what he knew was going to happen—he could *greet* chaos, *embrace* it. His mastery of the expected would enable him to better deal with the unexpected. You plan what you can so you can deal with what you can't. He knew it took a certain amount of time to get ready in the morning, to get to work, to prepare his mise-en-place. What good did it serve him to pretend that he didn't? He'd just assure himself a crappy day, every day—just like those commuters—exhausted before he even faced a real challenge. He wanted to greet the day.

WHAT CHEFS DO, WHAT CHEFS KNOW

Chefs put planning first

A restaurant is a promise: Walk in and we'll be ready. Select anything on our menu and we'll cook it for you quickly and well.

Because of that promise, chefs and cooks can't wing it. They must have all the resources (ingredients, tools, and personnel) to fulfill it. They must know the actions (recipes, procedures, and skills) needed to honor it. And this all must happen before the first order comes in, because once it does, they will have no time for *anything* but the act of cooking. Thus, for chefs and cooks, the act of planning takes precedence; it must *precede* cooking. Chefs become planning machines so they can become cooking machines.

Planning is primary for chefs in another way: It takes longer to plan and prepare than it does to cook. As a result, the mind-set of a chef toward both his personal planning and the planning of his entire kitchen is different from yours or mine. Because planning is "first thought," chefs invest much more time in the action of planning.

Chefs don't plan well because they are better than us. They plan because if they don't, their career is dead. We customers play a significant role in the chef's drama because we will wait patiently for almost anything but food. In restaurants, 1 minute can seem like 10 if we're hungry enough. Our blood sugar lowers and our temper flares. We actually *can't* wait for food without some kind of physiological reaction. We, alas, are the people with whom chefs must deal.

Chefs are honest with time

A chef can't change human physiology. She can't change the laws of physics. Cooking rice takes a specific amount of time. Heating a steak to medium-well will take a certain amount of time. Better and quicker processes may speed things up, but those processes also follow the laws of nature. Second, while human motion can be accelerated with mastery—chopping, carrying, sorting, flipping, and so on—those motions, too, take a certain amount of time, and a chef must be honest with both her abilities and her limitations. Because cooking takes time and because dinner starts on time, planning becomes imperative and forces chefs to develop a painfully honest relationship to time.

Being scrupulous with time means more than creating a list. Making a list is only half the job of planning. To complete the other half, the chef must square that list with the clock. *How much time will this take? How many things can I do in time given my resources? When, exactly, will I do them, and in what order?* Chefs cannot afford to take too many chances in the careful balance between time and tasks. Time forces them to make decisions.

It's hard to decide—literally, to kill off one thing in favor of another, as the word *decide* comes from the same Latin root as *homicide* and *suicide*. Chefs make good executives because they are executioners, killing off the nonessential.

Chefs schedule their tasks

The scheduling of tasks, negotiating between the list and the calendar, is at the center of the chef's approach to planning.

When new students enter the kitchens of the Culinary Institute of America, their chef-instructors present them with a blank form with which they'll become intimate over the next couple of years. Entitled "Mise-en-Place (Timeline)," this form will be their primary tool for learning the work of planning.

MISE EN PLACE (Timeline)

Name: _Student_   Station: _4_   Date: _3/13/14_

	Steps (a breakdown of tasks)	Foodstuffs

Equipment List
Check all that apply:

☐ -Small Sauté Pan
☑ -Medium Sauté Pan
☐ -Large Sauté Pan
☐ -Metal Spoon
☑ -Slotted Spoon
☑ -Cutting Board
☐ -Small Sauce Pot
☑ -Medium Sauce Pot
☐ -Large Sauce Pot
☑ -Sanitizer Bucket
☑ -Tasting Spoons
☑ -Ladle (2oz, 4oz, 6oz)
☑ -Paper Towel
☐ -Small Bowl (1)(2)(3)
☐ -Medium Bowl (1)(2)(3)
☐ -Large Bowl
☑ -Whisk
☐ -Rolling Pin
☐ -Scale
☑ -Twine
☑ -China Cap
☑ -Bain Marie
☑ -Spatula (rubber, metal)
☐
☐
☐
☐
☐

1:30	Mise-en-place
2:30	Lecture
3:00	Fish fumet
3:15	Roux
3:30	Veloute
4:00	Prep carrots
4:20	Cook rice / prep sauce
4:30	Poach flounder / cook spinach
4:40	Present
	Clean
6:00	Dinner
6:45	Start cleanup
7:30	Lecture
8:15	Checkout

Steps (a breakdown of tasks):
Chop white mirepoix
Start fish fumet-3
Make roux-3:15
Make veloute -3:30
Prep carrots- 4
Cook rice/prep sauce -4:20
Poach flounder,
cook spinach -4:30
Present 4:40

Foodstuffs:
1 cup jasmine rice
Saffron
Spinach
Shallots
Salt & pepper
Carrots
White wine
Fish stock
Roux
Cream - 2oz.
Sugar
Chicken stock
Butter

What's interesting about the mise-en-place form is that it's no simple "to-do" list. "Steps," the breakdown of tasks, takes up only a quarter of the page. Another two sections ask the student to list resources, "Equipment" on the left and "Foodstuffs" or ingredients on the right. But the most prominent of the four areas of the form is the daily "Timeline." It isn't enough to simply list the tasks. From their first days at the CIA students have to *order* those tasks in a timeline, deliberating how long each step will take and when to do them.

Sequence is everything. You can't make the sauce until you've made stock; you can't make the stock until you've roasted the bones and cut the vegetables; you can't roast the bones until the oven is hot; and you can't turn on the oven until you're in the kitchen. Experienced students unpack nested tasks and break them down into their component actions. Then they put them in sequence.

New students aren't used to thinking this way. They wrote their high school term papers the night before they were due without scheduling either a trip to the library beforehand or time for revision after. Most kids don't properly sequence their actions because nobody teaches them how.

For chefs-in-training the timeline becomes an integral part of their culinary coursework. When they find themselves running behind or missing things in the kitchen, their chefs refer to the students' timelines. Usually, the chef can point to the error in the students' planning that caused the error in behavior.

By the time they reach their turn in one of the college's restaurants, students have caught the planning bug. They stay up late and spend hours designing their own, more detailed timelines. They divide prep into lists of things they need to do, things they can prep well ahead of time, and things they've already done. They distinguish the equipment they'll need before service from the things they'll need during service. For their stations, they make maps showing where they'll place their ingredients and tools for the different phases of service. They draw them on paper and color code them with markers, print out spreadsheets made on their computers, or write them on a stack of index cards.

Students also come prepared with a binder containing special checklists of equipment and procedures for each specific dish.

Chances are you have a few of these in your home as well: They're called recipes.

The timelines and the recipes, macro-plan and micro-plan, represent the core of kitchen planning. Still, some of the better students, especially those to whom cooking feels natural, become flippant about planning. For CIA baking student Arbil Lopez, the value of making timelines became clear during her first practical exam. She didn't write out her equipment list, so she spent the first precious minutes trying to figure out what tools she needed to gather. She listed her tasks without the necessary timing. The lack of information made her nervous. Her nerves engendered more mistakes. Lopez's puff pastry collapsed on itself, and her éclair was dry. She delivered on time, but her product was not servable. The chef failed her. Lopez called her mother and cried.

"What could you have done better?" her mother asked her.

From then on, Lopez prepared. The culture of planning is such at the CIA that the students develop a remarkable ethical sense about it. "The only thing worse than failure," Lopez says, "is passing by accident."

When culinary students graduate and begin working in professional kitchens, they enter a world that often expects them to internalize that planning. Wylie Dufresne—the James Beard Award–winning chef-owner of innovative New York restaurants like wd-50 and Alder—developed his own approach to "becoming one" with his list. From the time he showed up on the doorstep of Alfred Portale's Gotham Bar and Grill as a culinary student, to working as a sous-chef for another young legend, Jean-Georges Vongerichten, Dufresne began a routine. On his way home from work, he'd take out a small pad and pen and write down everything he knew he had to do the next day. He'd finish the list, tear it out of the pad, and crumple the list up. Then he'd go back to his pad and write the list again from memory, and destroy it. The next morning, on the way to work, he'd reconstruct the list again. It became a game. Every day, Dufresne would scorch a list into his brain. Years later, he still has shoeboxes full of notepads containing his old lists. Occasionally, he'll look through them—each list a little movie of what he was doing on one evening, many years ago. Dufresne instructs his chefs to make lists, not only of the things they know they need to do, but everything they *might* need to do—telling them that he'd rather have them cross needless items off their lists than miss an item and realize it only when it's too late.

Chefs plan ahead, chefs plan backward

À la carte cooking turned the culinary arts into an industry, but it also made that profession a constant gamble. A successful chef must do more than cook well. She must predict what dishes her customers will want and when they will want them. The contemporary chef must stand on both sides of time: in the present, making projections into the future to calculate needed resources; and in the future, counting the minutes and hours backward to the present to calculate needed time.

One of the first things that Dwayne LiPuma tries to teach his students is the simple concept of menu mix: predicting how much of each menu item to prepare. Every day at American Bounty, students will have to prepare 10 portions of each item per every 100 reservations. For example, if their reservations are at 40, they'll have to prepare to make four of each menu item. All the ingredients that go along with those dishes have to be portioned accordingly. Experienced chefs know that certain days and times of the year favor certain menu items more than others. For off-site events, planning starts with the plate itself: a vision of the finished dishes on the table. Then, a chef counts time backward: *How long will it take to plate and serve those dishes? How much time to finish those dishes for service? How much time for transportation from the kitchen to the off-site dining room? How long will the cooking process for each thing on that plate take before that? How long will the prep be for each of these dishes? How much time do I need to allot to gather those tools and ingredients? And how much time can I shave off these times by adding more bodies, by getting help?*

Chefs' backwards planning skills are as applicable as they are enviable outside the kitchen. Before she became an academic and a noted scholar of culinary history, Amy Trubek began her career as a cook and caterer. She remembers the call she got the day her father got a job as dean at a prestigious midwestern university.

"Amy," he said, "I want to send all the associate deans to culinary school." Trubek, nonplussed, asked why.

"Because I have noticed how organized you have become since you worked in restaurants and went to cooking school," her father replied. "You know how to start and finish projects following a deadline." Trubek credited her transformation to mise-en-place and in particular the idea of working backward from time of service.

The constant for all great chefs and cooks is the effort they put into planning. The result of all that physical and mental energy they devote to planning is excellence and calm execution—in the face of both the expected challenges and the unexpected.

OUT OF THE KITCHEN

How do *we* greet the day?

Some of us relegate planning to the margins of our schedules and our psyche. We see planning as something that interrupts and delays our work. We plunge into our mornings with a quickly made list, if we've made one at all. We forget to consult our calendars for impending and future events. We make ourselves vulnerable to chaos. We get buffeted about by a timeline that is not of our own making. When we arrive at appointments, we're not prepared. When we're not in meetings, we forget what we should be doing. We neglect to handle the expected and thus have little bandwidth for the unexpected. We are *underplanners*.

Still others spend *a lot* of time planning, perhaps too much time. Our lists are sophisticated and endless, our expectations for our days excessive. We pack our daily schedules with back-to-back appointments with others and tasks for ourselves. We do too much and fight to fit in even more. We're disappointed with ourselves every day. We've created for ourselves a different kind of chaos, self-imposed. We, too, have no bandwidth for the unexpected. We are *overplanners*.

Underplanners surrender to time. Overplanners fight and curse time. What we need is the chef's mature sense of honesty about what we can and cannot do with time, and of the consequences of surrendering or fighting something that should just be met squarely. What we need is to *work clean* with time, where working clean with time means two things.

1. Determining our daily actions

2. Ordering those actions in sequence

The pages that follow contain some exercises and habits to help us do just that.

EXERCISES: SKILLS TO LEARN

MAKE AN HONESTY LOG

Kitchen folk have an easier time determining and ordering tasks because kitchen work is defined by physical processes. It's easier to know how long it takes a steak to get to medium-well than it is to know how long it takes to create a spreadsheet, write an article, or make a sale. Knowing how long our actions take is harder for us to determine, but that information is valuable. Creating an honesty log will help you understand how much time your regular, recurring tasks actually require.

Let's use a specific example to illustrate how a creative professional might do this exercise. Let's say you're a graphic designer. How long does it usually take you to come up with a logo concept? Sometimes you allow yourself 30 hours spread out over 3 weeks. At other times you can come up with a bunch of ideas in one intense, 4-hour session. You won't develop knowledge about this without *gathering data*. So for your most important categories of tasks, log your times for a month on a piece of paper, a spreadsheet, or a time-tracking app, and see if they average out in a meaningful way. Some more examples: For a teacher, how long does it take you to prep a class? For students, how many hours does it take you to read 50 textbook pages? For executives, how many small tasks, like returning e-mails, can you complete in an hour, on average? For insurance agents, how long does it usually take you to fill out paperwork on a new client?

Perhaps you will always have certain tasks that are particularly hard to nail down. But what you *can* do, even in those cases, is determine what the length of a "minimum session" might be. Maybe it's not worth working on a logo concept if you can't set aside at least an hour. Great. An hour becomes your baseline for that particular task. And knowing that a logo design might take up to 30 hours, it's your job to gauge and moderate other projects you accept so that you can deliver the one on hand. I know, for example, that for certain types of writing, I can usually get 500 words down in 2 hours. That's helpful information for scheduling purposes, but that information would never have been possible if I hadn't purposefully tracked it.

FIND YOUR MEEZE POINT

Here's an exercise for habitual overplanners. We're going to find your Meeze Point: the optimal number of Actions you can put on your daily list before you begin to overload yourself, an Action being either an appointment or a task. This will become your normal daily work threshold. Begun as a 1-day-per-week exercise, finding your Meeze Point can ease you out of the overplanning habit. Fridays are good days to reserve for this experiment because they are often the day wherein we feel the least pressure to overplan. To begin:

1. Select a maximum of three Actions to complete for this day. An Action can be as large as something that takes 5 hours or as small as 5 minutes. We want a nice balance of large to small actions, like a normal day.

2. Place those Actions on your calendar at the appropriate times.

3. Do not plan or schedule any other tasks for the day. You may do extra, unplanned tasks, of course, as long as you honor your schedule.

4. Honor your schedule. Show up for your appointments and tasks. If a real crisis arises and you can't honor your schedule, it may be best to do this exercise another day.

5. At the end of the day, log how many of your three tasks you accomplished.

6. If you completed all three, then the next week, on your designated day, select and schedule *four* Actions. If you didn't complete all three, stay at three next week.

7. Continue each week until you arrive at a number of Actions where you become unable to cross all the items off the list for 3 weeks in a row. For example, if you sometimes can get through a nine-item list, but can't *ever* get through a 10-item list, then your Meeze Point is 9.

8. Once you arrive at your Meeze Point, you can then begin to bring other days into this regimen, using your Meeze Point as a guide for your maximum number of Actions to schedule for your days.

From this practice, I know my Meeze Point is 10.

KITCHEN PRACTICE: MAKE A TIMELINE

The home kitchen is a great place to practice the principles of mise-en-place before you apply them to your work life. The next time you make an ambitious recipe in the kitchen, make a timeline similar to the one they do at the CIA. This is how you do it.

1. In the first column, write down all the ingredients listed. Determine what you don't have on hand and circle those items.

2. In the second column, transcribe the circled items into a shopping list.

3. In the third column, write the steps to the recipe.

4. In the fourth column, the actual timeline, write the start times for each of those steps.

5. In the fifth column, write the list of tools (pots, pans, spatulas, etc.) that you'll need for all those steps, and also the tools you'll need for service (plates, silverware, napkins, glasses).

6. As an extra step, you can make a diagram of what item goes on which burner, for example, or where you'll be setting up your cutting board.

You'll begin to notice that there's a world of things that many recipes don't tell you: What to buy. What tasks to do while other tasks are in progress. What tools to use. How to coordinate your cooking with your service.

Being honest with time is another difference between the

professional and amateur cook, but practicing that honesty in the kitchen can engender honesty in the planning you do at your desk or computer.

HABITS: BEHAVIORS TO REPEAT

CREATE A DAILY MEEZE

For chefs, a commitment to a daily practice of planning comes with their jobs. For us, the commitment to planning will have to come from within. The most important way to work clean is to keep dedicated, structured planning time. If you were to take only one recommendation from this book, creating a Daily Meeze is the paramount habit.

What is a Daily Meeze? It is a personal mise-en-place for your workday, a time to (a) clean your physical and virtual spaces, (b) clear your mind, and (c) plot your day.

How much time does it take? 30 minutes.

When should I do it? In kitchens since the time of the tenzo, tomorrow begins today. Many chefs begin tomorrow's planning in the evening, at the end of their current workday. Some like to do their planning in the morning because new and important considerations often appear at the start of a workday. It all depends on the kind of chef *you* are.

The Daily Meeze is so central to the practice of working clean that we've dedicated an entire section to showing you how to do it. See *A Day of Working Clean* on page 247.

SCHEDULE YOUR ACTIONS

An Action is *anything* you plan to do during the day. Any task ("Pick up butter," "Call Jeff," "Sketch designs for new campaign") is an Action. An appointment ("Staff meeting," "Conference call," "Lunch with Sam") is also an Action. There is no difference between a task and an appointment when it comes to thinking about scheduling because they both need your time and your presence. This difference has long been maintained by the two different tools we use for each: the "to-do" list and the calendar. But for the chef, as it should be for us, it is a false difference. The "to-do" list without appointments lures us into packing lots of tasks onto it without thinking about when they will actually get done; and a calendar with only appointments on it misleads us into thinking we have an open schedule when in fact we don't. This separation creates an unhelpful tension between our mental and spiritual goals (which usually end up on our list) and our physical presence (which is usually determined by our schedule).

The main reason we order and schedule Actions—tasks and appointments alike—is that we want to give ourselves the best shot at getting them done.

"A to-do list is useful as a collection tool," writes author Peter Bregman. "Our calendars, on the other hand, make the perfect tool to guide our daily accomplishments. Because our calendars are finite; there are only a certain number of hours in a day."

We schedule our Actions to help us make decisions about them—and as a device to force our hand. The calendar compels us to be honest about time. A list, too, can be a serviceable device for ordering your day—as long as your appointments are on it! This is the way that chefs think about time. We should, too.

PLAN "PLATE FIRST"

Plan complex, multistep projects as chefs do: with the end in mind. Just as some chefs begin a dish by drawing a plate, for your own projects, first envision the moment of delivery, then plan backward from it. What resources will you need to make it look, read, feel, or sound perfect? What time will you need? Have you accounted for possible delays, holidays, disruptions? Have you given yourself time to inspect and correct? What other things will you have to give up in order to deliver?

GET THERE EARLY

Where is "there"? Everywhere. How early? Fifteen minutes. Why? The dividends are serenity and opportunity. Entering a space calmly, under your own control, and without apology retains your power and dignity. So many of us hustle and stumble our way into a room after an agreed-upon time. When we do that, we forfeit a chunk of our energy before we even sit down.

Arriving early often unlocks opportunity. An old friend of mine recently had this epiphany. He had always been a "late person" until recently when he made a commitment to arrive at a weekly class before the designated start time. "I realized that there were all these other people showing up early, too," he said. He liked "early people." He made connections, he made friends.

Getting there early applies especially to the appointments you make with yourself because those are the appointments you are least likely to keep—having no one to answer to but yourself. Prepare early, make sure to disentangle yourself from whatever it is you happen to be doing beforehand, and you will ensure that you'll show up for yourself. Some of the most successful chefs and executives I know share this ethos and practice.

---

*Entering a space calmly, under your own
control, and without apology retains your
power and dignity.*

A chef's reprise: Riding the range

In 1999 Chef Dwayne LiPuma became a high priest of mise-en-place when he began teaching at the CIA.

LiPuma had mastered the painstaking planning that allowed him to open up his breath, greet every workday, and cook with love. But he had also discovered the limits of mise-en-place at home. He found that he had to temper his planning impulses at home or he'd drive his wife and his daughter Kaitlyn crazy. Once he realized that mise-en-place had its own right place, he valued and understood it even more. He began to see how his entire work practice of mise-en-place could allow him to relax, greet the evening and weekends, and let go of structure. A happy home was his reward for having compressed his work with mise-en-place. From this, he learned several things: Mise-en-place is not about focus, but rather the process of negotiating focus and chaos. Mise-en-place is an inside job—meaning that it's something you have to choose, to willingly take on. And mise-en-place is also a shared culture, meaning that while he could have his own mise-en-place in his home, that mise-en-place ended where his wife and kids began, unless he and his family agreed where they shared it.

His wife, Kareen, began laying her clothes out at night, too. And she found Dwayne's planning instincts handy, like when she organized a $300-a-plate fund-raising dinner in a fancy Park Avenue apartment. LiPuma loved to plan, and catering was the greatest planning challenge. If you forget an ingredient in a kitchen, you can always walk to the pantry; if you forget a pot, you can go to the storeroom. In catering, if you don't bring it, you won't have it.

On one piece of paper, he wrote his menu. On another, his ingredients and tools. On still another, he ordered that information into a schedule. After a day of planning and shopping, he assembled the tools and ingredients into a neat row of brown shopping bags, each divided and labeled by menu item: soup, pasta, foie gras, scallops, and so on.

Kareen walked by 2 days' worth of planning and said: "*Man, you are anal retentive.*"

"No," LiPuma said. "This is how chefs think." He was going to cook in someone's home, after all.

When the big evening came, LiPuma found it almost too easy. Kareen and his daughter Kaitlyn became his sous-chefs, but he hardly needed them. They enjoyed a nice, relaxed service, and it turned out to be a great meal. LiPuma had little to do but be present, joke, and smile.

Kareen smiled back. *My hero.* The Italian without a stallion, riding the range. Just a different kind of range than he had planned.

Recipe for Success

Commit to being honest with time. Plan daily.

ARRANGING SPACES, PERFECTING MOVEMENTS

A chef's story: The move maker

IN A KITCHEN at the New York Institute of Technology's Long Island campus, a chef taught his new students how to turn potatoes—"turning" being one of the basic techniques of knife work: peeling and cutting vegetables so that they have a smooth and uniform shape.

One student, Jarobi White, was neither novice nor slouch. He'd been working in restaurants since he was 14 years old. Stuck stuffing hot dogs into buns at an O'Charley's on Long Island, Jarobi muscled his way onto the hot line by convincing his boss to fire one of his coworkers because, Jarobi claimed, he could do both jobs at once.

Jarobi's problem was that he hustled too hard and moved too much. The chef watched Jarobi at his station, potato skins spilling over the table and onto his feet, potatoes rolling off his cutting board. The chef could see Jarobi's thoughts play out on his face: *Oh, shit, I need a bucket!* Jarobi crossed the kitchen to grab one. The potatoes now went into the bucket, graying as their moist insides came in contact with the air. *Shit, I forgot to fill it with water!* Jarobi crossed the kitchen again to fill the pail.

Finally the chef-instructor barked at him in German-accented French: "Mise-en-place!"

Jarobi turned around. He had no idea what the chef was saying.

"Mise-en-place! Mise-en-place!" The chef gestured to his own station: *tray, knife, pail of water, bowl for scraps.*

Jarobi's face lit up. Jarobi said: "Oh, word!" He meant: *What a great idea.*

The chef nodded: "Everything has its place," he said. "I don't go anywhere."

Jarobi White gathered his mise-en-place, resumed, and tried going nowhere, fast.

While Jarobi White tried to make smaller moves, thousands of people were asking why he wasn't making bigger ones. After all, Jarobi was the only person in that kitchen with a video on MTV. The year was 1991, and Jarobi was a member of a new rap crew named A Tribe Called Quest, along with three friends—Jonathan "Q-Tip" Davis, Malik "Phife" Taylor, and Ali Shaheed Muhammad. The previous year the group released their first video, "I Left My Wallet in El Segundo," and their debut album had sold hundreds of thousands of copies, making A Tribe Called Quest one of the most talked-about new acts in hip-hop. While the group worked on their second album, Jarobi had second thoughts. He'd been skeptical from the start. Jarobi hadn't signed the group's penurious management and production contract. Recording artists found it hard to make money even in the best of circumstances, and even with Tribe's success, they were still far from seeing real money to live on, not with four dudes in the group. With Q-Tip and Phife handling most of the vocals and Ali being the DJ, Jarobi was the unofficial member with the least-defined role and thus relegated himself to the margins. He had always been the silent one, with fans wondering aloud what he did. He soon became the invisible one—appearing, disappearing, and reappearing—fans wondering where he'd gone.

If they happened to stop into the Tacoma Station Tavern in Washington, DC, in the mid-1990s, they would have seen him running the small kitchen there, cooking soul food and burgers and wings. But if they caught Tribe on tour, or one of Phife's solo gigs,

Jarobi just might be on stage. You never knew. He kept moving. By the mid-2000s—married with a newborn son, and living in Charleston, South Carolina, where his wife was a teacher—Jarobi needed to plant some roots. He walked the town, handing his résumé to every restaurant on his path. The last one he visited, Pearlz Oyster Bar, was the only one with a black chef, Eric Boyd. Boyd took a chance on the boisterous quasi-famous rapper. "I want this guy in my kitchen," the chef said.

Jarobi still treated cooking like a competitive sport, his goal being to drill out food faster than the chef or expediter could handle, to put them in the weeds, in the shit, *dans la merde*—meaning inundated with orders. *Take that, motherfucker.* Jarobi cooked at a furious pace. Fury, however, was not all Chef Eric wanted from Jarobi.

"Mise-en-place!" the chef said.

Jarobi compensated for his lack of preparation and order as he always had, with extra movement, speed, and muscle. But his adrenaline-fueled drive ran right over the subtlety of the chef's dishes, like a delicate tempura tuna roll—raw tuna brushed with tempura batter; then rolled in panko crumbs and black and white sesame seeds; then quickly, carefully deep-fried, so that the outside was crusty but the inside remained nice, succulent, and rare. The time difference between perfection and destruction of this dish was maybe 10 seconds, after which, according to Jarobi, it became "tuna in a can." Jarobi kept destroying it. "What is this?" Chef said, smashing the plate to the ground. "Again!"

Jarobi repeated his failure, and the chef "plated" him once more. "Again!"

After his shift the chef asked Jarobi over to the bar and bought him a beer.

"So, you had kind of a rough day in there today, hunh?" the chef asked, as if he were the observer and not the administrator of that roughness. Jarobi had to laugh.

"I know it seems petty," his chef continued. "But if you apply mise-en-place to how you cook, you can apply that to your life."

Jarobi tightened his moves. He expended less energy and got more done. The chef began trusting him to run the kitchen in his absence, and Jarobi showed a flair for the administrative duties—inventory, ordering, analyzing food cost. The firm that owned the restaurant, Homegrown Hospitality, gave Jarobi the kitchen of its flagship steakhouse, TBonz. Staying put was paying off.

Then, just as everything came together, it fell apart. His wife lost her job. They had to move to Atlanta. The marriage dissolved. Jarobi bounced from job to job, including a gig as private chef to Lee Najjar, a nouveau-riche real estate investor who threw dinner parties where guests from the rap world would do double-takes seeing the fourth member of A Tribe Called Quest sautéing vegetables and slicing meat. Jarobi made lots of money and was miserable. He moved again, back to New York.

Thanksgiving dinner at Q-Tip's house in 2010 changed Jarobi's fortune. One of Q-Tip's friends dropped by: Josh "Shorty" Eden, the Jean-Georges Vongerichten–trained chef of a new restaurant in Manhattan called August. "If you ever move back from Atlanta," Eden said, "I could use your help."

"Well," Jarobi replied, "guess what?"

The next Monday, Jarobi White stepped into one of the most rarified kitchens in New York. He knew how much he *didn't* know, but he *did* know that the kind of career leap he had just made was impossible. He called Eden his "Yoda." Eden taught Jarobi about molecular gastronomy: foams and other subtle arts associated with modernist cuisine. Jarobi's education on mise-en-place began anew, too. When Jarobi relied on speed and brute force, Eden encouraged sensitivity. Most of all, Eden forced Jarobi to bring order to his surroundings and restraint to his movements: Where and how to stand. How to set his station. How to move his hands and arms.

Jarobi began to see the space around him geometrically, a triangle into which he fit quite naturally. In front of him was his focus point, the stove. Extending his left arm behind him, he grabbed a pan. Extending his right arm behind him, he could touch his mise-en-place. Pivoting on his right foot, he brought his pan to his mise, where he had arranged his containers and bottles by menu item, each ingredient in the sequence that he used them. His fingers moved from left to right: butter, salt, garlic confit, pistachios, mussels, wine. Pivoting back, he cooked. Reaching back and to the left, he grabbed a plate. In front of him, he plated the food. Pivoting right, he set the plate down and finished the dish from his mise. Turning right again, he placed the plate on the pass and grabbed another pan. A final turn and he found himself facing the range again. A circle within a triangle. No wasted motion. Going nowhere, fast.

WHAT CHEFS DO, WHAT CHEFS KNOW

Chefs gather their resources

The heart of mise-en-place is "place" itself: the cook's station.

In the professional kitchen, mise-en-place arises from the grim reality of cooking-on-demand for a lot of customers, each choosing her own dishes. A cook cannot prepare dozens, perhaps hundreds of dishes in the span of a few hours without her resources—her tools and ingredients—being within literal arm's reach. In a job where 60 seconds can be the difference between a satisfied or enraged customer and 10 seconds the difference between perfection and destruction of a dish, leaving one's station to grab something from the storage area can throw off a cook's rhythm; taking minutes to cut vegetables can disrupt the entire crew; and running out of a prepared ingredient like a sauce that takes hours to create can wreck an entire service period. The first task of organizing space is that the resources be in place, so that the cook himself can *stay* in place.

"Theoretically," award-winning chef Wylie Dufresne says, "if you have enough mise-en-place, you can just cook forever." As Dufresne speaks, he mimes the actions: feet planted, but arms swirling, fingers pinching ingredients, an upper-body ballet.

Chefs arrange their spaces

That upper-body ballet must be constrained, too, to preserve the seconds that matter for hungry customers. So a chef's tools and ingredients must be arranged in a precise, predictable, economical way to allow a cook's motions to be precise, predictable, and economical.

Chefs hold a few governing principles: Ingredients should be close by and close together. Ingredients for each dish should be arranged in the order that they go into the pan or plate, and they should all be grouped together in "zones," as Chef Dwayne LiPuma calls them. A cook can't root around for ingredients scattered all over the place. A cook's hand should move inches, not feet. And the arrangement of ingredients and tools needs to be constant from day to day, so that the cook can learn and internalize the movements in her space.

Arrangements should make sense both for the cook's body and for the ingredients and tools she uses. LiPuma's old chef, Charlie Palmer, tells cooks to put dry ingredients *behind* wet ones, so that water from, say, a container of sliced radishes won't cake a crock of salt in front of it. When Chef Alfred Portale checks the line at the Gotham Bar and Grill, he often rearranges the mise-en-place of his cooks to get more economy of space. "You'll see a cook and he'll have a bain-marie on his station with five spoons and three pairs of tongs," Portale says. "And I walk by and take out everything except one spoon and one pair of tongs. Why do you need *five* spoons? You can only use one at a time!"

Cooks construct their mise-en-place in different ways, but the icon of modern mise-en-place is the *fractional pan*. To limit motion, cooks want the smallest containers possible, so they'll

often use what they call nine-pans—which means a steel pan that is one-ninth the size of a full steam table pan, into which nine nine-pans will fit snugly.

Mise-en-place arrangement also changes with time, because space around cooks is limited. There are phases of mise. A cook's setup for heavy prep changes for preservice cooking. Their setup for preservice changes again for service. Each phase of work requires a different mise-en-place, and the previous mise needs to be broken down before the station can accommodate the next.

Chefs train and restrain their movements

Pretty as it might look, the point of arranging spaces is not beauty, but to allow movements to be free, small, rhythmic, and most important, automatic. Repeated often enough, a movement will train our brains in a process called automaticity that allows us to execute that movement without consciously thinking about it. Chefs sometimes call this phenomenon muscle memory, but muscles don't actually remember anything. What's actually happening is that the part of the brain that thinks about what we're doing, the prefrontal cortex, cedes control to the part of the brain that governs nonconscious reactions, the basal ganglia.

Movements in the kitchen run from simple procedures like cutting vegetables, to complex processes like multistep recipes, and then to the ballet of an entire service period. Each of these levels engenders its own choreography, as Michael Gibney calls it in his book, *Sous Chef*.

> *(A) Left hand picks up pear*
>
> *(B) Right hand peels pear*
>
> *(C) Left hand places pear in acidulated water*

. . . and repeat. The specificity of the choreography is important. You can't cut a pear a different way each time and expect a similar result, nor can you expect to ever gain speed.

The choreography of the entire workflow must support the choreography of the task. In many cases, the flow will move *across* the cutting board, the right-handed example being: Unprocessed ingredients move in from the left side of the cutting board, cutting happens in the center, and processed ingredients move to the right. Knife and towel go back to their original places when the task is done.

But depending on the size and nature of the ingredient, this workflow may change. "One's physical orientation during a given task is the product of the task itself," Gibney says. "If I were sectioning lemons, I might have a tipped-over container of lemons to the north of my cutting board, the storage container to my left, and the refuse receptacle to my right." In this case—similar to the pear example above—the nondominant left hand holding the fruit will also move the fruit, once processed, to the left instead of the right, to avoid another inefficient move that chefs abhor: hands crossing *over* the body's central axis.

"You'll see somebody who's right-handed peeling a carrot and reaching across themselves and putting it in a container on the left," Chef Alfred Portale says. Sometimes Portale not only arranges his stations, but arranges his *cooks:* "They're trying to cut something square and they're standing at an angle, or their cutting board is at an angle. I'll say: 'What are you doing? You've got to square your whole body up if you want to cut a perfect dice.'"

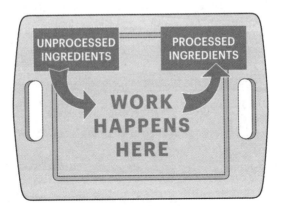

"Nobody is naturally disposed to move this way," Gibney says. "You don't often think, 'I'm going to put my groceries away in the most efficient way possible today. Let's start with the fridge open, squat down, bag on the ground in front of me, and pull items out shelf by shelf to minimize excess movements.' Unless, of course, you're a chef."

Indeed, chefs and cooks spend their careers rehearsing and refining their "moves," and they regard good moves in other cooks as basketball players might revere the hook shot of Kareem Abdul-Jabbar.

Every cook in some way makes an internal map of his or her movements. It took more than a decade for Jarobi White to conceptualize what he calls his Magic Triangle.

The triangle itself is an ergonomic shape, matching how we're built: When planted, our attention can be on our front and sides, but not behind us. Sometimes a triangle is as simple as Gibney's cutting board workflow: input, work, output. And a circle within the triangle enables our primary focus to change with minimal movement, allowing for a more complex workflow like Jarobi's: action, beginning/finishing, input/output. The Magic Triangle is the holistic assembly line of any craftsperson, a path in and out of any task.

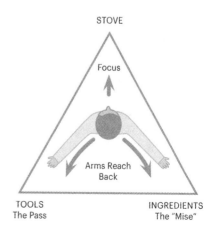

Chefs greet space

When chefs like Mario Batali, Masaharu Morimoto, and Eric Ripert need to create a new kitchen from scratch, they call Jimi Yui.

Yui (pronounced "You-eee") isn't a chef, but he grew up in a restaurant. His parents ran The Guest House, serving gourmet Peking-style Chinese meals in the Roppongi district of Tokyo, where Yui developed a visceral familiarity with the rhythms of a kitchen. So when Yui takes on a new project, oftentimes he will go to an existing kitchen run by that chef, watch how cooks move, and listen to what they're saying and doing. *How many burners does a particular station need? How many people need to fit there? What are the most common actions on those stations and movements around the room?*

When Yui walks into a new space, he watches and listens to the emptiness.

"You embrace it," Yui says. "You try to make the most of what it can do for you, or you realize that the space doesn't want to be what you want it to be." Once, Yui entered a vacant space for a new Gray Kunz restaurant on New York's Columbus Circle and found it shaped like a flattened triangle. The most logical place for the kitchen—where the space *itself* wanted that kitchen to be—was against the wall of gorgeous windows looking out on Central Park, where the most desirable dining tables would normally be. Yui put the kitchen by the windows.

"I believe in trying to solve puzzles, but in a way that doesn't fight the space," Yui says. "Fighting space is a really bad thing."

In the same way that chefs try to be honest with time—to greet the day—Yui strives to be honest with space.

Yui's designs also follow another principle: Make the kitchen and the spaces within it *as small as possible.* This is a counterintuitive notion to many Americans for whom the holy grail is a spacious kitchen, with their stove, refrigerator, and sink set up in a perfect triangle—because a triangle, they've heard, is efficient.

"It's not efficient if you have 10 to 12 feet of space between each of those points," Yui says. "I hate those kitchens."

Instead, Yui tries to make the points on his triangles much smaller.

"I try to do things so that you don't have to take a step," he says. "We make things as small as we can make them."

How small? "Until you can't physically fit all the stuff and people that you need in order to work. Until the point of no return where you know you're gonna die."

Chefs know they don't need a lot of space because they are smart about why and how they use it.

Chefs use all movements

Inside Jarobi's Magic Triangle, he's not just moving one arm, he's moving both simultaneously. While his left hand shakes a pan, his right hand grabs onions from his mise. When he reaches for plates, it's two at a time, not one at a time because, well, he's got two hands. It's what Chef Fritz Sonnenschmidt, dean emeritus of the CIA, calls "using both sides of your body. Your left and your right side have to become one."

Balanced movement is a key part of ergonomic movement. It's something I realized at home after spending a lot of late nights in professional kitchens. One bleary-eyed morning, I leaned on the countertop with my left hand as I unloaded the dishwasher with the right; grabbed one plate, put it on the counter; grabbed another, put it on the counter; grabbed another, etc. *What I wouldn't give for a helping hand*, I thought. I looked dumbly at my left hand, still propped against the countertop. With that, I drafted Lefty into service. Now I'm emptying the dishwasher in half the time. Life lesson learned: Use both hands. But I'm also still emptying the dishwasher one rack at a time: top one first, then the bottom. To do that, I'm crisscrossing the kitchen constantly: put glasses over here, cross the dishwasher, put cutlery over there, cross the dishwasher. Lefty said: *Wouldn't it be better to stand on one side of the dishwasher, pull out all the things that go on that side, and then stand on the other side and do the same?* Another lesson learned: Use both sides of a space.

Chefs don't only use both sides of their bodies, they use both sides of their motions. *If you're headed to the dishwasher's station to drop off dirty pans, use the opportunity to stop in the walk-in refrigerator nearby to replenish your supply of proteins or vegetables or sauces. If you're headed toward the pantry to pick up onions, take trash with you on the way there.* Good servers and food runners excel at this practice: Take a plate of food out, bring a dirty plate back. Jarobi White calls this "hands in, hands out."

Every day, chefs cultivate the use of *both sides of the body, both sides of a space,* and *both sides of a motion.*

Chefs chain tasks

Planning is thinking *before* moving. Movement is that thought embodied. But the culmination of perfected motion in the kitchen is the cook's ability to intertwine planning *and* movement: thinking *while* moving. We might call it dynamic planning, but some cooks refer to it as task chaining or task stacking.

While cooks are handling task A, their minds envision task B. As a result, as they finish task A, their body begins to move toward task B. While they are on task B, they think about task C. An apt metaphor for this would be the monkey bars at a playground, where you must grab onto the next rung before releasing the current one.

Michael Gibney writes about this phenomenon in *Sous Chef*: "Like a skilled billiards player, you begin anticipating your next move and the one after that, so that when one task is done, you don't waste time trying to figure out what follows. You move seamlessly between activities, shaving precious seconds off the overall time it takes to complete your mise-en-place."

CIA baking graduate Arbil Lopez explains task chaining this way: "You're always thinking, 'What am I doing next? I'm mixing now. When I take this off the mixer, I have to pipe it. When it goes in the oven for 45 minutes, I can put something else on the mixer. While that's on the mixer, I can boil syrup for this other thing.' You have fewer moments of, 'Umm, what am I doing?'"

The crucial, seconds-saving elimination of lag time between actions is what Dwayne LiPuma calls *flow*: an internalization of the sequence and order of tasks, derived from an active mind that is always thinking one or two steps ahead. Cooks develop a nose for tasks that can be done simultaneously, chained together, or stacked within each other. Over time, they make mental maps of those routines.

Making every movement count is an unattainable ideal. Still, chefs and cooks stretch toward it every day—not just to save time, but to save their minds. If a cook can use one movement to get two things done, that's one less thing to worry about, which in turn makes her movements more focused and less fraught. It also turns mise-en-place into a game of sorts, a competitive sport wherein a chef plays against herself.

"Even when I'm at home, I'm always thinking," says Lopez. Cleaning her apartment has become a feat of task chaining and stacking. She puts the laundry in the machine and is already thinking about grabbing the mop as she shuts the door. "You end up saving so much time," she says.

OUT OF THE KITCHEN

We arrange spaces—and perfect movements within those spaces—to *remove resistance*. The less friction we have in our work, the easier it is to do, the more we can do, and the quicker we can do it; and thus the more physical and mental energies we can preserve for other things. We want the absence of friction, or as Dwayne LiPuma says, to move through our work "like oil on glass."

In the kitchen, chefs and cooks *work clean* with space and movement because even a slight amount of friction—not knowing where an ingredient or tool is—will slow them down, physically and mentally, and undermine their ability to be excellent. Arranging spaces for economy of motion pays extra dividends in the kitchen because most motions in the kitchen are repetitive. But the behavior can be just as helpful in our homes and at our workspaces, too.

Our offices may not have the physical demands of the professional kitchen, nor quite the degree of repetitive motion, nor the moment-to-moment need to save and shave time. But we all feel the psychological and physiological results of disorganization; we've all lost minutes, even hours, of our time looking for tools or resources, or re-creating lost work. Our keyboards and screens require all manner of repetitive, automatized movements; and we all suffer from time wasted by failing to apply our mental capacity to our daily movements, and to the execution of complex processes, which are also movements on a macro level. A project that ends up sidetracking managers and workers for days or weeks or longer is just one big, bad wasted move to be looked at with the same skeptical eye.

In the office world, we not only devalue space and motion, we hardly think about them at all. Mise-en-place encourages us to look at the human, physical side of work—even virtual, digital work—and to apply those same concepts of eliminating resistance to higher orders of motion and process.

We arrange spaces to remove resistance.

EXERCISES: SKILLS TO LEARN

AUDIT YOUR SPACES AND MOVES

In this exercise we're going to inventory friction points in your physical and virtual spaces.

Step One. List three tasks that you find difficult or resist doing.

1. One physical task at home or work (for example: taking out the trash, putting project materials away)

2. One digital task on a digital device (for example: answering e-mails, backing up the computer)

3. One complex process or errand at or between home and work (for example: prepping to teach a class, taking stuff to cleaners)

Step Two. For each of those tasks, list one action you can take to decrease that resistance. Some suggestions:

1. For difficult physical tasks, look for ways to arrange your space to make the motion easier. For example: If reaching the file cabinet is a problem, try positioning your desk another way or purchasing moveable file boxes or bins to get your "desk piles" off your desk but keep them together and available. Think also about ways to move more efficiently, using both sides of your body, both sides of a space, and both sides of a motion.

2. For difficult digital tasks, look for ways to use software to automate tasks (see "Digital Declutter, Software Shortcuts" on page 79) and consider purchasing new hardware and software to smooth your way.

3. For complex processes (for example, onboarding a new client or vendor, editing a piece of work), pinpoint the steps in the process where you get hung up. Then make a checklist to guide you through those steps (see "Checklists: Recipes for Processes" on page 78).

4. For difficult errands, consider a larger-scale version of balanced motion. For example, a run to the cleaners needs to be paired with another motion on a regular basis to make both more efficient.

Ultimately you want to create workflows for each of the important tasks or processes you do. Michael Gibney describes what happens in the kitchen if this choreography is not set up before the task begins: "Occasionally you'll see this beautiful moment of frustration on a cook's face when she's doing something and—'*ugh!*'—rearranges something on her station really quickly. It's embarrassing for the cook and super brief, but you realize that 3 minutes into doing this task she realized, 'Oh, shit, I'm not doing this the right way. I'm not working as efficiently as possible.'"

DRAW AND BUILD YOUR WORKSTATION

Whether building a new kitchen or creating a new dish, the first action many chefs take isn't making a list, but drawing a picture.

In this exercise you will draw your own perfect workspace, and yourself within it.

Step One. Get a sheet of paper and a pen or marker. Set a timer for no more than 5 minutes.

Step Two. Begin your drawing with yourself. Are you standing? In a chair? Draw a circle around yourself.

Step Three. Begin placing work objects around you. Some guidance:

- **In front of you.** The thing(s) you need to see and touch the most. In some cases this might be a computer or laptop, but for others it might be a drafting easel or an empty space for books and papers. Control devices like keyboards go here.

- **On the side of your dominant hand.** Control devices, mobile devices, phones, paper, stapler, tape, pens.

- **On the side of your nondominant hand.** Resources, files, fasteners, references, inboxes/outboxes. The principle behind this, says Jimi Yui, is to limit "crossover," i.e., your hands crossing your body.

Step Four. Stop when the timer goes off. Now look at your current workspace. Take note of everything that you didn't draw. Write those items down. Ask: *Why are they there?* Sometimes stuff just stays on our desks because we neglect to move it, or we want to use it as a placeholder, or it has some sentimental value. Now think about using height—a shelf—to take less essential items out of your immediate field of view but within arm's reach.

After this exercise make a list of items to gather or purchase to create this workspace. Invest whatever time and money you can spare in setting up your workstation as ergonomically as possible: the right desk, the right chair, the right tools. Are big, L-shaped desks with plenty of drawers better? Not necessarily. Small, as we've seen, is often better. Are fancy ergonomic chairs good for you? Sure. But sitting upright at the edge of a metal folding chair might be just as healthy for your back. And if you have a computer, should you have a pull-out tray to keep the keyboard parallel to your forearms, and a screen at eye level? Probably.

Consider removing anything you didn't draw in your picture; you don't have to trash it, but try your workstation in its most spare, uncluttered form for a week and see how it feels.

KITCHEN PRACTICE: TASK CHAINING

Whether you call it task chaining, task stacking, or flow, being able to conceive and envision your next move while making your current one can save time and turn even drudge work into a moving meditation.

One of the ways I practice both task chaining and balanced movement together is in the kitchen. For example, when I make a fried egg, my first action is to reach up and grab a pan. But while my right hand is reaching for the pan, my left is turning the gas knob on my stove. While I'm bringing that pan to the heat, my mind is already thinking "butter and eggs," so there isn't any hesitation between steps. My head has already swiveled and my feet are moving toward the refrigerator. And I know my left hand will grab the butter while my right hand grabs the eggs. As I move back toward the stove, I shut the door with my foot, and my mind is already thinking about grabbing a butter knife from the drawer and a bowl from the cupboard once my ingredients are set down.

Task chaining, in a way, is a kind of *moving mise-en-place* for the experienced cook. Sara Moulton, who assisted Julia Child for years before she rose to run the kitchen at *Gourmet* magazine and became a noted TV personality and author, wrote a blog post called "Mise-en-Place Is a Waste of Time for the Home Cook"— and worried that it might seem heretical to her colleagues at the CIA. But she's right: When it takes more time to assemble ingredients beforehand than it does to assemble them on the fly, the *latter* is true mise-en-place, not the former. It takes, however, both knowledge of a recipe and familiarity with your space to make the latter more efficient.

HABITS: BEHAVIORS TO REPEAT

CHECKLISTS: RECIPES FOR PROCESSES

We've formed mental maps and memorized movements for simple physical tasks (left hand grabs the carrot, right hand grabs the knife). But for more complex processes (making sales calls, completing a spreadsheet, or writing a proposal) we often miss something or make mistakes. Each of these mistakes or omissions is a *friction point*. Just as chefs diagnose and adjust their movements to be as free and efficient as possible for the simple tasks, we can identify and remedy friction points for complex processes as well. The solution for what author and physician Atul Gawande calls "the problem of extreme complexity" is something that chefs and cooks create and use all the time: checklists.

Checklists are the chef's "external brain," and they can be ours, too. They concretize thinking *before* movement, assist thinking *during* movement, and enshrine knowledge gained from mistakes in thinking *after* movement.

Begin this habit by creating the first of many handy checklists to smooth your way through your day.

Step One. Select a task, errand, or routine that you do often.

Step Two. Break it down into 10 steps or fewer. Checklists are more effective when they are shorter; if your task has too many steps, try this exercise with another task that has fewer.

Step Three. Determine the kind of checklist you need. Gawande divides checklists into two distinct groups.

■ Read-Do—*read the checklist item, then do the item*

■ Do-Confirm—*do all the items and then use the checklist afterward to confirm*

You can also think of these as *preflight* and *postflight* checklists.

Step Four: Test your checklist by using it three times.

Step Five: Each time you finish the checklist, note any additions or modifications you realized you need to make.

Unlike task lists, which we use to remind us of the actions we have to accomplish throughout our day, checklists guide us through the *interior* of the more complex processes that we must repeat without fail. Task lists change every day; checklists don't change. Writing and following checklists is particularly helpful during prep times, daily routines, and transitions from one project or location to another.

Whether we're internalizing movements through repetition or externalizing them through checklists, both mechanisms free the brain to think about other things.

DIGITAL DECLUTTER, SOFTWARE SHORTCUTS

Our digital devices—computers, laptops, tablets, and phones—are virtual spaces that function like real ones because we must view and manipulate objects within them. And because we spend much of our time in these virtual spaces, clutter and chaos can be sources of friction in the very same way. Some tips for reducing resistance in your digital world include the following:

Choose your organization approach. When "graphic user interfaces" were invented for personal computers decades ago, they were designed to resemble familiar objects in our physical workspaces. So the screen became the "desktop," which in turn became the home for files that could either be "nested" neatly within each other in a pseudo "cabinet" or else strewn about the virtual desktop as we might do in real life. But unlike in the physical world, the computer's search, tagging, and flagging functions make instant access possible and render moot the need to click and scroll to find objects; if, of course, we can remember what terms, tags, and flags to use in our search.

Our approach to our virtual spaces tends to be similar to that of our physical ones. Some people can't imagine not creating an organized system to file documents on their computer and would find it chaotic not having documents housed in relevant folders. But it is also possible to pile your documents, just put them anywhere, and still be able to access them instantly *if* you keep a consistent convention for naming files. The reality is that if you are the kind of person who resists filing, you might also be resistant to naming things consistently.

The cost of not doing one or the other, I guarantee you, is hours of lost time. If you take either consistent filing or naming seriously, getting some of your life back seems a pretty good dividend.

Consider iconography geography. Both our computers and mobile devices require us to work with icons. And because we use these virtual "buttons" so often, it is vital that we develop automatic reactions linked to where these things are. Invest some time to place and/or nest your icons, with the most frequently used placed to one side or another. It's worth the time, but will also require periodic reinvestment as you add and delete apps.

Learn gestures. Many digital devices now enable powerful shortcuts called *gestures*—manipulations you can do with different combinations of your fingertips. For example, on some computers you can clear all the open windows off your desktop by spreading your fingers. Take some time to learn these gestures, and that time will be returned many times over.

Automate. Software and apps automate so many processes now—like turning business cards into entries in your digital contact list or shunting unwanted e-mail out of the way. Using these can be complicated for the less-advanced user, but there are plenty of online tutorials. Consulting with an expert can save a lot of future keystrokes.

Learn to type. Keyboard use in the developed world is now nearly universal in both the workplace and outside of it. Yet it boggles the mind that so few people have developed automaticity for the one device they use the most. Not knowing how to type well makes about as much sense as a chef not knowing how to wield a knife.

Your devices are important spaces to arrange and make as ergonomic as possible. They are extensions of your nervous system, and you can only be as responsive as your technology.

A chef's reprise: Keep on moving

If you happened to stop into Bed-Vyne Cocktail in Brooklyn in the summer of 2015, and waited in a long line that snaked from the door to the rear courtyard, when you finally got to the front of the line, you'd find Jarobi White serving his food.

"Tribe Taco Tuesdays" began as Jarobi's version of the Los Angeles street food tradition, powered by the continued popularity of A Tribe Called Quest. On the first Tuesday, Jarobi brought enough mise-en-place for 75 people; 100 came. The next Tuesday, he brought enough for 100 people and 200 came. The following week, his girlfriend Kamilah and a culinary extern cooked alongside him. Throughout the summer, the event grew with local and national media attention. When the crowds swelled to almost 300, neighborhood complaints forced the bar to shut the party down. Jarobi felt that old frustration. He wanted a place of his own, but being at Shorty's August had spoiled him. After working amid marble counters and cobblestone floors, every other place looked like a dump.

An offer from Chef Roy Choi diverted Jarobi's worries. Choi had pioneered the food truck movement in L.A., later inspiring and consulting with Jon Favreau in the making of the actor-director's 2014 movie *Chef*. Choi opened a slate of restaurants; a trip to one of them the previous summer had inspired Jarobi's taco experiment. Now Choi asked Jarobi to take over the pool deck of L.A.'s Line Hotel for Labor Day Weekend. Choi provided the mise-en-place; Jarobi secured the celebrity DJs, including hip-hop legends Jazzy Jeff and Cash Money. The success of the 3-day poolside barbecue dwarfed anything Jarobi had done.

One evening Jarobi removed his apron and was approached by a posse of thick-necked, tattooed OGs from the 'hood. "I brought everybody here," the leader said, "to show them how you always have a chance to redefine yourself." On another, Jarobi looked up from his mise to see Favreau and his teenage son walking toward him. The actor turned out to be a fan. After service, Choi and Favreau cornered Jarobi: *This was fantastic. What's your next move?*

"Food truck," Jarobi said, as much a question as it was a statement.

If that's what you want to do, Favreau said, nodding to Choi, *you're sitting with the expert. But that's not for you. You don't need to be on some food truck slaving away for 14 hours a day. You need a spot, a building to contain all the things that are about to happen to you. You need to be in the business.*

Kamilah, however, suggested something different. *You loved the event. You love to travel. Why not keep doing this?* She meant: cooking one-of-a-kind meals at different spots around the country and getting a nice fee for it.

Jarobi went to the beach to think about the right move. After driving a while, he found himself in front of a huge sign. "Welcome to El Segundo," it read. Funny, after 25 years, to have come all this way to find his wallet. To be touring still, not rapping but cooking. Maybe he was going somewhere after all.

Recipe for Success

Commit to setting your station and reducing impediments to your movements and activities. Remove friction.

CLEANING AS YOU GO

A chef's story: The bloody *stagiaire*

ONE MORNING in the summer of 2006, Wylie Dufresne walked through the downstairs prep kitchen of his restaurant on Manhattan's Lower East Side, wd-50, to find a young *stagiaire*—a kind of "guest employee" in the kitchen, there to learn a bit and leave—standing in the midst of what looked like a bloody mess.

"What are you doing?" he asked her.

"I'm juicing beets," she replied, her apron, the floor, and the counter spattered with the results.

"Oh yeah?" Dufresne asked. "Who's winning?"

"I think it's a draw," she said.

Dufresne raised an eyebrow. "You think? Maybe not."

The chef shook his head and walked away, leaving Samantha Henderson to ponder the implications of the chef's sarcasm in the sticky red pool of her own making.

Unlike most other *stagiaires,* Henderson had not come from a culinary school. A willowy, quiet 25-year-old, she had never worked in a kitchen and possessed few culinary skills. She had waited tables at a restaurant and hated it. Henderson still worked a full-time job just 16 blocks away on Broadway—at Scholastic, the multi-billion-dollar children's publishing behemoth and the home of Harry Potter and Clifford the Big Red Dog. It was the type of gig her fellow graduates in the English department at New York University coveted. Henderson had moved from Georgia to Green-

wich Village to write fiction and study Shakespeare, Nabokov, Paul
Auster, Keats, and Donne. She adored Irish poetry because
although it could be sad, it wasn't defeatist. They took their sor-
row, transformed it, and moved on.

But the job at Scholastic hadn't matched her dream of reading
through a slush pile of manuscripts to find the next great novel. She
worked in the editorial offices of *Math* and *DynaMath* magazines,
matching five-digit multiplication and long division equations with
formulaic copy and kid-appropriate adjectives like "wacky" and
"cool." She liked her bosses and colleagues—all of them smart,
funny, interesting people. But after 3 years, Henderson withered
from boredom. To give herself a challenge, she ran marathons. The
exercise made her ravenous. She started cooking for herself. Then,
from cooking, a surprise: the genuine satisfaction of having made
something from start to finish. She watched episodes of Jamie Oliver's *The Naked Chef*. She bought the *Larousse Gastronomique*, a
1,000-page technique and recipe encyclopedia with a forward by
Escoffier himself. Henderson wanted to know how things worked.
What, for example, do butter and flour do to milk if you keep
cooking them together? She experimented. What little money she
had, she splurged on trying ethnic cuisines and new restaurants.
She'd eat something new and try to figure out how to make it.
Finally, she called her parents and told them she had made the
decision to apply to culinary school.

"You don't know that you want to do this for a living," her
mother warned. "Why don't you see if you can hack it in a kitchen
first before you spend another 20 grand on school?"

Mom had a point. So on her lunch breaks from Scholastic,
Henderson walked to different restaurants in Manhattan and
asked whomever could be lured from the kitchen if they'd let her
come in and work for free. She had no idea that she was asking to
stage; she had never heard the word. But she did realize how
unlikely it was for a good kitchen to employ someone with her
lack of experience. Nevertheless, she pushed open the front door
of wd-50, a restaurant that received two stars from the *New York
Times* when it opened in 2003 for its "intellectual approach" to

food, "exhilarating" experiments, and Wylie Dufresne's "total lack of fear."

A sous-chef named Mike Sheerin emerged from the kitchen to receive Henderson. "Can I come and hang out for a couple of days a week in the kitchen?" Henderson asked. "I'll do anything you want. I'll pick herbs. I'll peel potatoes."

"We don't use that many potatoes here," Sheerin replied, looking for a way out. Dufresne later remarked that Sheerin must have been in a good mood that day, because Sheerin went on to say: "Come next Saturday. Wear some comfortable pants and clogs, and bring a chef's knife."

Samantha Henderson went to a housewares store, bought the cheapest knife she could find, and showed up for work. Sheerin put her in the downstairs prep chamber, far from the expansive, gleaming service kitchen upstairs.

Henderson honored her promise. She juiced beets. She picked spinach. She cut vegetables. And despite the messes she made, eliciting the occasional quip from Dufresne, she loved the work. Henderson decided that she wouldn't go to culinary school; she'd quit Scholastic, find a real job in a restaurant kitchen somewhere, and learn by doing. Dufresne and Sheerin offered to help her find a gig. A few months later, on her last day at wd-50, Dufresne called Henderson into his office.

"I know where you're going to work," he announced.

"Where?" Henderson asked.

"Here," Dufresne said. "We're going to give you a job."

Henderson secured her place in wd-50's kitchen on reliability and attitude alone. Dufresne was saying *I will be your teacher,* just as Alfred Portale and Jean-Georges Vongerichten had done for him.

In the months that followed, the hardest thing for Henderson to learn was the fundamental lesson behind those mangled beets, one that Vongerichten himself taught Dufresne.

"If you can't clean, you can't cook," Jean-Georges told him. "You cook the way you look."

For Dufresne, that maxim meant more than making one's bones

with menial work, though earning the privilege to cook was a time-honored practice. It signified something more than sanitation, though that, too, was of particular importance. It involved more than the physical repercussions of clutter in one's workstation, of not having the room to cut and cook. Rather, the act of cleaning spaces maintained an optimal *mind state* for a cook. Thus the most important notion about cleaning was *when* cooks were supposed to do it: *all the time.*

Cleaning as you go, not waiting to clean, separated true chefs and cooks from everyone else. If Samantha cleaned her cutting board and station as she made messes or mistakes, her environment would always be optimal for success and her system would remain intact. If she waited to clean and let things accumulate, she'd lose her attention to detail in a restaurant where the details mattered. You can't tend to the details if you can't see them. If she waited to clean, she'd also make cleaning harder and more time-consuming with every passing minute, as the detritus of her workday began to ossify into a culinary archaeology that she would have to excavate herself. New cooks make more messes than seasoned ones, so cleaning wasn't only doubly difficult for Sam, it was doubly important.

When Henderson worked at Scholastic, she kept a tidy desk. In the kitchen she put stuff everywhere—on herself, the cutting board, the counter, the appliances, and the floor. The floor thing made Dufresne crazy, especially when he saw cooks *deliberately* sweep a mess off their station and onto the tile instead of into their cupped palm. He'd send a dishwasher right in there with a broom, sweeping right over their feet. If a cook dared complain—*Hey! I'm working here!*—Dufresne would tell him: *I won't make him come over here if you don't give me a reason to.*

Sam Henderson learned by watching the other cooks. She picked up little techniques. Like if she was peeling a bunch of parsnips, instead of peeling them onto her cutting board or into a garbage can—a risky, unsanitary habit—she put a half-sheet tray down on *top* of her cutting board and peeled the parsnips over the tray. Then when she finished, she could pick up the whole tray and toss the peels in the trash. *Voilà*, clean cutting board. She learned that the tighter she arranged her station at the start, the cleaner she could keep it. And working clean meant that she had to be assiduous about putting every ingredient and tool back where it had been before she grabbed it. The moment she stopped cleaning, things spun out of control. If she made a mess on the counter—where it could be transferred to her sleeve, her apron, a bottle, a plate—she wiped it down right away and left nothing behind. She slowed her overall pace to clean better, because although delay was bad, it wasn't as instantly observable as a messy station. Wylie and Mike would bust her chops the minute they caught her slipping into disorder, and Henderson found the kitchen's social pressure potent. If the guy next to you was working clean and you weren't, that hurt your pride. If you spilled stuff onto his station, you were being rude. A messy station was *shameful*.

As Henderson cultivated the cleaning reflex, she noted the more subtle changes that Dufresne knew she would. *You cook the way you look.* The cleaner her station, the faster she worked. The cleaner her station, the better her product. Her attention to detail deepened. The aesthetics of a clean station pleased her. She liked folding her side towel and replacing it at the top of her cutting board. She liked the look of the spotless counter. She strove to make it through an entire service without a spot on her apron, to look just like her fellow cooks. It made her feel better about her food, about herself. Plus, she stopped getting blasted by Wylie and Mike. They could teach her things now that she didn't have to figure out what to do with her body and her space. She learned to taste, to deconstruct recipes, to *make* them, becoming part of wd-50's engine of innovation. Dufresne now asked her to teach the things she knew to the new *stagiaires*. *Make a mess, clean it now, move on.*

After 3 years, when Dufresne figured Henderson had learned all she could at wd-50, he sent her off to *stage* elsewhere. She cooked for a while at Mugaritz outside San Sebastian in Spain, and then in some renowned restaurants in Chicago. But in 2011, when Dufresne needed a sous-chef, he called Sam.

For 2 years Henderson was Dufresne's right hand in the kitchen, until he opened a second restaurant, Alder, that needed his attention. That's when he promoted Sam Henderson to *chef de cuisine*. In the *New York Times*, he dubbed Henderson a kitchen ninja.

"Super strong," he called her.

She needed to be: The beet-bloodied *stagiaire* would now be running his kitchen.

WHAT CHEFS DO, WHAT CHEFS KNOW

Chefs work clean

For the chef, the first stage of mise-en-place is readiness—make your plan, gather your resources, arrange your space.

Then you cook.

What happens in these next moments is the second stage and true test of mise-en-place. Do the objects you've so carefully arranged go back to their rightful places, or does the station you've set become chaotic?

Even the most refined systems become useless unless maintained. It is not enough to find a "right place" for everything. Cooks can't use a static system; the system must move. So the real work of mise-en-place isn't *being* clean, but *working* clean: keeping that system of organization no matter how fast and furious the work is.

For chefs, cleaning as you go is a commitment to keeping order through disorder.

Chefs clean everything

The cutting board is the holy of holies, with its own articles of faith. Chefs believe nothing but food should ever touch the cutting board—not plates, not pots, not pans, nothing that can contaminate the board or spread a mess elsewhere. (Many Japanese cooks consider the cutting board sacred; when Bobby Flay jumped atop his board during a televised battle in 2000, his competitor Masaharu

Morimoto retorted that Flay was "not a chef.") Cooks constantly wipe the board with a moist towel; some chefs use a mild bleach or vinegar solution to avoid cross-contamination—for example, when salmonella bacteria in the juices of a chicken breast come into contact with raw vegetables.

Chefs extend this meticulousness from the cutting board to the objects around it. Michael Ruhlman devotes a section of his fond monograph of Thomas Keller's The French Laundry in *The Soul of a Chef* to the cooks' practice of wiping down bottles of cooking oil. *Why*, Ruhlman intimated, *be this fanatical?* Keller answered: Oil from the outside of the bottles transferred to fingers that then transferred to nice clean plates, making them not so nice and clean. The longer a cook waited to clean the bottles, the harder it would be to get them back to their original state.

Chefs clear their minds by clearing their space

The kind of cleaning that great chefs and cooks do transcends hygienic or aesthetic concerns. When a cook falls behind in her work—"in the weeds" or *dans la merde* (French for "in the shit")—the first thing that her chef will look for is the cleanliness of her station. Often the chef will find a cutting board littered with food scraps and juices, dirty tools lying around, garbage everywhere. *Messy station equals messy mind*, chefs say. *Clean station equals clean mind.* In the kitchen, chefs train their cooks to wipe down their stations at the first sign of confusion or panic.

When chefs and cooks talk about cleaning, the conversation often shifts to cleaning's psychological and spiritual merits. Dwayne LiPuma teaches these benefits to his young students with an analogy that hits home.

"Say you have a roommate," LiPuma begins, "and your roommate's a pig, really sloppy, unorganized, all over the place. . . . Tell me, how are you gonna feel knowing that the sink's full of stuff, there are clothes all over the place? You start to build this anxiety, your mind starts to get cluttered, you start to get a little flustered. But you won't pick it up because it's not yours, because it's not your job, right? But you get so frustrated that one day when your room-mate is at work, you clean the whole house. Now it's the way *you* want it. You sit in that chair, how's your mind? How do you feel? You're decompressed! You feel better."

LiPuma takes his students back to the kitchen: "Now you're trying to cut something and you're working around a box. You're working around dirt. All this stuff and your mind starts to close down. You start to feel closed in. You get claustrophobic. But if I can keep my station open and clean, my mind stays open and clean. I breathe beautifully, and I just cook fantastic."

It's no mistake that LiPuma cites the breath as a reason for cleaning. The breath powers athletes and artists. It underlies the great spiritual and holistic traditions of the East, like martial arts, yoga, and tai chi. In some traditions, connecting with the breath is not only healing and centering, but the highest aim of life itself.

What many chefs seem to be aiming for, then, is not cleaning for the sake of cleanliness, but rather cleaning as a spiritual prac-tice. Chefs see a direct correlation not only between the condition of one's station and one's mind, but also between the tolerance of dirt and the tolerance of distractions, and between the disposition of oneself to cleaning and to responsibility *in general*. Thus the idea of "working clean" is not only personal but collective. Our roommate's mess becomes our mess. Our mess becomes our coworker's mess. This collective responsibility is why our best kitchens often look and feel cleaner than our best hospitals. The chefs *themselves*—the "doctors" of the kitchen—do the cleaning.

This holistic view of cleaning—that it should be integrated into every moment of a chef's work, and that cooks clean not just for one but for all—creates the foundation for excellence in the profes-sional kitchen.

OUT OF THE KITCHEN

No chef works clean primarily for the spiritual benefits. He works clean because unclean food can kill people.

The chef's fastidiousness may seem foreign to those of us who work in offices because we aren't forced to clean. And many chefs don't clean when they're not forced to, either. Wylie Dufresne's kitchen was among the most pristine I had seen. But Dufresne didn't apply mise-en-place to his other workspace, his office—not only because his considerable willpower was tied up in maintaining the kitchen, but also because the physical imperative to clean his office simply wasn't there. No one will die because our desks are messy. But we, the deskbound, miss the huge mental and spiritual benefits of *working clean* in our spaces and systems.

Remember our friend Jeremy? (See "Chaos: How We Work without Mise-en-Place" on page 23.) So many of his problems during his dark day in the office could be solved by this one behavior, cleaning as you go. Jeremy fixates so much on *drilling the work out* that he doesn't take care of his own physical, virtual, psychological, and physiological territory, the places from which all that work arises. He's never conceived of working clean. Why take the time for something so frivolous when each minute spent tidying is a minute of good work lost?

But when Jeremy "works dirty," he loses time: 2 minutes looking for his notebook, 15 minutes finding that sheet of price quotes, 20 minutes solving someone else's computer problem, 10 minutes searching for one e-mail, 5 minutes sifting through his inbox for receipts, 15 minutes walking around without thinking about where he's going, plus all the delays and extra work he's caused himself through carelessness, from chasing those release forms to an impending and tense meeting with Stephen, who is now troubled by Jeremy's performance. Some brief moments taken to restore order (returning things to their proper places, putting paper in marked files) totaling no more than 10 minutes' time could have saved him nearly 90 minutes, plus the harder-to-calculate but significant cost of the tension between him and his boss and colleagues. Working clean on a regular basis would likely take only seconds in transitions between tasks. But those seconds can make the difference between supporting and disappointing people, between success and failure.

I recall how my desk used to look before mise-en-place, and I see piles of work left in place for weeks and sometimes months, work that I let ossify. I left those objects on my desk—papers, books, envelopes, random household items—with the best of intentions, to remind me to get them done. But these things clogged my professional arteries. They made my desk a place that I was slightly but perceptibly more reluctant to go. They also made my organization tools—my list and calendar—less effective because I knew that they weren't comprehensive, that there were some items I deemed "too important" to go there and thus left lying about where I could see them. They made the job of cleaning more difficult because exceptions to cleaning breed ever *more* exceptions to cleaning. That's the reason why the game of counting seconds and minutes spent or saved by cleaning misses the point. One simply cannot foretell the cost of chaos and mess.

A story: I came home one day and went to throw something in the kitchen trash can while my wife was cooking dinner. My wife had placed an empty baking pan atop it. I grabbed the pan to move it and felt my flesh sizzling. I spent the next 24 hours dealing with second-degree burns on four fingers, time and pain that could have been spared if I'd had the *presence* to think before I grabbed the pan, or if my wife (whom I adore and who felt horrible about this) had taken the extra few seconds of *process* to put that hot pan in a safe place. The incident left us both feeling stressed and distracted. A few seconds of cleaning can save hours of trouble.

In the office, working clean is a choice, not an imperative. But when we know the true benefits of cleaning as you go, our choice to do so can transform everything about our work lives.

EXERCISES: SKILLS TO LEARN

COME TO ZERO

The essence of mise-en-place is *everything in its right place*. But if we don't move and use those things we've so carefully arranged, we can't work. And we can't maintain our system if we don't cultivate the discipline to replace those things where they belong.

In yoga, practitioners develop a habit of coming back to a neutral posture between each exercise. We'll call this neutral state *zero point*. The concept of zero point can help us maintain our systems.

In the previous chapter, you established your physical and digital workstations. You arranged them in the manner that best helps you do the work. This is your "zero point" for each of these workspaces. Now try this exercise to get you in the habit of coming back to zero point.

For 1 day, every hour on the hour that you are at your desk, take 1 minute to reset both your physical and digital workspace, no matter what you are currently doing.

In the physical realm, your tools (stapler, phone, pens) return to their homes; your papers slide back in your folders or file

boxes, your folders go back in the files, your books back on the shelves.

In the digital realm, zero point means closing windows, folders, or applications.

You will, of course, have to resist the temptation to keep things out or open because you may use them again "soon." Many times, "soon" isn't quite soon enough, and you end up with a messy desk again.

KITCHEN PRACTICE: CLEANING AS YOU GO

The next time you prepare a meal, challenge yourself to do the following:

- As you cook, replace ingredients and tools exactly where you picked them up. Pot holders go back on the hook, not on the counter. Tongs remain near the stove, not across the kitchen by the sink. The sugar returns to the shelf right after you use it.

- Between cooking actions, clean whatever pots, pans, and dishes have accumulated in the sink.

- Every few minutes, wipe down the counter and stove, and straighten your tools and ingredients.

Because our movements can become so unconscious in the kitchen and elsewhere, it's effective and even fun to have a friend watch and coach our moves. We can learn how difficult it is to maintain a system, but that we can develop strong habits to do so.

HABITS: BEHAVIORS TO REPEAT

PRACTICE PROJECT HYGIENE

Develop a clear sense of the borderlines between individual projects and between the segments of your day by *resetting the table*.

Try not to begin a new project without putting the old one

away. Keeping your e-mail program open while you focus on a creative task may seem harmless. But odds are you'll hear a chirp from the program and you'll be tempted to check it. Closing e-mail takes a few seconds, as will reopening it. But it will likely save you time and headspace.

On to the next transition: Let's say you don't finish your creative task by the time your next appointment arrives. You'll be tempted to leave the papers on your desk or leave that document open on your computer desktop. Don't do that. Will you lose a few seconds closing the document? Sure you will. But you stand to gain much more than that in your return to zero point: You'll have the clear headspace that comes from a clean workspace. You won't have that report yelling at you from your desk. You won't risk it being buried under other projects and documents. You won't be able to fool yourself—*look at me, I'm so busy!*—into thinking that work is actually being done when it isn't. You will have to put projects away, thus encouraging yourself to schedule more discrete time to actually finish them.

Making distinctions between discrete tasks by resetting the table creates important boundaries between individual tasks and is a great way to clean as you go.

DEVELOP A REPERTOIRE OF CLEANING TACTICS

We don't wipe down our workstations like chefs do their cutting boards. But giving our desks an occasional dusting or straightening can do wonders for our state of mind and our work.

Dusting and wiping. The difference between a clean and a dusty desk is subtle, but the subliminal effects are huge. Always have a duster and a wiping cloth in your tool kit. Buy a duster that's easily washable in soap and water, or else buy a disposable duster system like Swiffer. You can also keep a cloth or disposable wipes at the ready.

Kichiri, or straightening. In the Japanese culinary tradition, the apprentice, or *oi-mawashi*, must demonstrate proficiency in *kichiri*, or making things perfectly straight, with objects at parallel or right angles to each other. *Kichiri* means "exactly."

Straightening the items on your desk, especially during transition times, is like a beginner's cleaning practice. Pile-o-maniacs and sticky note addicts, if afraid to actually put their work away, can begin their cleaning practice by simply straightening the items on their desk: You just take all that stuff and make everything neat. You create visual order out of disorder.

New York–based designer and artist Tom Sachs practiced straightening while working in famed architect Frank Gehry's furniture workshop. According to Sachs, a janitor named Andrew Kromelow had taken to cleaning cluttered work surfaces by spreading everything out and then arranging tools and other objects either parallel or perpendicular to each other, everything at right angles. Since Gehry was designing furniture for a company called Knoll at the time—and since that furniture was angular itself—Kromelow called the technique *knolling*. Sachs later codified it as follows:

1. Scan your environment for materials, tools, books, etc., which are not in use.

2. Put away everything not in use. If you aren't sure, leave it out.

3. Group all "like" objects.

4. Align or square all objects to either the surface they rest on, or the studio itself.

Sachs made knolling a part of the system of organization for his own studio.

Straightening creates quick, visible structure and reveals things that would have otherwise remained hidden.

Containerizing. For tools and loose items that make a regular appearance on your desk but need to be handy—like headphones or cell phones or wallets—purchase small boxes or trays in which to quickly place and retrieve those objects.

A chef's reprise: Exit the *stage*

Chef Wylie Dufresne transformed a Lower East Side bodega into a Zen monastery of molecular gastronomy. But by 2014, the Manhattan neighborhood that Dufresne helped revitalize with wd-50 was rapidly gentrifying. Developers snapped up empty parcels and old buildings around him to erect a condominium. Dufresne wanted to stay. The developers wanted him out.

While Dufresne fought, Sam Henderson and the staff at wd-50 tried to ignore the rumors, both in the restaurant and online, and keep working. Henderson had another job on her mind, one she had to keep secret from Wylie: coordinating a surprise dinner party for him in April, celebrating the restaurant's 11th anniversary. This epic modernist feast would be cooked by nearly two dozen of the world's finest chefs, including Iñaki Aizpitarte, René Redzepi, Gabrielle Hamilton, Daniel Boulud, and David Chang, each creating his or her own version of a Dufresne dish. Henderson felt like a *stage* again, surrounded by icons she had dreamed of meeting, and yet she had to tell these men and women where to stand and when to cook, and to make sure that they didn't make a mess of her kitchen.

The surprise party was a smash, with Wylie's mentor, Jean-Georges Vongerichten, in attendance; but it also turned out to be the prelude to a long goodbye. In June, Dufresne announced that he would fight no more: wd-50 would close in November. What happened in those intervening 5 months astonished Sam Henderson.

"Instead of the crew donning their life vests and jumping ship," Henderson recalled, "everybody stayed put and did their job better than ever." Alumni like Mike Sheerin, Simone Tong, and J.J. Basil returned to cook, and Dufresne's chef friends came to dine. "The last two nights were some of the best services we've ever had."

On the last night, the cooks hugged, cried, cleaned, and drank. Many of them returned in the days that followed to help Dufresne tear the kitchen apart, and attended the auction where the plates they wiped with care were sold for 50 cents apiece and the appliances they scrubbed until gleaming were dragged out by gloved laborers. It broke Henderson's heart to watch.

But being a former writer, she knew that an ending gives a story its meaning. The way wd-50 ended—in its prime, surrounded by family—earned it an indelible spot in the history of global cuisine. Sad but not defeated, Henderson saw the ending was a new beginning. The restaurant would remain with her in more ways than one. Former sous-chef J.J. Basil was now her fiancé, and they planned to open up a place of their own.

She cleaned up, moved on, left nothing behind.

Recipe for Success

Commit to maintaining your system. Always be cleaning.

MAKING FIRST MOVES

A chef's story: The pan handler

DRIVING BACK to New York City after a Thanksgiving dinner upstate, Chef Josh "Shorty" Eden took a detour. He pulled off the Palisades Parkway in New Jersey and headed toward the home of his buddy Kamaal—the name that the rapper Q-Tip's closest friends now called him. Eden dropped off a tray of leftovers, some roasted root vegetables. He left with a new employee.

Eden didn't think twice about offering Jarobi White a job. The chef needed bodies for his kitchen at August, the restaurant in Manhattan's West Village where he himself had just been hired. Eden liked helping friends. He met Q-Tip at his previous restaurant, Shorty's 32, and he had gotten to know Tip's erstwhile bandmate soon thereafter. They had all haunted the same downtown clubs in the 1980s and '90s, and they shared mutual friends, including Michael Rapaport, the actor who would soon direct the documentary on Q-Tip and Jarobi's group, A Tribe Called Quest. Eden wanted to help Jarobi go legit.

"If you're going around New York telling people you're a chef, don't just *say* you are. Do it," Eden told him.

Hiring Jarobi meant breaking him down, forcing him to unlearn all the bad habits he had accumulated in the course of his career. *Wear an apron, Jarobi. Make sure your braids are up, Jarobi. Don't eat breakfast at your station, Jarobi.*

In the heat of service, cooks pursue the quickest route between taking an order and putting a plate in the window. Like all cooks, Jarobi took shortcuts. Eden tried to show him what shortcuts he could and couldn't take. Eden went for as many corny analogies to the music world as possible: *How many times did you cut that song before you put that record out? Slow down.* Or: *Learn how to fix things. When the show starts and you forget a line, do you stop and start over? No, you find your way through it.* Eden didn't care about Jarobi's semi-celebrity. When Jarobi messed up, Eden yelled at him just like he would anyone else. *You're supposed to be making my job easier, not harder.* Then he taught Jarobi the right way to do it.

Eden invested months training Jarobi, but the hours expended early on started to pay off. Eden put him on lunch service. The apprentice improved. Jarobi climbed through the stations. Then came the morning that Eden decided he could sleep late. Why? Because *Jarobi was in the kitchen, handling things.*

Jarobi worked for Eden for 3 years, until August closed. He left a bona fide New York cook. More than that, Jarobi had joined a noble family of chefs, a direct lineage that Eden could trace for him all the way back to France, beginning with Fernand Point, viewed by many as the successor to Escoffier in the evolution of French cuisine. Point trained Louis Outhier and Paul Bocuse. And a student of Outhier and Bocuse—a young Alsatian chef named Jean-Georges Vongerichten—brought that training with him to America, where in 1993 he met a hustling 23-year-old cook just out of the French Culinary Institute named Josh Eden. Now Eden had passed that training on to Jarobi White.

Eden mentored White in the same way that Vongerichten had mentored him. Jarobi called Eden his "Yoda"; Eden worshipped Jean-Georges: At the age of 29, Vongerichten earned four stars from the *New York Times* for his cooking at the Drake Hotel's restaurant, Lafayette. Then he took that food out of the hotel and into his first restaurant, JoJo, leaving the stuffiness and the high price behind. After Eden secured a spot low on the totem pole in JoJo's kitchen, he convinced Vongerichten that he could be useful by scouring the farmers' markets of New York every day for the freshest produce. Vongerichten bought a van for Eden's errands. Eden drove that van until he totaled it.

Eden hadn't ripened yet and still required more energy than he generated. In Vongerichten's kitchen, *chef de cuisine* Didier Virot dubbed the stocky, compact cook "Shorty." The nickname stuck. Vongerichten relentlessly criticized Eden's skills and moves. On fish station, Eden overcooked a piece of salmon, and the chef was all over him for the rest of the week. But Vongerichten always followed a slap with a caress. On Friday night, Eden cooked an end-of-service meal for Vongerichten, Virot, and the sous-chefs. The chef came down the line and threw his arm around Eden.

"I've been screaming at you every day. You're doing a good job. I just want you to learn."

"Chef, you never need to apologize to me," Eden replied. "I'm here to learn."

Vongerichten produced a bowl of mousseron mushrooms. "Let me show you how to cook these like my chef taught me," he said. Thus Josh Eden inherited the knowledge of another culinary legend and Bocuse contemporary, Chef Paul Haeberlin.

Above all his lessons, Vongerichten taught Eden the value of time. Rather than the simplistic notion that "every moment counts," Vongerichten implied a more esoteric concept: The first moments count more than later ones.

On a busy night when the kitchen got pounded and the orders flew in, Vongerichten repeated a mantra: "Guys, pans on!" *Before you do anything else, make the first move: Get some damn pans on the stove, turn on the heat, and get them hot.*

The first reason for Vongerichten's admonition was mental: Working at such a fast pace, cooks need reminders. Each pan, in effect, becomes a placeholder for an order. A cook can look at the stove and see, at a glance, a proxy for the work that needs to be accomplished. The second reason was physical: To properly brown vegetables and proteins—to get that wonderful, crisp, and delicious external texture—the pan and the oil in it need to be hot *before* the food goes in. It takes a certain amount of time to heat a pan, a minute or two. There are no shortcuts when it comes to that process. So if a cook puts a pan down the moment an order comes in, he can get it hot while preparing or seasoning the ingredients that will go inside of it. But if he doesn't get that pan on, and preps the ingredients first, he'll still have to wait around for a minute after seasoning, like a jerk, for the pan to get hot. Those 2 seconds just cost him a minute later on. *The first moments count more than later ones.*

It took a while for Eden to catch on, even after he had graduated from JoJo to become saucier at Jean-Georges. One evening Eden was getting crushed on his station. Working his way through a backlog of orders, he wasn't getting the food out fast enough, and tables were waiting for their meals. Upstairs came Jean-Georges's recently promoted sous-chef, Wylie Dufresne.

"Shorty," Dufresne said, "when you're getting beat like that, you've got to throw a couple of extras in the pan. If you lose one at the end of the night, you lose one. Would you rather get screamed at or would you rather have the food ready to go?"

Dufresne was telling Eden that if the orders were coming in faster than he could manage, and he couldn't even manage to get new pans on the range, then at the very least throw some extra portions in the pans he did have cooking. It was a shortcut, yes. "Sandbagging," crowding the pan and thereby reducing the heat, might change the texture and flavor of the dish. Cooking off too much protein in advance might waste food and money. Dufresne was counseling Eden that it was better to get screamed at by Vongerichten at the end of the night for raising his food cost than to enrage the staff and the customers by not having the food ready when it needed to be.

To be ready, you have to make first moves.

WHAT CHEFS DO, WHAT CHEFS KNOW

Chefs move now

How do we start? The principle of making first moves is the chef's answer to that question, but it's universal wisdom about how to begin any project that involves a series of tasks.

My own chef—the master from whom I learned to practice and teach yoga 20 years ago—had a saying: *When the time is on you, start, and the pressure will be off.* I thought he was talking about momentum—like writing the first sentence, making the first phone call, or rising up out of my chair to have a difficult conversation. I didn't grasp what my teacher was truly saying until years later when I started spending hours in professional kitchens. He was trying to teach me a more subtle and profound notion about the nature of time: *The present has incalculably more value than the future.* An action taken *now* has immeasurably more impact than a step taken later because the reactions to that action have more time to perpetuate. Furthermore, because our mind state has a huge effect on how we perceive time, acting in the present releases psychological pressure and opens up more time. *Starting is, in effect, a shortcut.* To mash metaphors: A stitch in time causes a wrinkle in time.

"We're in the weeds all day long," Eden says. "But when service begins, service is easier, because we've done all our hard work already."

The first few moments of your day or minutes of your project are crucial. They matter more than any others. A minute spent now may save 10 minutes, 20 minutes later on. The seasoned chef or cook—with an unquenchable thirst to shorten the distance between "here" and "beer"—seizes those first moments for everything they're worth.

Chefs move by marking

In the kitchen, orders don't arrive in a nice, steady stream. The work comes in waves, often at a pace that is too much for the mind to handle. At some point during a busy service, orders will flood in faster than a cook's ability to process them. Cooks in the weeds barely have time to reference the printed orders, on little curls of paper called dupes. Nor can they remember all the chef's or expediter's verbal commands. So cooks make first moves by setting reminders of the things that need to be done, especially when the things that need to be done arrive all at the same time.

To do this, cooks place a marker object in their visual field for each item to be accomplished. Getting a pan onto the stove is one way to make that first move. Placing raw ingredients on a platter or plate or cutting board is another.

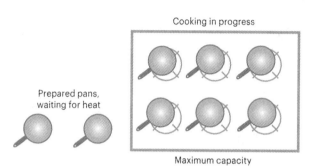

Cooking in progress

Prepared pans, waiting for heat

Maximum capacity

Chefs move in dual time

Many of us live by the anti-procrastination aphorism, "Do the worst first." Organization guru Stephen Covey gave us a related mantra, "First things first." The thought behind both of these phrases is *do the thing that's the hardest or most important early, while you have the time and energy*. It's in this spirit that new culinary students rush into the kitchen thinking about executing the most difficult tasks—intricate knife cuts and complex preparations that need extra time and attention. Then, having done the "worst" first, their stomachs drop when they realize they should have done something *else* first, something rather quick and easy: *Turn the oven on.*

We hold a linear, one-dimensional concept of time. Along this timeline, we order our tasks: *First we do this, then we do that.* Much of the literature about productivity focuses on *how* we do this ordering. Do we put the most urgent items first, or the most important? Do we do first what can be completed quickly, or do we give our first moments to things that need quality time?

In contrast, chefs and cooks cultivate a two-dimensional concept of time. A chef thinks this way: In the foreground are the projects that need my presence: my hands, my mind, my body. But in the background are the projects that don't need my continued presence, but need me to start or maintain them.

I call "hands-on" time *immersive time,* because the projects that happen in it are wholly executed by me and happen largely independent of external processes and other people. *The vegetables won't chop themselves.* Hands-on, immersive time aligns with *creative* work—activity with which we engage fully. I call "hands-off" time *process time,* because the tasks and projects therein are dependent on and linked to external processes. Some of those processes are impersonal: *The rice needs a certain amount of time to simmer;* other processes are interpersonal: *Joe needs the chicken stock from me so he can prepare the sauce.* Hands-off, process time aligns with *management* work—engaging with external objects, processes, or people.

Immersive time is worth its face value. Five minutes of my energy now equals 5 minutes of my energy later. *I can chop the vegetables for garnish now, or I can chop them 5 minutes before service.* Process time, however, can be worth much more than it seems. Consider the consequences of not jump-starting a physical process: *The 2 minutes I save now by not preparing the rice is not just 2 minutes I must still spend later on, but also the 15 minutes I will have to wait for the rice to cook if I wait until I need it, plus the cost in minutes, energy, and resources of all the other delays in the kitchen arising from that absent pot of rice.* When a task in the present unlocks a cascade of work that other people do on our behalf, the worth of process time increases and becomes harder to measure. *If I don't take 5 minutes now to show Joe how to work the equipment, and instead show him 5 hours from now, he will spend 5 hours not doing that work. And, in 5 hours, my 5 minutes will be worthless because there is no more time for Joe to do the work. The delayed 5 minutes cost me 5 hours.*

Great chefs maintain a constant if often unconscious awareness of the dual nature of work time: hands-on and hands-off. Immersive time and process time. Creative work and management work. Chefs know the importance of making time to immerse themselves in creative work. But they also understand that some small and

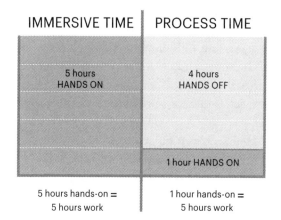

tedious tasks have the potential to launch powerful processes—unleashing huge amounts of energy, time, and resources—as long as they start those tasks *first*. Chefs perpetually make first moves on those two levels.

Some tasks, however, can be done *too* soon. "You have to know what to prep first," says Jean-Georges Vongerichten. "You start by butchering—deboning, filleting, making your portions. All that has to be done first thing in the morning. Then you peel the vegetables, make sauces with bone and vegetable stocks. Then the last thing you do is chop your fragrances: the lemongrass, mushrooms, and fresh herbs." Sometimes Vongerichten sees young cooks working in reverse. "They'll fill up a container with chopped parsley at 8:00 a.m., and by dinner service the parsley is dry." The handling of fragile, fragrant herbs can make the difference between four stars and no stars, and speaks to the power of even a small dose of mental mise-en-place. Everything has its right place *and* its right time.

OUT OF THE KITCHEN

Who hasn't felt the sting of a forgotten e-mail—one that would have taken us a few seconds to answer when we received it but now because of our delayed reply has cost us an opportunity or created extra work? Or realized we could have that thing we need right now if we had only made a simple phone call earlier? Or delayed giving our quick feedback on a project only to realize later that the whole thing stagnated for days, with everyone waiting for us to act, while we worked on something supposedly more important?

Even if we haven't articulated the concept for ourselves, we've all experienced the dual nature of immersive and process time and its repercussions. Making first moves engages the power of time in three ways and helps us work clean with priorities.

First, a first move can serve as a placeholder or a *mark*. When we don't have time to execute in the moment, a mark put in the right physical or digital place ensures that we won't forget an action and can subtly tilt us toward the task to be done.

Second, making first moves creates *momentum*. The first move compares to a *beachhead*, a military term signifying the most difficult first step of an invasion by sea. In our case, making the first move creates an initial staging area for a project, a foundation necessary for further progress. If you can't act in full now, make one small move toward completion.

On the highest level, making first moves results in *multiplication*. Investing the present moment with action can save multiple moments in the future. Mastering the art of compounding time requires a fluency in time's dual nature. Making first moves, cultivating a sense of *immersive* and *process* time, means acting immediately to set processes in motion and multiply your power and productivity.

EXERCISES: SKILLS TO LEARN

DISCERNING IMMERSIVE TIME FROM PROCESS TIME

How do you know if a task needs immersive or process time?

In principle, any task that requires you to be "hands-on" is immersive; any task that you can briefly start or maintain and then be "hands-off" is process.

In practice, however, the difference may not be so easy to discern. How brief is that "briefly" I mention above? For me, it usually takes 10 to 15 minutes before my brief attention to a "hands-off" project becomes something that feels "hands-on." Or here's another way to discern "hands-on" from "hands-off": Does the activity demand enough time to merit an entry on your schedule? Again, I find this threshold to be around 15 minutes.

Process time includes replies, quick decisions, short personal interactions, or small errands. Process tasks are the little management "noodges" that keep projects and people around you going. Process work also includes the work of delegation.

But when brief instruction becomes a longer education, when decision becomes analysis, when practical replies become a deeper conversation, those tasks require immersive time.

Process time unlocks work on your behalf; delaying process tasks will delay their benefits to you and others.

Immersive time can accord larger benefits than process time, but delaying immersive tasks doesn't necessarily delay other people or processes on your behalf.

Quickly discerning whether tasks require immersive or process time is crucial for being able to habitually make first moves, because process work is most effective when it happens *sooner*. The following quiz will help you get into that habit.

Which of the following tasks are immersive and which are process? Ask this question of each: If I don't act now, do I stop a process on my behalf? Do I stop other people's work on my behalf? If the answer is yes, write "Process." If no, write "Immersive."

1. Answer an e-mail asking for your approval on a brochure

2. Answer a request for an invoice from you

3. Come up with ideas to be pitched in a meeting happening next week

4. Write a recommendation letter for a student

5. Answer a friend's invite to a dinner party

6. Make a cold call to begin a negotiation for a partnership with another company

7. Review an e-mail containing a one-page summary of weekly sales numbers for your department

8. Read an attachment containing 10 pages of marketing recommendations for your department

Answers

1. Process—Your approval of the brochure unlocks work on your behalf. Delayed approval shuts work down.

2. Process—Your invoice unlocks payment to you. Nothing happens on your behalf until you send it.

3. Immersive—Brainstorming requires quiet, reflective, personal time. You don't block any work by doing this on your own time as long as it is completed by the meeting.

4. Immersive—Writing a thoughtful letter typically takes some dedicated creative time. What's more, delaying writing this letter doesn't block work on your behalf, though missing your student's deadline may hurt your relationship.

5. Process—Though a dinner party—and anything recreational—is by nature immersive, your decision to attend is one that can and should be made quickly to preserve the relationship and your time.

6. Process—The time needed to make one cold call is usually brief, and it unlocks potential work. Several of these calls together signify longer-term benefits and may need an immersive session.

7. Process—A one-sheet e-mail that can quickly be scanned and translated into one or two personal action items unlocks potential benefit.

8. Immersive—A long read is immersive by nature. To the extent that not reading it blocks a process from happening on your behalf, it should be completed sooner rather than later.

All the above actions have value. The purpose of this exercise is to get you to see the *hidden value* in some actions because they link to larger processes that are dependent on you.

Process tasks don't necessarily demand *immediate* action, but by their nature, they should be done or delegated in the short term. Immersive tasks can be delayed, but if left unscheduled for too long, they become blocks to your work and career.

KITCHEN PRACTICE: FIND THE SEQUENCE

Have you ever served a meal and messed up the timing, wherein one or more dishes weren't quite ready? Started the pasta too early, so it overcooked and became soggy by the time the sauce was finished? Served breakfast, but forgot to start the coffee? The next time this happens to you, take 2 minutes at the end of the meal to write out a new sequence of actions. Commit the sequence to memory and test it. The kitchen provides a laboratory for learning how process and immersive time work together.

HABITS: BEHAVIORS TO REPEAT

SCHEDULE BLOCKS OF IMMERSIVE AND PROCESS TIME

The really good stuff happens in immersive time, especially if you are in one of the creative professions. Immersive time is time to think, time to write, time to experiment, time to explore. But process time—because much of it happens with your "hands off"—actually produces more results in some cases. It's true, we need to make and honor time for immersive work. But we shouldn't undervalue process work. Here are tips for scheduling our work in dual time.

- Get in the habit of determining what tasks require immersive versus process time, as in the previous exercise. In your Action list or calendar (which we detail in Course Three of this book), denote each process task with a small "℗." Remember, anything that needs your input or feedback on a project to keep it moving forward is process work.

- Begin each day with 30 minutes of scheduled process time—starting, unlocking, and unblocking the work of others.

- Use your process time for communication, requests, and the like. Try to constrain check-ins during immersive time.

- Alternate blocks of process and immersive work throughout your day. The more management responsibilities you have, the more process time you need in your day.

- Given your responsibilities, try to attain a perfect ratio of process to creative work. A ratio for a writer will be different from that of a department manager. Start with a 1:1 formula for creative and process time, and adjust your schedule from there.

- Schedule process time directly after meetings. After a long, immersive meeting, make process time to digest and set action items in motion, whether by marking them on your schedule or Action list or by delegating them.

MAINTAINING A MOVING AND MARKING MENTALITY

Cooks move fast. They're able to process incoming requests and execute tasks with speed because they've cultivated a system for moving on tasks immediately or marking them for later.

You can also become a moving and marking machine. Here are the habits.

1. Carry a notebook and pen with you everywhere. Even if you carry a smartphone, you should always have an alternate, easy way to mark down tasks.

2. Get in the habit of marking down *every Action,* whether an incoming task is given in person or via electronic communication.

3. Move immediately on small process tasks (quick answers to e-mails, signing papers), especially during your process times.

4. Mark tasks in two ways: either directly onto your schedule or—if you don't have enough perspective on your priorities— onto your Action list for ordering and scheduling later, during your Daily Meeze. (See *Third Course: Working Clean as a Way of Life* beginning on page 221 for more details.)

5. Develop a flagging system for e-mails to mark them for action and to more easily move on those action items. For many of us, e-mail is our main channel to receive incoming tasks. In the middle of a busy day, we may not have sufficient time to mark every action item that we receive via e-mail, so the e-mails themselves must serve as marks until we are able to process them by moving on them or else transferring the action item to our schedule or list. In whatever e-mail browser you use, the flagging function can help you make first moves. The rhythm, repeated several times per day, is as follows:

    a. Scan your inbox for e-mails with action items.

    b. Flag those e-mails.

    c. Archive *all* the e-mails in the inbox, even the flagged ones. Your e-mail inbox is now empty.

    d. Now check the flagged folder for urgent items to act on immediately.

    e. Keep any flagged item you don't have time to address in the flagged folder for your Daily Meeze, where you'll either schedule the item or put it on your Action list.

    f. Unflag an e-mail once you've extracted the action item from it.

6. Remember that any action item that remains in your notebook, or your flagged folder, or on a paper or digital list, you will process during your 30-minute Daily Meeze.

With a strong Daily Meeze, you will build confidence that all your marks will always be processed later. You will also develop a sense of which tasks you can move on immediately and which seemingly "small" tasks are actually big ones in disguise. You will become a master mover and marker!

The present has incalculably more value than the future. Starting is, in effect, a shortcut.

A chef's reprise: No shortcuts

By the time Eden opened his first restaurant, Shorty's 32, the idea of making first moves had become instinctive—as it remains for him now at the reincarnation of August on Manhattan's Upper East Side. An order comes in—*bam!*—Eden's hand slaps a pan onto the stove by reflex. He doesn't think, doesn't realize it's happening. Every 2 seconds now saves him a minute later. Every pan down is the first move in a series of moves that need to happen to complete a dish. Without the first move, none of the other moves can happen. Eden tries to make as many first moves as he can. When he goes down to the storeroom, he returns with armfuls of ingredients and tools he knows he'll need for his mise-en-place, that he knows his other cooks will need. The newer members of the kitchen look at their chef like he's crazy.

But Eden knows: *Do it now, don't wait for later. Now I'm calm and steady and energetic; later I'm stressed and jittery and exhausted. Now I'm moving perfectly, which saves me time; later I'm making mistakes, which cost me time. One easy shortcut now can force me into any number of bad shortcuts later.* In service Eden urges his cooks to make the first moves, as his chef reminded him to do, and as his chef's chef did—*Guys . . . pans down!*—a lesson about time handed down through time.

Recipe for Success
Commit to using time to your benefit. Start now.

FINISHING ACTIONS

A chef's story: The delivery woman

CHEF CHARLENE JOHNSON-HADLEY was buried in mushrooms, eight cases in all. Hundreds upon hundreds of musky expressions of earth covered every available work surface around her. Charlene needed to examine and sort each of them, tossing the unusable ones and arranging the rest on sheet trays. Then she'd have to plunge batches of them into cold water, removing loose soil, twigs, and other impurities—another painstaking task. After that, they'd need to be sliced and roasted. The mountain of mushrooms would reduce to almost nothing—caramelizing, crisping, sweetening, losing their water and most of their mass—ending up as tasty slices in the mushroom soup devoured by the lunch guests at Chef Johnson-Hadley's restaurant, American Table in New York City.

Charlene couldn't focus. Her mind leapt to the other projects she needed to accomplish that day. There was a pecan tart. There were sherbets to make. A couple of times Charlene caught herself walking away from her station to start something else—the act was completely involuntary—but turned herself around before she got too far.

"Stop, Charlene," the chef said aloud. "No, you need to finish sorting these . . . "

Those mushrooms. Her subconscious was doing anything it could to get her away from them. She talked herself through the task, like her chef would have talked her through it, like her mother would have.

When the younger Charlene Johnson announced to her mother Hyacinth—a Jamaican immigrant with a master's in education—that she didn't want to finish college, she worried. After the death of a grandmother with whom she was particularly close, Charlene's pursuit of a psychology degree had left her feeling increasingly empty. She told Hyacinth that she wanted to leave academia and learn how to make pastry, and braced for the worst. Instead, her mother gave Charlene her best: "Why limit yourself? Get a culinary degree. That way, you'll get cooking as well as baking."

After attending the French Culinary Institute, Charlene moved through jobs of escalating responsibility: working with Francois Payard at his famous bistro and patisserie on New York's Upper East Side, rising from line cook to sous-chef at designer Nicole Farhi's restaurant, and taking the top chef's job at Farhi's 202 Cafe in Chelsea. But in late 2010, she saw that the former chef of Aquavit, Marcus Samuelsson, was opening a new upscale, concept restaurant in Harlem—a neighborhood whose most famous culinary attraction until that point had been the down-home soul food restaurant Sylvia's. Samuelsson, an Ethiopian raised in Sweden by adoptive parents, climbed out of some of the best kitchens of Europe into New York City. He was now making an equally improbable leap on behalf of his adopted locale: to bring fine dining uptown in a way that honored Harlem's particular cultural and racial legacy. Charlene got herself an interview and a chance to "trail" in the kitchen, meaning she could observe and have the chefs observe her, too. She had never seen so many chefs of color in a high-end kitchen. Even though she was already a full-fledged chef, she took a line cook job at the new restaurant just to be a part of Samuelsson's enterprise. He named it Red Rooster, after a speakeasy from Harlem's Renaissance period in the early 20th century.

Through the opening in 2011 and beyond, Samuelsson watched Charlene and came to know her as calm, dependable, and disciplined. One evening in the winter of 2012, about a year after she began working at Red Rooster, she felt a hand on her arm. It was Chef.

"Come with me," Samuelsson ordered.

Oh God, what did I do? Charlene wondered.

In a secluded corner of the kitchen Samuelsson told her, "I want you to know that I've noticed all of your work. I've got some things happening this year, and I want you to be a part of it. I just want you to prepare yourself."

Samuelsson made Charlene the executive chef of his restaurant in the sleek new home of the Juilliard School at Lincoln Center. The name itself was a mouthful: American Table Cafe and Bar by Marcus Samuelsson. And that job came with a catch: The kitchen was located in another building across the street, and finished food would have to be carted back and reheated for service. The operation would call on all of Charlene Johnson-Hadley's mental and physical mise-en-place.

After the opening, one food critic visited twice and enjoyed his meals before discovering that American Table was a restaurant without a kitchen on premises, a feat that he credited to "the menu created by Samuelsson and his fellow Swede-in-crime Nils Norén."

Meanwhile, in the bowels of Lincoln Center, the uncredited chef Charlene Johnson-Hadley ran the engine that made American Table go. Being chef today meant clawing her way out of this pile of mushrooms. She couldn't do it if she didn't stand still and deliver.

A half-hour later she was still coaching herself: "Yes, now we need to plunge these."

Even after years in the business honing her discipline, she found this was the hardest part of the gig, but one of the most crucial: maintaining a finishing mentality. It was too easy to give in to fatigue and frustration. It was too easy to stop or pause a project as the finish line came into view with a deluded confidence that it could be completed later. She knew that if she indulged her restlessness—even with the intention to get another project started—she would end up throwing her entire day off. If she didn't start the mushrooms, complete them; start the short ribs, complete them; start the pecan tarts, complete them; none of them would have gotten done. Charlene Johnson-Hadley respected the iron law of the kitchen: A dish that is 90 percent finished has the same worth as a dish that is zero percent finished.

WHAT CHEFS DO, WHAT CHEFS KNOW

Chefs deliver

Just as chefs have a philosophy about starting, they have a doctrine of finishing that springs from the distinctive character of their work. The very nature of the kitchen's product demands that chefs develop a finishing mentality. Dishes, for the most part, are all-or-nothing. A chef cannot serve a steak au poivre without the peppercorn sauce, at least not if she expects to keep customers who know the difference. A menu cannot promise fries on the side and fail to deliver them. And let's presume, just for the sake of argument, that the customer isn't so discerning. The customer can't be served at *all* unless the cook puts a plate in the pass. A bunch of dishes in various stages of completion are useless until at least one of them is finished. Ninety percent done is still zero percent done from the perspective of the customer. So a cook must develop a delivery mind-set.

Chefs avoid the hidden costs of stopping

The finishing imperative comes from the nature of kitchen production—churning out massive quantities of high-quality food. Finishing all that food requires a lot of repeated motion. The economy of repeated motion is the principle on which the industrial assembly line is built. Individual workers can get more work accomplished, and faster, if they do the *same* action or job repeatedly. If a worker stops, the whole line stops. We can measure the cost of the stoppage not only in minutes lost during a pause, but also in minutes spent ramping up production again. Think of someone like Chef Johnson-Hadley as an assembly line unto herself. She has a number of jobs to do. But she knows she will be more efficient if she does *one* job at a time—to *aggregate alike actions*—than if she stops and does something else, skipping from one action to another. Momentum and aggregation are key rationales for continuing with an action until it is done.

Chefs finish to clear workspace and headspace

Aside from the goal of delivering the product, the virtues of finishing are twofold.

In the physical realm, finishing yields precious space. Most cooks work in tight spaces, and their workstations must move through several phases of mise-en-place throughout the day: prep, cooking, service. A clean and efficient service is impossible when your station is still covered with the remains of bulk prep work. Finishing those actions conserves space and clears space for the next actions.

Finishing actions clears the mind as much as it clears the plate. An action once finished does not need attention or memory. An unfinished action still needs both to be completed. An accumulation of unfinished actions creates a mental clutter and a brain drain. Whether we possess the kind of mind that deals with that clutter easily or not, the cataloguing and prioritization of those remaining actions demands mental energy that could be spent elsewhere.

Jarobi White recalls cutting carrots in Josh Eden's kitchen at August, placing them in a container, and sealing the lid. *Done.*

Not done, said Chef Eden. *The container isn't labeled. It's still on your cutting board. It's not in the refrigerator. It's still on your metaphorical plate. Clean your plate.*

"I say it all the time: You start a job and you finish a job," says Eden.

Chefs begin with the end in mind

Chefs say two seemingly contradictory things. On one hand, they counsel the importance of making first moves immediately. On the other, they loathe the incomplete: *Don't start what you can't finish.*

But how can we start *and* finish everything? We can't. Chefs are saying something more subtle: "Starting" is less about doing *everything* immediately and more about creating a triage system to prioritize current and future actions. "Finishing" is not so much about completing *everything* and more about not being distracted by the periodic "starting" of other things. "Finishing" can also be stopping a project while it's incomplete but taking just an extra few seconds to wrap it up for resumption later so as to not leave loose ends hanging. What chefs attempt to avoid are *orphaned tasks*— things that take up physical and mental space because they haven't been tied up in the easiest possible form to be resumed later. And since the polarities of starting and finishing generate tension between them, we must always begin with the end in mind. When you start a project, ask one question: *How and when will I finish?*

Chef Eden has seen the consequences of failing to account for finishing when starting: "You're stuck in a kitchen 2 hours past the time you were supposed to go home because you've started 16 projects and you haven't finished one of them. And then you can't leave. Or you're throwing it all in the garbage."

The principle of finishing actions asks us to *work clean* with obligations and expectations, those that others set for us and those we hold for ourselves.

OUT OF THE KITCHEN

Finishing actions might not seem so important to those of us who work primarily with words, numbers, images, and people rather than perishables. If I don't finish an e-mail, I don't have to trash it. A half-drafted memo doesn't "go bad." But it occupies space on my physical or virtual desktop. It preoccupies my mind now, and later when I remember it's not finished. And it can slip my mind until someone or something reminds me that I'm late, that I've failed a commitment.

Better to confront the reasons why we stop before finishing and learn mental and physical techniques to push through.

Better to enjoy the temporal, physical, and mental dividends of finishing than pay the price later for not doing so.

Better to not open too many projects at a time so that I keep orphaned tasks to a minimum and give myself a fighting chance at finishing them.

And better to deal with the incomplete by finding a way to tie it up, temporarily, so that it doesn't crowd precious physical and mental space.

Says chef-author Michael Gibney: "Every time you cross something off of your list, you get a little endorphin rush. Every time you deliver, you get that thing out of your life."

The perishable and holistic nature of kitchen products and the limited time frame and repetition of kitchen production yield a culture of finishing like no other. We can integrate the principle of finishing actions into our own lives by applying ourselves to the following strategies.

Excellence is quality delivered.

EXERCISES: SKILLS TO LEARN

DEVELOPING A NOSE FOR THE FINISHABLE

Conscious finishing begins with conscious starting. Our chances of success grow when we ask ourselves "What's finishable?" at the start. We judge the finishable by two parameters: *ease* and *expectation*.

Ease is time plus energy: How quickly can we finish something, modulated by how much or how little energy we expend in that time? *Expectation* is deadline plus stakeholders: Who is waiting for our product, and when do they expect it?

- High-expectation and high-ease tasks are *finishable*.

- Low-expectation and low-ease tasks are *delayable*.

- Low-expectation and high-ease tasks are *distracting*.

- And high-expectation and low-ease tasks are the *complex* tasks that most need scheduling.

When you put these together, they form a different version of the Eisenhower Matrix.

Now remember our principle of "hands-on" immersive time and "hands-off" process time? We can complete immersive tasks on our own; process tasks require us to interact with physical

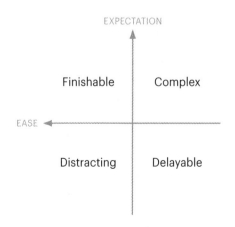

processes or other people to get benefit. Thus process tasks usually have higher expectation and, because they often take less time and thought, are easier to execute. They tend to be more "energy efficient" or productive than immersive tasks because the work that we unlock from them is actually done partly by others. Process tasks are among the "low-hanging fruit" that we should look to pick when conducting a triage for tasks to start or to finish. They compete, however, with immersive tasks that are lower in ease and expectation but higher in long-term benefit. In other words, there are beneficial things we must do that aren't easy and finishable, and those must be weighed alongside the easily finishable. The key in conscious starting is to cultivate a balance between the finishable tasks (high expectation/high ease) and the complex tasks (high expectation/low ease). This balance is the recipe for survival in the contemporary workplace.

What would a day look like that had this balance? Let's examine the "to-do" list of Sheila, a schoolteacher. Sheila has 4 hours in which to do some combination of the tasks below.

- Lesson plan for tomorrow (3 hours)

- Student assessments, half-finished, due last week (2 hours)

- Class trip forms due tomorrow (30 minutes)

- Compose e-mail for parent-teacher meetings to send later in week (1 hour)

- Go to bookstore to buy book for next semester (1 hour)

What actions should Sheila choose?

The tasks with the greatest ease (measured by *time*) are the class trip forms, the e-mail for parent-teacher meetings, and the bookstore errand.

The most expected tasks (measured by *deadline*) are the lesson plan, class trip forms, and the student assessments.

So the most finishable task (high ease/high expectation) is the class trip forms.

The most complex (low ease/high expectation) are the lesson plan and the student assessments.

Sheila can't do *both* complex tasks, so she has to choose one of them. Because she cultivates a delivery mentality, she considers both the political and practical repercussions of her decisions. On the political side, she decides that since she's already late on the assessments, *staying* late would be preferable to delivering them but then being late on a *new* piece of work (lesson plan), thereby reinforcing a track record of late work with her colleagues and superiors. On the practical side, she doesn't want to trade being prepared in the classroom tomorrow for delivering something that's already late. So she decides to deliver on the most finishable task (the class trip forms) and the more complex project (the lesson plan), for 3.5 hours of work. After slam-dunking those two, she will spend the last half-hour to deliver one-quarter of the assessments, because in this case one-quarter is better than nothing. So she's delivered on two projects and partially delivered on one, which is the best-case scenario for her both practically and politically. She has executed the finishable and complex in a balanced way for maximum benefit.

Try this thought exercise for 1 day's work, marking each task on your daily list with one of the four categories listed in the delivery matrix above, and then choosing which actions to deliver based on what yields the best combination of practical and political benefit.

KITCHEN PRACTICE: STAND AND DELIVER

The next time you find yourself struggling to get dinner on the table by a certain time, ask yourself the following questions:

■ What part(s) of this meal *can* I serve on time?

■ Can I create or prepare something quickly to let people eat while they wait?

■ What is the best sequence of actions I can take that will get the rest of this meal delivered?

A delivery mentality means constant triage: keeping a nose for the deliverable and a sense of the expectations into which you're delivering.

HABITS: BEHAVIORS TO REPEAT

WHY WE STOP AND STRATEGIES FOR CONTINUING

The problem of not finishing actions is actually a *failure to continue*. The reasons we fail—why so many of us stop a project halfway through or within sight of the finish line—vary, and each reason requires a different kind of solution.

Fatigue drains us. Facing a mountain of work can exhaust our physical and mental resources. The solution for fatigue is rest. I cannot counsel working through exhaustion as a sustainable life strategy (even though a lot of professionals both in and outside of the kitchen treat it as if it were). Pushing through, as a delivery tactic, should be occasional or temporary. If extra toil is a periodic burden, then periods of extra rest should be your reward. I do advocate the following: First, *discern fatigue from fear.* Fear often masquerades as fatigue, with a similar physiology: heavy eyelids, sore muscles, even sleepiness. Real fatigue is to be respected. Fear-related fatigue often needs a cup of coffee, a pep talk, or a kick in the pants. Second, *calculate the value of a pause.* Will your work be so much more efficient after a pause that it will make up for the time it takes to ramp up again? Or will stopping now—just a few minutes or hours away from the finish line—create even *more* work for you later? Will the mental benefits of pushing through now allow you to rest easier when the work is done? Or will working through exhaustion create more frustration and bad work? Of all the reasons to not finish, fatigue is the most legitimate. We need a consciousness of the reasons for fatigue and a measured response to it. For more strategies, see "Intentional Breaks" later in this chapter.

Fear, anger, and despair sabotage us. Sometimes we lose confidence in our ability to complete a project. At other times anger or despair about our circumstances can drain our energy and drive us from our work. Whether we doubt our skill or our will, the solution in the face of fear, anger, or despair remains the same: to *take small forward steps,* to literally put one foot in front of the other, or move your arms and keep the fingers moving. Move slowly. It takes a while to discern whether our feelings are warranted or not, or whether those fears merit a course correction. In any case, you can't correct your course without movement. So keep moving. For more strategies about grappling with fear or despair, see "Combating Perfectionism" later in this chapter.

Ambition compels us. Ambition is our inner executive chef run amok. The solution for those moments when our inner chef begins ordering us to do the next two things before we've finished the first is to *give ourselves a temporary "demotion."* The chef needs to chill out for a bit. Put yourself in the mind-set of the employee, not the boss: Until these mushrooms are done, I'm a prep cook, not a chef. Until my project is done, I'm the assembly-line worker, not the executive. Remove your freedom to do something else.

Scatteredness confuses us. We often leave tasks unfinished because our minds can't prioritize what's important. Somebody approaches us with a crisis—*their* crisis, really, not ours—and we leave to help her while our time to finish dwindles. We're struck with an idea, something that can wait, and what ends up waiting is the original project we intended to finish. Or we get giddy upon receiving a bit of inspiration for our project, and in our excitement, we can't sit still to execute. The solution for confusion is *focus:* When you feel scattered, keep your eyes, literally, on your work. Make your body steady. Keep your feet planted. Try to block out or avoid external stimuli as much as you can.

Overconfidence tricks us. We engage in magical thinking, an overestimation of our personal power and an underestimation of the rules of time and space. Overconfidence leads us to believe that we don't have to estimate the time it takes to complete a project, nor deliberately set aside the time for that work. Overconfidence is why we don't start a project until it's too late and also why we get that "finish line syndrome" mentioned earlier—for example, writing an e-mail but leaving the last few sentences or details for later. Two days later that e-mail remains incomplete and unsent on our desktop. Overconfidence rarely remembers that it takes time to ramp back up on a project once we've stopped it. The solution for overconfidence is *honesty with time,* the realization that we are all ruled by the laws of physics. Yes, sometimes we can do the impossible—fitting a week's worth of work into a day, or being hit with a stroke of genius that simplifies or transforms the tasks before us, seemingly bending time and space to our will. Don't bank on those surreal moments. They come frequently only to those who've attained a degree of mastery in their field. Time and space do bend, but they bend for the engaged, not the disengaged.

When we examine our week and see many incomplete projects, we need to realize that one of the above emotions is likely preventing us from solidifying a delivery mentality.

TIE IT UP

Sometimes we can't finish, the truly urgent arises, or we just plain run out of time. When we know that we're going to be leaving loose ends, we try to find ways to tie them up for ourselves so that our physical and mental ramp-up time is minimized.

Some strategies:

- Collect all the materials for the project and keep them in one place until you resume.

- Jot down any thoughts that are at the top of your mind that you want to remember.

- Schedule your session to resume the work, or set a reminder now to schedule one later.

- Communicate your progress to partners or stakeholders to assess what remains to be done and whether help is available now or upon resumption.

The maxim to remember: Just as you want to begin with the end or stopping point in mind, you also want to end with the beginning or resumption in mind.

For example, author Ernest Hemingway made a habit of ending every writing session with the first sentence of the section he intended to write in the following session. In 1935 Hemingway wrote: "The best way is always to stop when you are going good and when you know what will happen next." This goes not only for writing but for a pause in any kind of project, something to reduce ramp-up time at the start of the next session and continue your momentum so that no task is altogether orphaned.

ALWAYS BE UNBLOCKING

We should always be unblocking stuck projects so we can finish them. For every major goal, project, or mission, we should ask the question: What's stopping me from moving forward? What has stopped the process?

Sometimes an external process (for example, waiting for an approval) blocks us, and we must stop. But if we have the power to remove that block (for example, by sending an e-mail), our own hands can get that project rolling again. When we maintain a delivery mentality, we develop a nose for potential external blocks and try to avoid them. And if we cannot avoid them—if we must cede control—we try to work *with* those processes, removing or avoiding as many blocks as possible to our forward movement.

A great way to illustrate the concept of unblocking is something city dwellers deal with daily: commuting via mass transportation. When we travel by subway and bus, we face a succession of blocks to our forward movement, like turnstiles and lines. When we pass those blocks, we remain at the mercy of the intervals between trains or buses. So our goals at any stopping point are: (1) *minimize* the time spent waiting; and (2) *redeem* any time we must wait by using it to minimize our wait period at the next stopping point.

This *sounds* complicated, but my son grasped this principle by the time he was 5 years old.

"Daddy," he said one day on the subway platform, pulling my arm toward a set of benches. "Stand over here." Why the benches? Because he knew, like most New Yorkers do, exactly where to exit on the platform at our destination station. And why do New Yorkers memorize that? So that when we get to our destination, we reach the staircase before it gets blocked by a crowd of people. At 5, he knew that he could *redeem* the time we spent waiting at our origin in order to *minimize* the time we spent waiting at our destination. That's a combination of balanced movement, making first moves, and finishing actions. That's mise-en-place!

COMBATTING PERFECTIONISM

Perfectionism comes from either of two emotional sources: fear of failure, or despair over its impending arrival. And there are two kinds of perfectionists: those who quit their projects, and those who keep working on them forever. Both are afraid, but the former copes by stopping work, and the latter by working indefinitely.

Remember: *Striving for perfection* and *perfectionism* aren't the same thing. Both the striver and the perfectionist aim toward an ideal. But the striver knows that excellence is not about *creating* something of the highest quality; it's *delivering* something of the highest quality, with all the constraints that delivery entails—deadlines, expectations, contingencies, feedback. The chef cannot tinker forever with a dish: Customers get hungry. Food spoils. The chef *must deliver.*

In our society we've come to see speed and urgency as antithetical to quality. For the chef, the deadline is *integral* to quality. Without delivery, there's no feedback, severing the improvement loop that creates excellence. *Excellence is quality delivered.*

Deadlines compel excellence. Lorne Michaels, who has been delivering 90 minutes of influential TV comedy for more than 40 years with *Saturday Night Live,* has said: "We don't go on because we're ready. We go on because it's 11:30." And while *SNL* has produced plenty of less than perfect moments, a comedy sketch still needs to be ready by 11:30 p.m. to have a chance to be perfect. Don't let perfectionism make you miss *your* moment.

CHUNKING TIME

Try to break large projects into chunks that are finishable in the time you allot for them. Set benchmarks. For example, I know I can usually write 500 words in 1 to 2 hours. So I break writing projects down into chunks of that size, and try not to assign myself more than that amount so I can actually finish what I've started. Smaller goals lift the spirits because they make it easier for us to see the end. To recap:

1. Figure out the discrete parts of each project.

2. Build your pause points with intentionality.

3. Work intently toward those points.

INTENTIONAL BREAKS

When so many of us beg the Universe for a chance to *just get some work done,* why is it that when that time finally arrives, we often do anything we can to *escape* it?

Here's why: The process tasks we complain about are often easier to do than immersive work, and we get a little endorphin rush every time we deliver on one of those process tasks. Immersive work is harder. It doesn't yield those little rushes as often. Because it's creative and thus a reflection of ourselves, it puts our own demands and emotions front and center. Is it any wonder, then, why we abandon our creative work to chat on social media or browse the Internet?

Creativity—what we do when our hands are shaping something, whether words or numbers or designs or images or music—isn't linear. Booking yourself into some immersive time and then treating it like a 2-hour prison to attempt to squeeze every second out of it is a huge mistake. Our creative sessions need to breathe, as we do. We need mental, physical, and social breaks. Working clean with obligations and expectations means that we should strive to make breaks *intentional* ones.

The rules:

1. Any time you enter a creative session, *take as many breaks as you like* within it.

2. On a piece of paper or a spreadsheet, begin an *intentional break* log.

3. At the top, write down your start time.

4. For each break, log your in and out times on a new line.

5. Beside each break, put the reason for the break.

   - Mental (e.g., when you want to chat, browse, or when you just can't think)
   - Physical (e.g., bathroom breaks, snack breaks, stretching, or walking around)
   - Social (e.g., interruptions, chats with friends or colleagues)
   - Work (e.g., other projects)

INTENTIONAL BREAKS
TIME IN: 10:00 AM   TIME OUT: 1:00 PM

BREAKS TAKEN			
START TIME	**FINISH TIME**	**REASON**	**MINUTES**
10:10 AM	10:15 AM	Mental	0:05
10:29 AM	10:31 AM	Physical	0:02
10:45 AM	11:05 AM	Work	0:20
11:30 AM	11:35 AM	Social	0:05
12:02 PM	12:06 PM	Physical	0:04
12:20 PM	12:30 PM	Mental	0:10

WORK COMPLETED		
TOTAL TIME	**BREAK TIME**	**WORK TIME**
3:00	0:46	2:14
WORK PERCENTAGE: 74%		

6. When you are finished with your creative session, log your end time.

7. Calculate the time between your start and end times, and subtract the amount of time you took for breaks.

You could also use a time-tracker app for this habit. For my own creative sessions, I've created a spreadsheet that automatically calculates the percentage of my time I've spent working within that session. And I know that if my number is below 75 percent, the session has been a difficult one.

The point is *not* to get that percentage up! The point is that we understand *why* and *when* we need breaks, so we can better know how to schedule and encourage our creative process.

A chef's reprise: A strong finish

When Charlene Johnson-Hadley left the restaurant each evening, she returned to a home teeming with her 11-year-old daughter Chloe's colorful art projects—paintings, drawings, sculptures—all of them unfinished.

Charlene's training as a chef made Chloe's creative process difficult to watch. For each of these objects, Chloe had a plan, yet another addition or improvement she was going to make. But the incomplete projects only seemed to accumulate. Finally, in a quiet moment, Charlene decided to say something.

"Chloe, you are a very smart girl, but you have a problem focusing."

"I know, Mommy," Chloe replied. Charlene's jaw dropped.

"But," Chloe continued, "sometimes I have to do more than one thing at a time."

"That's fine," Charlene replied. "There are times you have to multitask. But you can't start five things and then have five things not finished. You can't have 70 percent done, 80 percent done, 20 percent done, 30 percent done, 90 percent done. Even 90 percent finished is still unfinished. So if you need to do more than one thing at a time, do two things, and don't go on to that third thing until you're done. If you do that, by the time you're 14, you'll be able to do five things and then you will complete them. The key is completing."

Charlene watched Chloe, hoping she'd take it in. If Chloe could deliver, she'd have a powerful life skill. She might not be a chef like her mommy, but she'd be the chef of her own life.

A few months later summer came. On the morning of her Brooklyn neighborhood's annual block party, Charlene walked outside and saw Chloe, who had set up a table on which she displayed a number of finished paintings. Beside them she had written a price list with a Sharpie. Chloe had done it all by herself.

She sold all her pieces by the end of the day.

Recipe for Success

Commit to delivering. When a task is nearly done, finish it. Always be unblocking.

SLOWING DOWN
TO SPEED UP

A chef's story: The base runner

ANGELO SOSA, center fielder for his high school baseball team, the Xavier Falcons, looked for a head start. He was halfway between second and third base before the opposing pitcher noticed, and Sosa tagged third milliseconds before the ball hit the third baseman's glove. Sosa stole a lot of bases.

Sosa, while shy in social situations, competed fiercely on the field. His father—a Dominican US Army captain-turned-psychiatrist—ran Angelo and his six siblings like a troop around their rural Connecticut home and corrected them with a hard hand. When Angelo did his chores, he ran. When he left home, he kept running.

After high school—when he had traded his pro baseball aspirations for a culinary career—Sosa spent his first days at the CIA like, he says, a dubiously trained rookie cop looking for action: trying out for the school's Olympic team and demanding a meeting with the president of the college, Ferdinand Metz.

Metz's assistant stared at the first-year student. "The only time students meet with Dr. Metz is at graduation," she sniffed. Sosa persisted. One morning he found himself on the doorstep of President Metz's campus residence. What was Sosa so desperate to say?

"President Metz, I'm Angelo Sosa. I want you to remember my

name, because I'm going to be one of the most famous chefs in the world. Thank you for your time."

Sosa graduated from the CIA with a fellowship that propelled him into the kitchens of Christian Bertrand, where he rose to sous-chef. After 3 years, in 1999, Bertrand asked Sosa if he'd like to meet the one chef whom every young culinarian in New York seemed to want to work for: Jean-Georges Vongerichten, who had just opened his latest four-star restaurant, Jean Georges, in a hotel off Central Park.

Sosa remembers that meeting in a corona of white: gleaming ivory-colored tiles in a spotless kitchen; Jean-Georges himself in his white chef's jacket, reading the *New York Times*. When Vongerichten spoke, Sosa understood only half of what he said, but the chef's voice sounded like liquid silver. Jean-Georges motioned for Sosa to come with him, leading the young apprentice to a new Bonnet oven from France as if showing him a Ferrari, placing Sosa's fingers on the handle so that he could feel the weight of the door. Jean-Georges smiled. *You see?* Sosa, blinded by the light, accepted the chef's offer of $6.25 an hour to take a demotion to the entremetier station. Sosa floated all the way to Grand Central Terminal. Only at the end of his commute to Stanford, Connecticut, did Sosa realize he would now make less than half of his current salary; and that his new weekly paycheck would barely cover his monthly Metro North train pass, let alone his rent. Sosa debarked, walked past his house and into a nearby bank, and talked his way out of there with a loan for $13,000 to fund his shortfall.

Later that week, Sosa asked to speak with Jean-Georges. "This is the biggest investment of my life," Sosa informed him. "And I want you to know that I'm going to be the best chef who has ever worked for you." Jean-Georges bumped him up to $12 an hour just for having the balls.

Back when he played baseball, Sosa figured he could make it to the minors. Now here he was, in the majors of a different league. As he had both on the field and in previous kitchens, Sosa relied on speed for advantage. He fancied himself a martial artist, a ninja, exploding on his station and leaving others dazzled.

Except they weren't.

Vongerichten liked to put his cooks in the shit; he'd drop a new lunch menu 1 hour before service just to watch his brigade scramble. Sosa ran, but in his mad dash, he got sloppy. Much of what he cooked did not meet Vongerichten's or his sous-chef Jacques Qualin's exacting standards. He forgot simple things, like seasoning the water in which he blanched asparagus. *Throw it out, do it again.* He cut his vegetables in inconsistent widths. *Throw it out, do it again.* He panicked, and panic made him rush even more. The more he rushed, the more he fell behind. The more he fell behind, the more hell he caught.

The crew began to tease him. Josh "Shorty" Eden gave Angelo a nickname: *Hurry-Up-and-Make-It-Twice Sosa.* Qualin would toss Sosa's mise-en-place every evening. Sosa started coming in earlier in the morning, sometimes sleeping in his uniform, when he could sleep at all, trying to regain that head start. One day during service, after Qualin reamed him for another underseasoned dish, Sosa's entremetier partner piled on: *Your station is shit, dude. You don't even deserve to be here. You are the worst partner.*

That's it, Sosa thought. In rage and frustration, he ran through the kitchen, past the coffee station, toward the door. His wallet and street clothes were still in the locker room behind him. *Fuck it,* Sosa thought. The wallet was empty anyway. But right below that red exit sign, Sosa felt as if he had walked into an invisible wall. He couldn't leave. Instead, he walked back to his station, grabbed his partner, and said: "Don't ever fuck with me again."

The mere act of talking tough ended Sosa's hazing period, which in turn relaxed him. As he relaxed, he began to behave in a way that didn't come naturally to him: He slowed down. As he slowed down, he made fewer mistakes. As he made fewer mistakes, he regained the finesse he needed to compete in the kitchen of Jean Georges. Sosa acquired what he refers to as *equilibrium*—an elegant balance of speed and refinement. Now his movements *were* becoming ninja-worthy: less lurching, more smooth. When he caught a mistake, he didn't panic. If he didn't cut the carrots correctly, Sosa stopped, took a breath, cleaned up, and began again, cutting them to perfection.

One day Jean-Georges walked past Sosa's station right before service. While everyone else scurried, there was Angelo Sosa, serene, polishing a set of copper pots. Jean-Georges's mouth twisted into a smile.

"Okay, Chef," Vongerichten said, and walked away.

WHAT CHEFS DO, WHAT CHEFS KNOW

Chefs don't run

Chefs have a paradoxical relationship to time. Every day they race the clock, but at other times they seem to be able to stop it. Time is rigid until it's malleable, finite until it's infinite. Chefs know some moments count more than others. And they know that one's perception of time has a lot to do with one's relationship to space. Those concepts of time and space merge in the almost quantum notion of *slowing down to speed up*.

Angelo Sosa didn't learn that principle until well after he had left the CIA. Melissa Gray began learning it while she was still there, dashing around the kitchen of her High-Quantity Food Production class while Chef David McCue watched.

Finally he spoke: "Chefs never run."

Gray stopped and looked at him.

"Do you ever see any of the chefs here run?" he asked her.

Gray thought for a moment. In her 4 years, not once.

"Chefs never run because they're always in the right place at the right time," he said.

The implication was clear: If you're running, it's because you aren't prepared. If you're running, you're wasting energy. If you're running, you're not thinking. If you're running, you're acting like a *cook*.

Many professional chefs wear the title of "cook" with humble pride and abhor the honorific "chef"—which Gray herself believes is a title earned by mastery and not by declaration or diploma. But among Gray's classmates, "cook" was a shame word, as in the insult, "Stop acting like a cook!" At the CIA the difference between "chef" and "cook" measured a culinary student's mastery of physical and mental mise-en-place: *Chefs plan, cooks don't. Chefs see the whole kitchen, cooks zone in on their own station. Chefs move calmly and smoothly, cooks rush.*

Gray remembered what her skills instructor, Rudy Speckamp, counseled before her first big practical exam, the test that determines whether students can move forward.

"*Pretend* that you are calm," he said.

Chefs don't panic

The basic concept is this: The natural human tendency in the face of imminent deadline is to rush or panic. Don't rush; when you rush, your movements become sloppy. Don't panic; when you panic, you forget things. When you find yourself rushing or panicking or both, just stop. Breathe. If your anxiety compels you to move, then clean. The act of cleaning, of wiping down your station, will force you to take some breaths. Look around you. Think about where you are and where you need to be. Think of the next step to get you there and take that step, slowly.

Chef Sam Henderson recalls a panic in her early days at wd-50. The restaurant had just initiated its first lunch service, and Dufresne put everyone in the weeds. The kitchen crew worked two shifts. "We were all tired and grumpy," Henderson remembers. Distracted by some family problems, she went to the farmers' market to pick up strawberries and got the wrong ones. Then she had to create an *amuse-bouche*, and nothing she tried was working. The clock ticked. In her rush to cook family meal for the entire staff, she burned the cauliflower she intended to use. With almost no time left, Henderson broke down and ran outside. A minute or two later, Dufresne appeared by her side—"Sammie, what's wrong?"—alerted by her fellow cook J.J. Basil. "Let's focus," he said. "I'll help you with family meal. We'll sort through the *amuse* together." Dufresne deconstructed her tasks, and he guided her through them. They made it through service just fine. *Sometimes it's the panic about the work that's in your way, not the work itself.*

Chefs put precision before speed

Slowing down does two important things for a cook. It steadies the body, allowing for smoother, more precise movements. And it helps the mind break down a series of movements into their constituent parts. Those two elements give slowing down its ultimate value: *Slowness is the only way a cook can access quality velocity.* The wiring of our brain makes this so.

All human movement and thought result from neurons—our brain cells—communicating in synchrony with each other. That communication happens through physical pathways called axons, which signal other neurons, and dendrites, which receive those signals. The brain creates a substance called myelin that quickens that transmission. The more a particular connection "fires," the more myelin "wires" that connection by adhering to the firing axon. This process, called myelinization, is the physiological result of repeated motion, repeated thought, repeated practice. It is how we learn and how we achieve mastery.

Here's the interesting part: Myelinization "wires" the *quality* of our movement, thought, and practice. So if you're repeating an action sloppily, that sloppiness will be what myelinization preserves. And if you're repeating an action precisely, that precision will be what myelinization enshrines instead. Adding speed to the "precise" movement may compromise that precision, but adding speed to the "sloppy" movement won't make that movement any more precise. In the duality between speed and precision, precision must always precede speed, like that adage attributed to football titan Vince Lombardi: "Practice does not make perfect. Only perfect practice makes perfect."

Chefs slow their bodies to slow time

Chefs believe that the state of their physical space not only has an effect on their minds, but on their perception of time. If your station is dirty, your day *itself* becomes compressed. If your station is clean, your day springs open. If you're worried about time, that worry will show up in your physical space. If you're calm about time, your workspace will be clear.

Chefs are practical people. But when they talk about the principles of mise-en-place, they often wax metaphysical. Remember Chef LiPuma? When he talks about the benefits of planning, he invokes peace: "You want to greet the day." When he holds forth on the wages of working clean, he alludes to life force: "I breathe beautifully and cook fantastic."

Chefs need every second they can get. But they don't wonder, as we do, whether planning and organizing take valuable time away from their real work. They *know* the wisdom of taking a moment to clear their spaces. They *know* how to save time and make time. Slowing down and moving smoothly, for chefs, is a behavior of the highest order.

When we are "in the shit" of our own life, with a deadline looming, we can't imagine slowing down. I find it comforting to know that chefs deal with this impulse daily. Are they afraid of failure? Of course. Are they fighting the clock? Absolutely. But the most seasoned among them know that there's a big difference between hustling and rushing, between a sense of urgency and panicking. They calm their minds and extend time by moving their bodies smoothly, and cover the distance to the finish line by moving them steadily. They *work clean* with their emotions.

OUT OF THE KITCHEN

When we talk about slowing down, we've referred here in large part to physical movement—how we move our legs and arms and hands and fingers. But slowing down can also refer to the cognitive—how we think—and also interpersonal and theoretical realms—how we engage a new project, how we embark on a new relationship, how we invest money and resources.

Outside the kitchen, we can practice and integrate the principle of slowing down to speed up in all its dimensions: physical, mental, and social.

EXERCISES: SKILLS TO LEARN

SLOW AND STEADY MOVEMENTS

Before we can master the swift, we must master the steady, and to master the steady, we must consciously reduce our speed. Here are some useful exercises to master the art of slowing down.

- When you feel the urge to physically rush, *elongate your movements* instead of quickening your pace. When you are moving your legs, don't run—just *widen* your stride. When you are moving your arms, imagine yourself gracefully extending them as a dancer would.

- Practice *interval breaths:* Get a stopwatch or an app that has an interval timer. Select a task that you do with regularity. For 5 minutes, every 60 seconds, stop what you are doing and take one full and deep breath.

- Whether on the phone or face-to-face, conversation can often induce the kind of impatience that causes us to be more brusque with other people than we'd like. This is a good opportunity to exercise your own speed control. When you hear yourself overtalking or interrupting someone, just begin to *talk slower.* Chances are it will have a calming effect on you, force your partner to pay attention, and actually let you wrap up the conversation in a way that is genuine, polite, and honest.

- In times of stress our thinking can get hasty. The next time you find your mind spinning, take a piece of paper and begin to *write down thoughts* as they occur. This "offloading" will slow you down, and you may end up with a "mind map" in front of you that helps you stay calm, gives you some ideas for action, and perhaps helps you solve your problem.

TASK BREAKDOWN

Select one task that you tend to rush—or drag yourself through, or dread, or bungle in some way—and break it down into its component parts.

1. *Perform the action once.* Let's say it's completing a "sales deck" or some other kind of common visual business presentation. Time it from start to finish.

2. Note the *time you took* to complete it and also jot down the *resistance you encountered* while making it: Trouble locating images or data, perhaps? Too much time spent formatting?

3. Then *list out the steps* for the action—being neither too granular nor too broad. Shoot for a number between 5 and 10 steps. Break down the action into discrete sub-actions that stand on their own. So for the sales deck example, it may end up being something like: (a) collect data; (b) write outline; (c) collect images; (d) create the slides; (e) tweak and finish presentation for delivery. Just looking at a task broken down in this way can tell you a lot. Maybe you spend way too much time trying to collect data. Perhaps then you need to allot more time for that step or delegate that work in advance to allow you to focus on other steps. Maybe formatting the slides is a problem because you haven't been able to take the time to create a style template that would make your workflow go much faster.

4. Where your breakdown tells you to create a process, fix a problem, or train yourself, *pause or slow down* by scheduling some time for that work.

The point of this exercise is to slow down a nonconscious process by consciously analyzing it so that, with practice, you can streamline it and make it faster. This exercise works like practice on a musical instrument. New York University professor and musicologist Jeff Peretz puts it this way: "For a particularly difficult piece, I tell my students to break the big task into microtasks—to repeat those smaller passages very slowly. Then when they get those microtasks down, they can move their fingers faster. Then you link all those microtasks together and work on the transitions. But you could never have done that long piece so well without breaking it down first."

Taking the time to slow down and analyze a complex task—even though it may feel like a waste of time and a pain in the ass while you are doing the analysis—will save you time in the long term.

KITCHEN PRACTICE: SLOW DOWN

Body calms mind, and for many chefs, a calm body and mind also make for better food. For one meal try making all your moves extra slow, steady, and smooth. Note the effect it has on your performance as a cook, on your food, your mood, and that of your diners.

HABITS: BEHAVIORS TO REPEAT

PROCRASTINATION KILLER

Slowing down to speed up gives us power over procrastination.

Yvette, an accountant, has a list of spreadsheets to prepare for her company's yearly audit. She has so much work to do that she begins to feel restless after simply opening and looking at the first document. So she clicks over to her Internet browser, to her e-mail—whatever it takes to not feel the weight of that work pressing on her.

Slowing down to speed up suggests another way to be in this moment. When Yvette feels like stopping, instead of distracting herself, she can just make her moves *very slow.* She can type slowly—one key at a time. If she needs to gather files, she moves very slowly in getting these, smoothly, like a ballet. When she calls someone for information, she dials lazily, even making her own voice relaxed. She opens each motion up. She breathes through each little thing. She still hates it, but now her tasks become more like a game or a moving meditation. The work is still getting done, albeit at a snail's pace, but the difference is this: (1) She hasn't given up her control, which is what she'd do if she decided to start browsing the Web; (2) She still has forward momentum, if languid; (3) She gives herself more time to think and be mindful of each action, which is the opposite of freaking out or shutting down in the face of an avalanche of work; and (4) She breaks down her actions into their constituent parts, which, as we did in the above exercise, is a time-tested method of getting large projects done, but *not* normally how we relate to smaller, more mundane activities like writing an e-mail or preparing for a meeting. But even tasks that are small in terms of labor and time can loom large for us, so using the same breakdown tools for small tasks can penetrate our resistance.

The more the resistance, the slower you move. But don't disengage. You can use this slow-but-don't-stop technique for just about anything that you don't want to do: getting out of bed in the morning (move left leg, move right leg, shift body, feet on floor), washing the dishes (move plate, turn faucet on, soak plate, grab sponge, move hand in a circular motion).

MAKE PANIC AND CRISIS CHECKLISTS

Each of us has triggers that cause us to panic in work or personal situations. If you find yourself in the throes of a crisis that tends to recur, use a variation of the checklist technique we suggested in *The Second Ingredient: Arranging Spaces, Perfecting Movements* beginning on page 78.

Here's an example: Whenever Fred makes a mistake that annoys his boss, Fred falls apart. His hands shake for the rest of the day, and he forgets things and makes additional mistakes, which makes everything worse. After a few hours, a friend takes Fred aside and calms him down. Why not enshrine that knowledge instead in a little crisis checklist Fred can keep at his workstation?

When the boss yells:

1. Listen to the boss and mirror her complaint.

2. Do not apologize or defend; the boss hates apologies and excuses. She will just say, "Get it done." So the only thing to say is "I will get it done."

3. Calm your body! No matter how urgent the problem, go to a quiet place for 2 minutes and breathe. Touch your toes and stand up and stretch 10 times. Go to the bathroom and splash cold water on your face.

4. Make a quick list of steps to remedy the situation. Determine how long those steps will take.

5. If pressed for time, don't forget to delegate or request help. Let your crew and your colleagues help you!

6. When the task is done, let the boss know. Say: "I fixed it."

7. If the task is not yet complete, before the end of the day, give the boss a status report and offer a delivery time estimate.

The checklist response can be effective for relationships at work or home. For example, if certain situations (a boss yelling, a child forgetting her chores) cause you to lose emotional control, you can make yourself a crisis checklist of reminders (breathe, know that it's not the end of the world, ask calmly for what you need, etc.), something to grab in those situations to reclaim some control.

Think that referring to a checklist in an emotional situation is a ridiculous idea? Then think about this: Pilots train to overcome their emotions when faced with situations much more dire. When an airplane is in trouble, the *first* thing a pilot grabs is his checklist, because pilots know that emotion can cause all kinds of counterproductive reactions and mistakes that could endanger the flight.

The aviation checklist industry exists to save lives in this manner. And when the worst happens, that industry's employees pore over the flight data recorders to see if they can change processes to save lives in the future.

It's not surprising, then, that some business literature refers to this kind of learning from failure as "black box thinking."

THE CLEANING REFLEX

In times of stress or panic, clean your workstation—your desk and/ or your computer—so that your visual field is clear. Put things where they belong. Close apps. Keep your hands moving, slow, slower. Now take another breath and look around. Think about the next thing you need to do. Chain your tasks together, chain your movements together. Now resume, slowly, steadily, smoothly. Keep breathing beautifully.

A chef's reprise: Velocity's cost

Sosa became a trusted lieutenant in Vongerichten's expanding culinary empire before leaving to *stage* in Europe and, thereafter, opening his own restaurant back in New York. But he continued to learn about the costs of speed.

When Angelo Sosa's child was born with a debilitating genetic condition, he figured it was time to slow his career climb a bit. But in the midst of his son's recuperation from heart surgery, he was pursued by the producers of Bravo's reality program *Top Chef.* He turned them down; they courted him some more. Sosa's competitive instincts kicked in, and he relented.

Oh, the irony of that very first "quickfire" challenge: a mise-en-place *speed* drill. In a finish that would have made Jean-Georges proud, Sosa came in second for speed, but won the overall challenge for his finesse. He cooked all the way until the last episode when—utterly spent—he was felled by a stomach virus. Hallucinating, Sosa oversalted his dish. After a season in which he cooked well but was portrayed in the narrative as a cutthroat—the kind of guy willing to wander off base for a head start—Sosa lost again later that year in the all-stars competition.

The young chef took stock of the costs of velocity. He had lept forward in name recognition but lost the subtlety of the real person behind the TV character.

Sosa took a breath, slowed down, and began again. You can find him at one of his three restaurants in New York, where the food is fabulous and the pace is relaxed.

Recipe for Success
Commit to working smoothly and steadily. Use physical order to restore mental order. Don't rush.

OPEN EYES AND EARS

A chef's story: The hungry cook

FROM THE START, no one wanted Elizabeth Briggs in the kitchen.

Her mother didn't. Briggs grew up poor, in New England. Whenever the young Elizabeth tried to watch her mother cooking, she'd get shooed out of the room.

Her first culinary teacher didn't. Briggs's instructor at a vocational school told Briggs that she would "never amount to anything" in the industry.

Her first chefs didn't. Briggs found a job at the Mountain View House in Whitefield, New Hampshire, in the 1970s, where she and a 69-year-old cook named Florence were relegated to working in a tiny room outside the main kitchen because—in the common manner of European-style operations of the day—women weren't allowed to cook on the "hot line."

This practice of deliberate exclusion continued when she became garde-manger at The Balsams—the famed luxury resort in New Hampshire—and then at the Everglades Club in Palm Beach, Florida, where she worked for a hostile French chef.

"He did everything he could to make it impossible for me," Briggs recalls.

While the men of the culinary world had the opportunity to apprentice at the right and left hands of their chef-mentors, women like Briggs were often kept at arm's length. Briggs had to steal her education like baseball players steal signs from an opposing team.

She did this by developing an acute sense of hearing and seeing.

The one preparation that the chef didn't allow anybody in the Everglades Club kitchen to observe was his pâté. He shielded the recipe and wouldn't let any of his cooks near him while he made it. But Briggs kept her eyes open. On the chef's day off, Briggs stepped into the walk-in refrigerator where he kept his ingredients. She measured everything carefully and wrote it all down. On her own she was able to successfully reproduce his precious pâté.

For Briggs the ability to see and hear things in the kitchen sprang from a hunger to pry open its secrets. Decades later as a chef-instructor for the CIA, Briggs teaches a generation of students for whom the culinary world arrives as an open book. Recipes and techniques abound online. With the abundance of information at their fingertips, it's no wonder that new students don't have to exert as much effort with their eyes and ears to get what they need. Briggs is the person who must teach them how.

Today, Briggs shoos her flock of novice students around her kitchen like a mother hen.

"Okay, stand out of the way. Out of the way. Stand out of the way."

The newbies look like chicks, too, all baby fat and wide eyes, bursting out of their stiff, newly issued, too-bright whites. Clustered in the narrow area between the entrance and the ovens, they don't move much upon her commands; they shift their weight from foot to foot like baby penguins, pushing each other around. They don't seem to understand language yet; why else would Chef Briggs have to repeat almost everything she says several times?

"Now, here's what a sanitor needs to do every day . . . " Chef Briggs looks around her and fixes her gaze on a student named Elena. "*You!* Walk out the door for a minute. Look down the hall. Walk down the hall, both ways." Elena pushes past the swinging front doors of kitchen K-7, turns to the right, and disappears.

"She's gonna come back," Briggs continues. "Stand out of her way, stand out of her way. Watch, watch."

But Elena doesn't return.

"Tell her to come back now. Where'd she go?" Briggs asks another student. "Oh, I hope she didn't go home. Tell her to come back. Just yell out, 'Come back!'"

A male student pokes his head out of the door and says, "Come back?"—more question than command.

Elena does not hear him call. She's down at the end of the hallway, confused by the chef's conflicting instructions to "look down the hall" and "walk down the hall."

"Okay, stand back out of the way so she can look down the aisle. Out of the way. Out of the way. Let her look down the aisle when she comes. Pull the bucket around. Pull the bucket."

Another student calls out: "She just went the other way."

"Oh my God, she's killing me," says Chef Briggs.

The student pokes her head out of the double doors: "Elena, come back!"

Within a moment, Elena is back in the kitchen, unsure of what to do. Chef Briggs directs her attention to the aisle on the right side of the room. "Now take a look."

Elena sees something she didn't see before she left: The kitchen is a complete mess. Nothing changed since Elena left the kitchen a few minutes ago except her perspective.

"When you leave the kitchen, it clears you of all the stuff going on, right?" Briggs says. "Because there's so much going on, you can't think or see. You go out, you stand at the door for a minute. You don't have to run to Poughkeepsie next time, all right? But you go out and you clear your head. You come back and you're like, 'Whoooh, what happened?'"

Chef Briggs has been teaching first-day students in this way for 28 years at the CIA. She's demonstrating the same mise-en-place principles as the other instructors, like preparation, arranging your station, and cleaning as you go. But the skill that's the hardest to teach—the one she's struggling with now, the one that's so fundamental to a cook's ability to execute all the other principles—is listening and seeing.

WHAT CHEFS DO, WHAT CHEFS KNOW

Chefs balance internal and external awareness

A chef's work requires concentration. Some chefs tell you that their work induces a meditative state so deep that it shuts out the chaos around them: the clatter, the heat, the movement, the shouting.

Yet in that tumult are signals that need to be heard and seen: voices making requests and issuing commands; printers clacking and spitting; bodies gesturing, moving, and prodding; pots of water boiling; pans making a certain sizzling sound indicating their contents' degree of doneness. In the kitchen, during the heat of service, new cooks can become so focused on the skills they've learned with their hands that they forget the other half of the job, which is to be a part of a functioning organism, responding not only to messages from people but from physical signals around them. The reverie of cooking is antithetical to the awareness that a cook needs to execute her job, a behavior that some call *kitchen awareness*, maintaining a constant consciousness of all five senses: sights, sounds, smells, tastes, and touch. We've discussed presence as one of three key values in the kitchen: Be here now. But cooking requires the cook to be in two places at once: in her head, and in the room. In essence we are talking about achieving two kinds of presence simultaneously, internal and external. Experienced cooks develop an ability that is perhaps one of the most enviable in modern society: to be focused and at the same time aware on multiple levels. For our purposes—cultivating a similar kind of awareness outside the kitchen—we'll call this behavior *open eyes and ears*.

Chefs don't space out

It's difficult to learn kitchen awareness. The most humbling moment for me in the kitchens of the CIA came when I was reporting inside American Bounty, observing students on their first day of cooking on the hot line. Here I was, trying to evaluate their ability to field and process incoming orders, and I myself was missing them right and left. I couldn't keep track of half of what was coming in, and unlike the students, I didn't have to cook a thing. My challenge resembles what Elizabeth Briggs faces with each new clutch of students in her classroom. Some students are naturally alert. And some are built for quick shifts in awareness. "We have people with ADD [attention deficit disorder] and ADHD [attention deficit hyperactivity disorder]. Those are the perfect people in the kitchen because they can multitask. But they hyperfocus, too, like tunnel vision. So what I need them to do is open up their vision."

When students don't respond to repeated calls for attention, a teaching tactic that Chef Briggs uses is what basically amounts to an incursion into their personal space. She moves in close—close enough for discomfort without touching them—and stands there. She whispers: "You know, it's really important that you hear me."

When she encounters a student who is particularly unresponsive to her commands, even those spoken into a microphone and amplified by her class PA system, she applies a rather unorthodox tactic: Chef Briggs sends them to the CIA's health office to get their hearing checked.

"I usually wait until lunch break so I don't interrupt their class," she says. "They think I'm kidding, but I'm not."

By the time the student returns to Chef Briggs's classroom, clutching a clean bill of health from the school nurse, three things have happened: He has recognized the gravity of kitchen awareness because he has seen the lengths to which the chef and the school will go to reinforce its importance, even to use student time and school resources to engage in a bit of theater; his insulation has been peeled back through a bit of indignity to expose that raw nerve of awareness; and he understands that it's his responsibility to continue to develop that sensitivity.

Chefs tune their senses

Beyond hunger and willpower, Briggs recommends techniques that any student can use to sharpen his or her awareness.

Attunement. Chef Briggs distinguishes between a focus-scattering openness and what she's really advocating, which is something more selective. "They need to tune in to my voice," she says. Eventually, she implies, the brain will create channels, loopholes in their wall of focus—the sound of their chef's or colleagues' voices, the hiss of a pan, the clack of a dupe printer, the clack of clogs on a tile floor.

Triggers: It helps to have your colleagues broadcasting on the same frequencies to which you're tuned. Chefs push certain words like buttons (or lean into them like car horns), a signal for everyone's attention on what's to come: "Ordering!" "Fire!" "Pickup!" Certain words, certain voices, certain sounds, certain movements—they can all pull us out of our reverie, as long as we're tuned to them.

OUT OF THE KITCHEN

Could we use attunement and triggers to cultivate open eyes and ears in the workplace? Or perhaps the first question to ask is this one: *Why in hell would we want more sensitivity to stimuli at work? We can barely concentrate as it is!*

Our ability to maintain focus at work is being challenged on three fronts.

Digital multitasking. Scientists and thinkers disagree about the effect of technology like digital screens, the nested hypertext of the Web, mobile alerts, and push notifications. One group believes that humans weren't built to sit gazing at digital screens all day. They say our brains haven't evolved to handle the amount of information that's thrown at us, nor to cope with the constant interruptions and digressions that technology foists upon us. They hold that humans aren't meant to multitask and point to studies showing that there is really no such thing as "multitasking" anyway, but rather a kind of rapid "task switching" at which few of us are good. As a result, they say, we may not only be hampering our brain's ability to focus, but also fostering a generation of humans who've lost some of that ability: Generation ADD, so to speak. The other group, however, holds that the brain is and has always been, quite on its own, a jumpy factory of distractions. Just close your eyes and sit, they say, for a minute in silence and know that truth. Our ability to create focus from chaos, they argue, comes from the potent functioning of our brain. "Attention blindness," the phenomenon wherein the mind concentrates on one thing and filters out other stimuli, can be cultivated. In other words, we can learn what to pay attention to, and what not to.

Digital mobility. Though the personal computer has been a part of work life for decades, the Internet, along with a proliferation of powerful mobile devices all connected to it, has demolished the walls separating our jobs from the rest of our lives. The same devices on which we work are a portal to the personal and vice versa. The impact of this connectivity depends on your perspective: Smartphones can destroy focus and participation in meetings, or they can more easily bring information and resources into them. Their presence during our personal interactions can help us share experiences or kill intimacy and trust. The increasing phenomenon of remote work—meaning work outside the traditional office—can give us an unprecedented freedom, or chain us to our jobs 24/7.

The open workplace. The walls have come down within the office, too. The old, hierarchical, siloed corporate layouts of corner offices and cubicles have given way to large, airy rooms with long, shared tables and all kinds of communal spaces meant to foster the same kinds of connectivity as the Internet itself. Some 70 percent of office employees now work in open layouts, and according to several studies, the change has been a dismal failure. The supposed benefits to workers—better communication, more collaboration, stronger camaraderie—have paled in comparison to the pitfalls: lack of privacy, more noise, more interruption leading to reduced productivity and diminished morale. For many older workers, the shift to the open office has been an indignity, reminding them more of industrial era sweatshops than a brave new world of work. And for many younger workers who've known no other system, the price of their satisfaction may be a lowered baseline of productivity. In other words, the young folks have no idea how much more productive they could be with some boundaries.

The modern office has become a laboratory for human attention.

THE OPEN KITCHEN

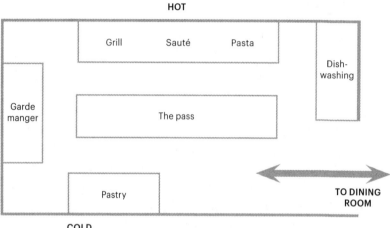

Ironic, then, that the professional kitchen is a great working model for an open-layout, multitasking environment. Everybody works together on the floor. The chef stands with them at the pass, like a maestro, orchestrating and evaluating the work. Noises, sights, and smells bombard the cooks while they try to focus on cooking.

But unlike that of the office, the cook's creative work is largely *nonverbal*. One of the reasons that chefs can communicate and create at the same time is that their verbal and nonverbal work— taking orders and cooking them—are not competing for the same brain space. Similar tasks, like e-mailing and talking, use the same parts of the brain, so they create what neurologists call interference and engender the kind of rapid back-and-forth task switching that studies have shown is so inefficient. But consider a study conducted by French scientists in 2010 that may show a refinement of this notion. They found that the geography of the brain actually *does* engender our ability to take on two similar tasks at a time—*just not three*. If we take this particular study to heart, then it does confirm not only the validity of the balanced motion and task chaining we've discussed in earlier chapters, but also suggests the usefulness of another model for an open-layout, *verbal* multitasking environment that works: the classic newsroom. So maybe our brave new world is just a sleek titanium-and-glass-mobile-phone version of our older one.

The kitchen demonstrates the tension between immersive tasks and process tasks in microcosm, but shows us that we can successfully be part of an interconnected system, be aware, be interrupted, *and still be creative.* Like chefs, we can work clean with our senses. We can use the common sense of chefs, combined with what we know to be true about the brain, to attune and extend our awareness.

EXERCISES: SKILLS TO LEARN

TAKE INVENTORY

To transform kitchen awareness into office awareness, we need first to take inventory.

What are the things in your workspace demanding more *awareness?* Make a list of the communication you tend to miss regularly or on occasion. Do you overlook e-mails? Do you mishear or space out in meetings? Do you take too long to hear when colleagues call to you?

What are the things in your workspace needing less *awareness?* Do computer and phone alerts interrupt you too much? Do nearby conversations distract you? Do you find that your inner thoughts and daydreams tug at your focus?

The goal of open ears and eyes is not to blast open your walls of focus, privacy, and sanity. Rather it is, as Chef Briggs said, to attune yourself, to set the boundaries properly and give the gate keys to the right people.

HUNGER GAME

Just as Elizabeth Briggs cultivated open ears and eyes as a young chef to acquire the skills necessary for her success, so can you. Survivors in a corporate climate have a kind of radarlike awareness. They ask more questions. They listen to people from other departments. They detect subtle shifts in tone and body language. They pick up cues that tip them off to things that take others by surprise. As a result they become like meteorologists of the political and business climate of the office. If you work in such an environment, ask yourself another question: *What do you want to learn and from whom?* Tune your awareness to those activities and people accordingly.

VIP CUES

For those with digital devices, pick three people you want to be more connected or responsive to at work: a boss, a colleague, or an assistant. For each of these three people, you are going to create "VIP" sonic and visual cues in your personal devices, to help raise your own level of alertness to them.

Unique alerts. Many smartphones allow you to set a specific ring for certain people. Many computer e-mail programs have "rules" settings that will play a unique tone when an e-mail from a designated person arrives, or let you set the e-mail to display in a particular color. For each of the three people in question, set specific sonic and/or visual cues, or one for all three. Humans are born with the ability to filter out certain voices and sounds. For our personal devices, it's important that we take a little time to program some intelligent, intentional differentiation into them so that we can aid our own ability to discern the important from the irrelevant.

Separate channels. Another way to differentiate important communication is to put it in its own unique channel, like forwarding these VIPs' e-mails to a separate address, or communicating in a private group on a closed service such as Basecamp or Asana. The most important thing about the separate channel is its exclusivity. Only those three folks have it, and it's the one that you might leave open to alert you when you've closed all the others.

Once you've set up these VIP cues, you can train yourself to be more responsive to them. Have one of your three VIPs help train you. For a day, have that friend call, e-mail, or message you every hour. Whenever you hear or see that friend's message, perform a *physical* action. If you are sitting, stand up. If you are standing, jump up or sit down. Begin to associate a behavior of intention and attention with that stimulus. Rest assured, you won't have to jump up forever! But from that day on, you should be more attuned to those particular sights and sounds.

KITCHEN PRACTICE: TEST YOUR AWARENESS

Test your kitchen awareness with these exercises.

- For 15 minutes while you cook, also listen to or watch the news on TV, the radio, or the Internet. Then, after those 15 minutes, write down the topic of every story you heard.

- While you cook, have a conversation with someone for 15 minutes. When time is up, summarize what he said.

- Try to cook with your ears and nose as well as your eyes. What sounds do you hear that tell you to give a pan some attention? Can you guess the level of doneness of a dish from its smell?

The kitchen is a great place to practice balancing internal and external awareness.

HABITS: BEHAVIORS TO REPEAT

UP PERISCOPE

Today's work environment demands constant awareness, and it takes great strength to pull away for even an hour or two to focus on an immersive project. The following habit is a great way to honor your need for focus by regimenting and constraining communication.

1. Set an hourly chime, either on a watch, your computer, or your phone.

2. Create a list of channels that you feel you must check when that chime rings to be in proper communication.

3. Turn off alerts and the ringer on your phone and close your e-mail and instant messaging programs. You can even disconnect from the Internet by shutting down your browser or turning off your Wi-Fi. Do whatever you feel you need for your own peace of mind.

4. When the chime rings, grab your checklist and check in quickly on all your channels. Give yourself 5 or 10 minutes to process that communication, unless something urgent has come up. At the end of that check-in session, retreat from your connectivity again.

You may already practice some version of this "up periscope/down periscope" habit. This exercise adds intentionality to these actions: *You—not other people, and not your technology*—set the rules for engagement with your work environment.

DUAL DEVICES

Some folks who possess more than one device might want to dedicate one of them to connectivity, and reserve the other purely for work. The act of physically turning from one device to another creates powerful shifts in attention.

PERSONAL NEGOTIATIONS

Let's say that you aren't in a position to make the rules for your workplace interactions. You may, for example, work at a company that insists all communications happen through a particular messaging system and mandates that you stay connected all the time. We can't control what companies expect of us in our communication. We can't control when people will approach us to chat. But we can all make and negotiate simple requests, even if we can't control people's responses to them. These kinds of requests may include:

- Asking people to honor a "Focusing: Do Not Disturb" card on your desk, wall, door, or computer monitor.

- Asking colleagues to say your name or touch your arm first if they want to get your attention during a moment of concentration.

- Asking your boss for permission for pauses in connectivity so that you can complete your work.

- Asking colleagues to contact you only during business hours.

The e-mail auto-responder is a powerful and often underused tool to set others' expectations about your availability. They're not just for vacations. Some college professors use them on weekends to set students' expectations. Some people use them for a few hours a day when they need time "off the grid."

RECOVERING YOUR FOCUS

Interruption is a fact of life in the workplace, but we can make peace with interruption. When our focus gets pulled, we can regain it by borrowing a technique from the Eastern tradition of mantra meditation. A mantra is a sound or vibration. A mantra meditation asks the practitioner to repeat that sound silently or aloud to herself for a certain period of time.

The main complaint of new mantra meditators is that "it doesn't work"—meaning that they start thinking the mantra and before they know it, they're worrying about work, or replaying a scene in their head from a TV show they watched the previous day, or thinking about where to get their car fixed.

To that we say: "Congratulations!" It's working.

Here's how it goes: You think the mantra. Your focus gets pulled. You notice after a while that you're not thinking the mantra anymore. You start thinking the mantra again. The process repeats. You don't get angry at yourself. You don't tell yourself and others that it's not working. You don't curse your wonderful, restless mind. You just accept that this is the way your mind works, with thoughts crashing in like waves on the ocean. Meditators commit to surfing those waves rather than getting pounded by them.

Keep a mantralike focus on your work, but accept the inevitability of interruption. When you are interrupted, you don't get mad. You give thanks that you are alive to be interrupted. You give a few moments to the person interrupting you. You stop what you are doing to help, or you ask them to wait. Then you come back to your mantra, to your work.

And in those times when your inner equilibrium becomes unable to compete with the interruptions, as with meditation, you go find a quiet place.

A chef's reprise: Mastery and awareness

At the end of Elizabeth Briggs's culinary fundamentals class, 15 weeks after her students first waddled in, their gait becomes a strut. Briggs notices that as her students' sense of confidence grows, so does their awareness—their ability to hear and see and be in the moment in her kitchen.

When they first arrived, the students "zoned in" on tasks because they were still learning the basics, just trying to get through class without cutting or burning themselves. "If I can get my students to work through that insecurity," Briggs says, "they usually have an awakening around day 18."

As they begin to get comfortable with their tasks, their sensitivity opens up. "They can begin to feel and see and hear more. They are more open to communication, and they have that sense of 'I've arrived.'"

She tells them: "If I had measured your height on the door frame on the first day of class, you'd see now that you've all grown 3 inches taller."

When she says this, they hang on her every word.

Recipe for Success

Commit to balancing internal and external awareness. Stay alert.

CALL AND CALLBACK

A chef's story: The mad scientist

BACK WHEN Rob Halpern ran Marigold, his restaurant in the Spruce Hill neighborhood of Philadelphia, he shopped downtown at the Reading Terminal Market. Halpern squeezed himself past the promenaders, browsers, and tourists, shouting "Behind!" from time to time to alert oblivious shoppers to his trajectory. It was kitchenspeak, but Halpern couldn't help himself. He liked the language of the kitchen, found it sensible. You give people information when they need it. When you receive communication, you let folks know you got it.

A produce vendor told him, "That's $4.25 for the tomatoes."

Halpern replied, "Heard!"

Everybody turned to look at him. *This guy is crazy.*

If they ever dined at Marigold or saw the kitchen, they'd understand. Halpern *was* a mad scientist. The kind to buy a fine-but-unremarkable à la carte restaurant in a sleepy Philly neighborhood and transform it into a 14-course, $80 prix fixe epicurean experience of molecular-gastronomy-meets-food-nostalgia with no menu and—aside from one course, the 10th—no choice for the diner. The kind to present a menu of pan-fried quail and lobster bao alongside "dippin' dots" of frozen pureed green vegetables, "push-pops," and popcorn arriving at the table in a cloud of evaporating liquid nitrogen. The kind to execute that vision while providing alternate vegetarian, allergen- and gluten-free meals in a restaurant where an average night might require 10 cooks to make dinner for 60 diners comprising nearly 800 plates of food. The kind to serve a bowl of truffled crab macaroni and cheese that inspired one customer, a young woman named Rinna Diaz, to vow she'd marry the person who made it. The kind to buy her an engagement ring not long thereafter.

Dining at Marigold inspired this kind of obsession; working there required it. Halpern's hodgepodge crew of culinary grads and externs—all of them in their twenties—toiled for 12-hour days, wiping clean plates in a water-and-vinegar solution to make them even cleaner, dotting them with demi-glace and painting them with puree, stacking them with perfectly cooked portions of protein. They didn't leave this obsessive way of life at the restaurant. On her way in to Marigold one morning, Kamal—who worked the cold station—stopped at Dunkin' Donuts for a cup of tea. She ended up at the condiment station sorting and arranging the store's packets of sweetener before she left. The "front-of-house" staff, too, was steeped in this culture of mise-en-place. Rachel, one of the waiters, saw her coursework at college improve after working at Marigold. At the preservice meetings, the front-of-house staff proved as engaged as the cooks, calling purveyors to verify, for example, the safety of certain kinds of cheeses for an incoming pregnant customer. The servers were an integral part of this intricate dance of plates out of the kitchen, into the dining room, and back.

For this kind of ballet, you need lockstep. To choreograph it, you need a code and a shared language. How else was Halpern going to manage this insane kitchen, a place where two dishwashers *and* one grill/sauté man were all named Alex, and his garde-manger guy was also named Al? Halpern gave each of them a designated "Alex number."

A waiter handed a foot-long, 3-inch-wide slip of paper to Halpern, a new ticket, for table 36, from which Halpern read the courses to the crew.

"Order in, table for four, please fire popcorn for four!"

"Heard!" said sous-chefs Tim Lanza and Keith Krajewski.

"Please fire dots for four!"

"Heard!" the cooks at the cold station shouted.

The command to "fire!" the first dishes for each customer was meant for both cold *and* hot plates, signifying that the cooks should prepare for imminent pickup. Now Halpern advised the crew of upcoming courses for table 36:

"This table's going to do four asparagus!"

"Heard!" Al Upshaw said.

"Three quails with one vegetarian egg!"

"Heard!" Alex Vittorio ("Alex 1") and Andrew Kochan, behind Halpern on the grill, replied.

Once everyone had the orders, Halpern clipped the ticket in a rack by the pass-through window. He circled the items that he just fired: the popcorn and the dots.

When the dots were ready, Kamal yelled: "Four dipping dots!"

"Heard that!" Halpern said. "Food runner please!"

As one of the floor staff arrived, Halpern said, "Four dots are for table 36!"

And as the server ran off with the four plates, she said: "Thirty-six walks!"

Halpern made a slash mark through the circle around "Dots" on table 36's ticket. Then it was on Halpern to time the meals of table 36 and all the others that came in. He did this with a combination of intuition and input from the floor staff. When the server returned and said, "Dots back from 36," Halpern acknowledged that and fired the next course.

This continued all night. The chef and the crew in both the back and front of house remained locked in with each other. When they said something, they expected a reply. When they didn't receive a reply, they made sure they got one.

A waiter returned with a plate and told Halpern, "I have sweetbreads back from 30."

Halpern didn't reply, distracted.

"I have sweetbreads back from 30," the waiter said again, louder.

"Heard," Halpern replied.

The verification went both ways. Halpern called for a food runner. A voice replied, "Heard!" But no one came to pick up the food. "Food runner please!" Halpern repeated. "Don't say 'Heard' and not come over here!"

Here was what Halpern called Station Four—the small table in the doorway between Halpern's hot line and the cold kitchen on the other side. Why he called it Station Four no one seemed to know. It didn't matter. They knew where it was and what he meant. The same held true for the dozen or so times during a service that Halpern said something like this:

"I need two Phil Collins and one Peter Gabriel, Station Four please!"

"Heard!" a server yelled.

Standing nearby, I turned to look at Halpern. *What the hell?*

Halpern laughed, an endearing, nervous, nerdy chuckle. He clarified: He was telling the servers whether they needed to bring a tray or not. "Peter Gabriel" meant "bring a tray." "Phil Collins" meant "no tray required."

Here's how absurd this reference is: After Phil Collins, a member of the 1970s progressive rock group Genesis, went solo in the 1980s, he won a Grammy for his solo album *No Jacket Required*. At some point, Halpern probably got tired of saying "no tray required" and hit upon this quick substitute. And for the opposite of a Phil Collins, "bring a tray," he defaulted to Collins's former bandmate in Genesis, Peter Gabriel.

Ridiculous. But for the crew of compulsives at Marigold—Robert, Keith, Tim, Andrew, Kamal, Rachel, Emily, Solomon, Alex 1, Alex 2, Alex 3, and Al—it worked.

WHAT CHEFS DO, WHAT CHEFS KNOW

Chefs confirm communication

The heartbeat of the kitchen has always been the *call and callback* between a chef and her cooks.

Even in this gilded digital age of computer keypads, screens, and printers, the communication in many of the world's finest kitchens remains completely verbal and manual.

Here's how that traditional system works:

Servers write orders on paper and hand them to the chef or whomever is acting as the *expediter*—the person giving orders to the cooks and gathering finished plates to serve.

The chef says "Ordering!" and calls those orders out to the cooks. Sometimes those verbal commands are supplemented with duplicates, or "dupes," of the order ticket. The cooks confirm to the chef that they've received the order by repeating the items and quantities. They then find a way to keep all that information organized: They memorize; they put raw ingredients in pans; they read the dupes again. Sometimes they lose their place and ask the chef for an "all day," a refresher on all the orders currently working. When the cook on grill says, "What do I have all day on steak?" the chef might reply, "All day: two rare, two medium-rare."

When the chef says "Fire!" on a particular table or dish, the cook repeats the command, takes those ingredients in hand, and brings them to temperature—in other words, the cook makes all the moves necessary so that she can plate the dish when asked.

The chef officially asks for those plates when she says "Pick up!"—meaning that the cooks should plate the dishes in question and bring them as quickly as possible to the "pass" or shelf between the chef and the cooks. The cooks confirm the command and do just that. Then the chef may call for a food runner or back waiter, who rushes the food out to the tables.

Chefs coordinate communication

The profusion of "stations" in a kitchen—grill, sauté, vegetable, appetizer, fry, dessert, and more—adds to the complexity of that communication system, especially when you consider that one plate may contain ingredients from multiple stations. Something as simple as a steak with fries and salad demands coordination between cooks on grill, fry, and garde-manger stations. Those

cooks, in turn, must communicate with each other to make sure
that all the elements on the plate are finished at the same time; fries
can't get soggy on the pass while a steak finishes on the grill; a
steak can't get cold in the window while it waits for a salad order
that the garde-manger didn't hear.

Call and callback is not just vertical, from chef to cooks; it's
also horizontal, between cooks. A cook might ask his fellow, "How
many minutes on that steak?" "Five minutes," might come the
reply. And the cooks in turn gauge and adjust their speed to coordinate their finishing times.

"Sometimes as a line cook, I'd repeat somebody else's order, even
if it wasn't my station, just to make sure we all heard," says Michael
Gibney. "What you trust each other to deliver is inviolable."

"I would run that shit like a fucking ballet," Jarobi White
remembers. "I'd say, 'Don't pay attention to nothing else, just hear
my times. I need such-and-such in 4 minutes. If you need an extra
3 minutes, let me know.' And sure enough we'd all be turning
around with our finished plates at the same time."

Most kitchens generate a huge amount of ambient noise: the
sounds of flames, the clatter of dishes, the spray of water, and the
constant whir of the venting system. In the midst of this racket,
different kitchens have different communication styles, depending
on the will of the chef. Many roil with cooks' banter; others are
quiet save for the sound of call and callback, because for chefs that
information is vital and paramount.

Call and callback, a system of communication and confirmation,
is a vital behavior and principle of the kitchen environment because
there is so little tolerance for mistakes and so much blowback from
making them. Nothing can be lost. One order missed, and an entire
table's food can be delayed. In some high-end restaurants, if one
plate is wrong, all the other plates must be redone. One table's delay
can throw off the rhythm of a kitchen and an entire restaurant. One
bad night can generate dozens of bad experiences for customers.
Dozens of bad experiences can spell bad word of mouth, bad
reviews, lost revenue, and—eventually—a closed restaurant.

A kitchen like Marigold in Philadelphia, with its oral fixation approaching the ornate, can seem fussy or pretentious to the casual visitor, its cooks neurotic and nerdy. But that complicated call and callback provides a manifestly practical bulwark against a failure that can happen at any moment.

Chefs demand specifics

Believe it or not, Halpern's vocabulary is not precise enough for some culinarians.

At the CIA, Melissa Gray and her fellow students kept a running joke. *If your friend tells you something, anything, you reply, "Heard!"*

"We said it just to be ridiculous," Gray recalls. "People *hated* 'Heard.'"

When someone shouted "Heard!" in her skills class, Gray remembers her instructor Chef Rudy Speckamp would reply: "Herd? What herd? Herd of cows? Don't tell me 'Heard.' Tell me *what* you heard."

Even "Yes, Chef!"—that mantra of honor, reverence, and deference—isn't enough for some people.

"You got four bass on order," Chef LiPuma calls to one of his students on sauté at American Bounty.

"Yes, Chef!" comes the reply.

"Don't '*Yes, Chef*' me," he says. "Say what I say. You've got four bass on order."

"Four bass, Chef!"

Specific communication has been a part of the professional culinary heritage for more than a hundred years, and in military cultures for longer than that, but it came relatively recently to other disciplines. Now often used in psychotherapy and counseling and well represented in the teachings of corporate communications consultants, the technique is called *active listening,* or sometimes mirroring: the process of repeating or paraphrasing communication from someone else, be it a partner or colleague. Active listening verifies to the sender that his message has been received; it gives him the opportunity to catch an error or omission early; and it helps the receiver retain that information better, taking the words "into the body." As a result, active listening builds trust, important in battle, whether during war or dinner.

Chefs get respect

In the kitchen and the military, respect matters. The honorific of "Chef" can and does instantly communicate hierarchy. In the best kitchens the term *Chef* communicates something more subtle: not just "you are my chief," but "you are my teacher." To *accept* being called Chef confirms that obligation. It is a two-way promise: a pledge to learn and trust, and a vow to coach and be trustworthy. In these kitchens, the repetition of "Yes, Chef!" can be a beautiful thing to witness.

Chefs demand brevity

"Talk to me like you're texting," LiPuma tells his students. "Because I have absolutely no patience for the *Gone with the Wind, Godfather II*, 4-hour epic. Five words or less, tell me what you need. I'll start you with 10, but then you got to get it down to five so you can learn how to get to your point: *Chef, I need help straining the sauce.*"

Those seven words—perhaps two too many for Chef LiPuma— balance the social and practical. They communicate a measure of esteem and pare away everything but the most vital information. They show respect and also respect for time, the chef's most precious resource. In the kitchen, extraneous information is exiled. Sometimes, chefs issue a blunt edict: *Get to the point.*

Sam Henderson noticed this in her transition from the corporation to the kitchen, and welcomed the removal of what she calls the burden of being polite.

"There are very few industries like the kitchen where you just say what you need and what's on your mind," Henderson says. "You don't have to be nasty or mean, but you get to the point. If something's wrong, you say it's wrong. If you need something immediately, you say, 'I need this now. I needed this yesterday.' You just cut the nonsense out because there's no time to tiptoe. Running an efficient and a cost-effective kitchen is just a monumental task. Being polite can be a waste of time. It actually gets in the way of your getting work done."

While it's hard to imagine the self-effacing Henderson—if she were to somehow find herself back in the corporate world—telling her coworkers to *just shut up and get to the point,* she nails the social whimsies of the office world. In the kitchen, work can be fun and social, but work time is *time for work.* In the office, inefficient, escapist, and self-indulgent communication devalues the very thing corporations are purchasing at high cost from their employees: their time.

Chefs meet rarely

In the last few decades we've seen chefs leave the kitchen and create their own corporations. In 1992, Eric Bromberg and his brother Bruce founded a restaurant called Blue Ribbon in New York City. By 2015, the Blue Ribbon Group comprised 19 restaurants with more than 1,200 employees in four cities. Bromberg the chef had become Bromberg the executive. But Bromberg took the lessons of mise-en-place with him. In the office he could boast of a marvelous retention rate: Of the 14 people who started with him in 1992, 11 remained after 2 decades. One reason for this was Bromberg's no-nonsense approach to interoffice communication.

"We never have meetings," he says.

"Never?" I ask.

"Not in the corporate office," he replies. "We go months and months without a meeting. I find meetings a waste of everybody's time. Once they're at work, they need to be working. We communicate in a constant flow of texts, [one-on-one] e-mails, and in-person interactions to directly solve problems. We try to have a personal connection with everyone. E-mails and general meetings are impersonal. You send [bulk] e-mails, they don't read them. I'll say, 'Talk to your people.' If I felt that someone was dynamic enough to carry a meeting, sure. But I'm not interested in group therapy sessions. We try to take problems out of a general forum and address them from top down, because every failure starts at the top, with me."

Bromberg's anti-meeting, in-person policy might not work for many offices, but just as Sam Henderson's words about politeness illuminate a particularly wasteful aspect of office culture, so, too, do Bromberg's about meetings. For the most part, staff meetings in offices happen because they're good for the *boss*, not the staff.

Meanwhile, employees in the United States spend somewhere between 40 and 50 percent of their working hours in meetings that are estimated to waste $37 billion per year. A meeting of just a few managers can cost companies thousands of dollars per hour in salary. Meeting culture proves how common and acceptable tremendous, wanton time waste is in the world of the office. Chefs, once they establish their own corporate ventures, often have an unsurprising lack of tolerance for that kind of waste.

The office has much to learn from the professional kitchen: Don't act like you have all the time in the world, and that goes double for how you treat the time of the people who work for you. Endeavor to make the work lives of your employees, your colleagues, and your bosses easier, and the first way to do that is to treat their time, and yours, as a precious commodity. Strive, like chefs do, to work clean with communication.

OUT OF THE KITCHEN

The kitchen asks cooks to field a flurry of orders, confirm them, coordinate them with their fellows, and deliver them. This communication comes from only two sources: verbal or written orders.

Here's where it doesn't come from: phone calls, voice mails, text messages, video chat, e-mails, instant messages, shared task management software, Tweets, Facebook messages, FedEx packages, postal deliveries, and pop-in visitors.

In the kitchen, communication is complex. But communication in the office is far more complicated. Cooks have one stream of orders; we have a multiplicity. Cooks cook and talk; we talk, write, call, draw, illustrate, calculate, sell, measure, stitch, and more. Cooks work in one place; we work in many. Cooks communicate frantically, but simply; our pace matches theirs, but our correspondence is much more complex. For cooks, when service stops, communication stops. For us, it never ends.

Given the tremendous differences here, I've wondered at times whether the kitchen provides useful guidance for effective communication on the outside. Again, I've concluded that the differences between kitchen and office actually *highlight* the usefulness of the thought form behind mise-en-place and call and callback.

- Kitchens maintain one stream of information. Ergo, the fewer streams, the better.

- Communication should be *clear, concise,* and *respectful.*

- Coworkers should have a *common language.*

- Communication should be confirmed with specificity, and reconfirmed when needed, for accuracy and memory.

The kitchen offers these universal principles for excellent communication.

EXERCISES: SKILLS TO LEARN

CONSOLIDATE YOUR STREAMS

The proliferation of communication channels consumes most of our work life and mounts the most challenging obstacle to creating a functioning workplace mise-en-place. The best way to manage communication is to *contain* it. Though few of us will likely succeed in paring our communication channels down to one, we can do a number of things to reduce and simplify them. Options include:

Consolidate e-mail browsers and addresses. Many of us maintain multiple e-mail addresses. If you can't reduce the number of accounts you use, forward your e-mails to one address or program your browser so that you can check multiple e-mail accounts in one place.

Reduce the number of social media and communications services you use. Services like Facebook, Twitter, and LinkedIn keep us connected and entertained. But the more we use them, the more channels we leave open for input. It's better to maintain robust activity on two or three accounts than dabble with a dozen. As for the apps, services, and software that you use to record your thoughts, notes, and tasks, discipline yourself to use only one or two programs, thereby limiting the number that you have to check.

Redirect voice mail. Some services transcribe voice mails into text. Your outgoing message can ask callers to send messages to you via e-mail instead of leaving a message. Or you can simply turn voice mail off.

Discourage communication on particular channels. You can send auto-replies from particular e-mail addresses, or you can not respond to or check messages on selected social media services, so folks who attempt to contact you through them eventually get the message that it's a dead end. When an important person regularly uses a channel that you don't, that's the kind of situation that forces you to use a service even when you've tried not to. You can, of course, ask that person to contact you on another channel, depending on your relationship. Corporations, for example, may insist you use their chosen services. That's even more reason to restrict where and when you respond in the personal realm.

Establish forwarding and alert mechanisms. Many social media services can send you an e-mail alert when you receive a message, so you don't have to take the extra step of checking that Web site or app. Third-party services can consolidate messages for you. Your e-mail program and many social media services can also alert you to communication from selected people or on selected topics. The point is to give yourself fewer channels and fewer reasons to check them.

KITCHEN PRACTICE: COOK WITH SOMEONE

The next time you cook with a partner, don't simply chat: Confer about splitting the work and tell each other what's happening as you cook. Use your kitchen communication skills.

- When your partner calls, call back with specifics.

- Share space by alerting each other with kitchen vocabulary: "Behind!" "Hot!"

- Make requests ("When will the spinach be ready?"), and answer them with times ("Two minutes!").

You might be surprised at how regimented, specific communication imparts mutual trust and makes the experience of working together efficient and pleasurable.

HABITS: BEHAVIORS TO REPEAT

CONFIRM ESSENTIAL COMMUNICATION

Not all communication requires callback, but essential communication does.

Here's why: According to a number of studies on corporate e-mail, recipients interpret e-mails correctly only 50 percent of the time, while believing they interpret them correctly close to 90 percent of the time. The same divergence occurs with senders. Another study found "a link between e-mail misunderstandings and ego-centrism," meaning that senders aren't concerned enough with how their messages are being understood.

Confirmation is only the first of four levels of callback.

1. *Confirmation*—a simple reply to acknowledge receipt of a piece of communication ("Got it!")

2. *Routing*—a reply to delay, direct, deflect, defer, or refer the sender or issue in question ("Will reply by tomorrow.")

3. *Simple answer*—requiring nothing more than a yes, no, or a specific piece of information ("I will meet you at 5:00 p.m.")

4. *Detailed answer*—any reply requiring more than about a minute of your time

Consider confirmation as the easiest option, and routing and providing a simple answer as the most efficient, because these get the item off your plate. If there isn't time for a detailed answer, the item should ideally be routed to your Action list and/or calendar.

Who and what you deem "essential" is up to you. In general, consider the following *hierarchy of relationships* in your communications triage, with "1" being the most important:

1. Managers, partners, clients, teachers, family

2. Employees, colleagues, friends

3. Vendors, solicitors, acquaintances

Also consider the following *hierarchy of issues:*

1. Health related

2. Financial

3. Managerial/administrative

4. Creative

5. Social

Confirmation need not be immediate, but it should happen within a time frame that works for you and your relationships. Though many workplaces expect replies from within minutes to an hour, in most close work relationships, 24 hours is a reasonable time to allow someone to get back to you, or for you to get back to them.

In all this communication, the good habits of active listening and mirroring will go a long way to keep your relationships solid and your communication tight, help you remember essential actions, and put a lot of the small but deliverable process work behind you.

USE ACTION LANGUAGE

We can't control others' communication behavior, but we can influence it by setting proper boundaries and rules of engagement, and by developing and using action language: a persistent effort to distinguish discussion on one hand from requests for action on the other.

Action language helps in meetings where people need to make those distinctions. Direct those around you to those requests by asking the right kinds of questions: *What's the consensus here? What's the takeaway? What's the next step? Who needs help? How can I help?*

Action language helps in e-mail as well. Often you will find yourself engaged in a thread—an extended back-and-forth conversation—or find yourself included in one and completely lost. Again, the right questions can constrain the conversation to the essentials. You can, in a particularly long e-mail thread, call for the equivalent of an "all day," something like: *Apologies. I am having a hard time deciphering this long thread. Can you outline the original issue here and tell me what you need?*

When requests aren't clear or complete, you can create forms, which regiment what others need to give to you. These can be a time-saver for both you and the person making the request provided that your form is easy for the other person to complete and that you act on it promptly.

Be careful. Forms, like meetings, measure authority in the corporate world. To those with even a bit of power, they can become a power trip if unchecked. Chef Thomas Keller disdains forms in all forms, especially when a member of his executive team creates a new one for his kitchen staff.

Don't do this to them, he tells his corporate executives. *They're working 12 hours a day. They're in the restaurant at 1:00 in the morning. They come in at noon. The only reason you're here is because there's a kid working in the restaurant at midnight when you're in bed. Don't make their job harder. Your job is to make their job easier. You* fill out the form. *That's your job.*

A chef's reprise: Heard

For 5 years while he built the restaurant into one of Philadelphia's hottest, Rob Halpern lived at Marigold, and not in the metaphorical sense, either. Halpern slept in a small room upstairs not much bigger than a closet.

One day in 2014, however, the chef decided that his work there was done, and that he and his fiancée were getting married and moving to California. With that, Halpern left. Tim and Andrew bought Marigold from him for somewhat less than Rob's asking price of $300,000 and renegotiated the lease.

One year after my first visit, I dropped by to see how things were going.

Tim and Andrew promoted Keith to executive chef and kept as many of the crew as they could after a pause of several months for renovations. They simplified the cooking, removing most of the retro references and nitrogen-powered items on the menu. They focused on a more classical approach while retaining a bit of Halpern's whimsy. They simplified the stations; at the new Marigold, everyone was encouraged to be a "roundsman," meaning someone able to cook every dish on the menu if called to do so. And they simplified the communication, too. Gone were the references to obscure white male progressive rock artists. Gone were the annoying little sticky notes that Rob used to leave for them on their stations: "This could have been cleaned better." They did keep the reference to the pass—the place where waiters picked up food from the hot line—as "Station Four," even though there wasn't a Station One, Two, and Three, nor had there ever been.

Keith's cooking kept the good reviews and customers coming in. But the new chef had to swallow one bitter pill: It was he, and not Rob, who had actually prepared that truffled crab macaroni and cheese that won Rinna Diaz's heart. The guys in the kitchen break Keith's balls about it all the time. *Just think, Keith. If Rob hadn't taken credit for it, Rinna could have been yours.* Instead, it's Rob in California and Keith at Station Four.

At that very moment, Rob Halpern was likely enjoying the sunshine on his 30-acre almond orchard outside Paso Robles. Outside his 1,600-square-foot home, chickens were probably poking around in the soil among his persimmon, peach, and pear trees. He might be driving to the farmers' market, or else to the winery or retreat center where he was serving as exclusive chef for special events. And when Rinna returned from her job as an operating room nurse, they'd drink wine.

Back in Philadelphia, Halpern's old crew had no clue. "I think he has some land," Keith said. "He told us potentially he was opening a farm."

Is he gonna cook? I ask.

They shake their heads. They haven't heard.

Recipe for Success

Commit to confirming and expecting confirmation of essential communication. Call back.

INSPECT AND CORRECT

A chef's story: The laughing coach

THE CRITICS AGREE: Bill Telepan can cook.

Frank Bruni, a writer for the *New York Times*, shrugged when he first entered Telepan's eponymous restaurant after it opened in late 2005. The food press heralded Telepan for his seasonal cooking at fancier digs like the Judson Grill in Midtown; this new place, Telepan's first as an owner, was humble, tucked away on a residential side street on the Upper West Side of Manhattan. "An oddly configured series of rooms," Bruni wrote, "created from the joined first floors of adjacent townhouses." The menu looked "prosaic." But in his 2006 review, Bruni described being startled, again and again, by unpretentious food that burst with flavor, "none of it precious but all of it vibrant"—a vegetable bread soup, a juicy fillet of salmon, smoked trout on little blini pancakes. The food, Bruni enthused, "shuns trickery and puts its faith in fundamental virtues: its freshness; the pureness or punch of its flavors; the skill with which it's been cooked." Other reviews, like the one in *New York Magazine*, found fault with the restaurant's decor and pricing, but conceded there was "no doubt about Telepan's talents as a chef."

Of course, Bill Telepan didn't actually *cook* his food. As a chef-restaurateur, Telepan's job now was to *look* at his food. All the dishes were *his* recipes, but other hands made them, hands trained by Telepan. He watched his food and his crew as they cooked it, listened to his customers and critics after they ate it, and made adjustments.

Telepan resembled his food: brilliance in an unassuming package, his refinement evolved by watching, listening, and adjusting along his own journey from the kitchen of a New Jersey deli into what Bruni called the "top tier" of New York chefs. He had come from a working-class family—his dad employed at a General Motors plant, his mother doing odd jobs. He started cooking in high school, ending up behind the grill at Garfunkel's—what Telepan called a "glorified TGI Fridays"—but left the restaurant to go to college. When Telepan became bored by his classes and missed the kitchen, the chef at Garfunkel's drove him up to the CIA and gave him a tour. In his 2 years at the CIA, Telepan's world and palate sprung open. He trailed at Charlie Palmer's River Cafe, and soon Palmer introduced Telepan to the man who would become his mentor, Alfred Portale.

The Gotham Bar and Grill was only 3 years old when Telepan arrived, but by that time Alfred Portale had transformed it from a mediocre restaurant into one of the most important in the world. According to Ruth Reichl—one in a line of *New York Times* critics over the years to give Gotham a coveted three-star review—Portale and crew "figured out how to make Americans feel at ease with fancy food." At the forefront of "New American Cuisine," the diminutive Portale liked his food tall, and, though exacting, remained as composed as any of his famous plates. Telepan recalled: "It was a busy kitchen with 350 to 400 covers a night at a very high level of service. So everybody had to be on. But Alfred wasn't a yeller. Alfred would get *disappointed* in you."

Telepan worked on Gotham's line for 3 years, left for a time, and returned as Portale's sous-chef for 4 more years. The gangly Telepan—a Jersey kid prone to sudden bursts of full-body laughter—contrasted with the quiet, restrained Portale. He emulated Portale's dedication to ingredients, to uniformity, and crucially, to his role as chief inspector. Portale himself didn't make the food. The cooks did. Portale taught them how, inspecting and correcting their work until they got it right. Portale could do this because, unlike other chefs of his stature, he stayed in his restaurant, at the pass, the last line of defense of his three stars and his standards. To this day he stays. "I like it better when I'm there," Portale says.

The standards and refinement rubbed off on Telepan. And when his turn came to teach people how to cook *his* food, he followed Portale's example by constantly watching and training others to watch. At Telepan's restaurant, he always put three sets of eyes on every dish that went out: the cook's, the expediter's, and the head food runner's. Usually Telepan expedited, but when he stepped away, Darwin, his longtime back waiter, stepped in. After 8 years Telepan built a two-star restaurant with a rock-solid crew who cooked his food well. He had gathered great customers, a mix of regular neighborhood folks, foodies, and theatergoers for nearby Lincoln Center. He decided to open a second place.

Telepan chose a space in the upscale Tribeca neighborhood, where the food scene was hotter. Bill Telepan wanted to do an American version of a Spanish *tapas* restaurant with small dishes inspired by the comfort foods of his Jersey youth—haute versions of pizza, Buffalo wings, pigs in a blanket, shrimp poppers, grilled cheese, even gourmet Cheez-Its—along with plates of short ribs, sweetbreads, pork belly, and escargots. He called it Telepan Local.

The restaurant launched only for friends and family in January of 2014. Then Telepan decided that Local should stay open, quietly, and at least have some kind of income stream while they worked the kinks out. There were a lot of kinks. The restaurant hadn't yet installed enough natural gas capacity to run all the appliances, so many of the stoves and ovens remained inoperative. The kitchen didn't have heat lamps either, so plates went out as they were ready, and the kitchen and waitstaff had trouble nailing the timing. The waitstaff needed continual training.

Bill Telepan now spent more time downtown, nurturing his newborn. Telepan promoted his uptown sous-chef Joel Javier to run Local as chef de cuisine. Telepan coached him while Javier in turn trained a kitchen of new recruits on almost 30 recipes and techniques. On an icy evening in February, Telepan stood at the pass next to Javier, who called out orders to the line and received the plates, inspecting them and giving each a sprinkle of coarse sea salt and olive oil before handing them to a food runner.

Javier talked about the difficulty of getting consistency while also maintaining finesse or *soigné* (French for "made with great care")—the lesson that Telepan learned with Portale. "It's why fast food is so successful," Javier said. "They've found a way that you can get the same hamburger and same fries anywhere, anytime. Of course, it's not very good." One thing you couldn't do was automate *soigné*. That's why Javier and Telepan watched.

They both eyed a new extern, Diana, a Russian Studies graduate of Columbia University who had pivoted to become a culinary student at the nearby International Culinary Center. On her third day at Telepan Local, she still struggled with several of the six dishes for which she was responsible.

Telepan caught a glimpse of an order of mushrooms in parchment that Diana had just pulled from the oven and split open to plate. He saw that the food inside it wasn't cooked completely. There was no putting it back.

"Just start a new one," he told her.

Diana continued to rush things. Diana put an order of Telepan's *pan con tamate* on the small grill at her station to toast before brushing with garlic and topping with a spread of chopped tomato and garlic. A minute later, Telepan caught her pulling it off the grill prematurely.

"That's not done," Telepan barked. "Fire another one. Be *patient*. It's grilled cheese, right?"

"Right," Diana replied. "Can't rush the chemistry."

Javier counseled her. It should toast to a *good* golden brown, he said, or the garlic wouldn't release its essence when she rubbed it into the bread. And if she didn't toast it enough, the bread would get soggy faster when she spread the tomato on it. Telepan worried that the grill itself might not be getting hot enough. Another equipment problem, perhaps. "I know it's just a grilled cheese sandwich," he told Diana. "But it's got to be a great fucking grilled cheese sandwich."

"I'm Bill Telepan," he said later. "I can't fuck up a grilled cheese!"

Telepan heard himself and exploded with laughter.

WHAT CHEFS DO, WHAT CHEFS KNOW

Chefs remain vigilant

The restaurant business is hard.

A study published in 2005 found that 60 percent of new restaurants fail during their first 3 years. The challenge of feeding demanding customers meals prepared by hand from expensive, perishable ingredients is insurmountable for most entrepreneurs who try it. In fine dining the stakes rise: costlier ingredients, equipment, rent, and talent.

Failure can happen at any time. It can come as slowly as a season of half-empty dining rooms or as suddenly as a bad review. It can be sparked by a mistake in one dish, or caused by hundreds of mediocre plates. Failure may not arise from the food at all, but from the manner in which it is served.

A good restaurant requires constant vigilance. That watchfulness ensues not from a clichéd quest for excellence that one might see on a motivational poster, but from a fundamental, endemic, unending fear of failure.

Because the kitchen is the beating heart of a tough business that demands finesse from people who may not have much experience or many standards, the professional kitchen must always train and coach its staff.

Ergo the best kitchens are schools, the best chefs are teachers, and the best cooks are students.

Chefs approach perfection

Inspect and correct is how the chef approaches perfection, "approach" being the operative word in that phrase, because perfection is never achieved. At most, what the great chef can accomplish is *meticulous execution,* a phrase that kitchen designer Jimi Yui borrowed from Chef Gray Kunz. *Meticulous execution* encompasses the ambition of a chef, but also a bit of her stoicism: *You can only do what you can do.*

Chefs submit to critique

As a system of ongoing education dedicated to becoming better at one's craft, inspect and correct requires humility, a commitment to *submission.* The chef submits to her responsibility to teach the cook. The cook submits to the wisdom and guidance of the chef. The cook submits to her own discipline and to honing her own processes. The chef submits to maintaining a balance between her own instincts and the wisdom and guidance of the customers and critics. And both the chef and cook submit to the fact that this submission never ends.

Chefs prowl

Inspect and correct happens primarily at a place called the pass, or pass-through, a checkpoint between the kitchen and the dining room. Think of it as the narrowest point in an hourglass, through which all orders from the customers pass through to the cooks, and all dishes pass from the cooks on their way back to the customers.

The person who runs this checkpoint is called the *expediter.* Many times it is the chef herself who stands here, but you may find a sous-chef or an experienced food runner expediting as well. The expediter acts in several capacities, first as a defender of the cooks— evaluating and pacing the incoming orders so that the kitchen doesn't get overwhelmed; second as a monitor of practices, processes, and habits as the food is being cooked; and third as the defender of the customer and the restaurant, evaluating each dish before it goes out.

In this work, the expediter draws on her sense of the restaurant's rhythms. She employs reconnaissance from the dining room to make decisions. She will use all her senses: mostly sight, but also sound, touch, smell, and taste.

"I taste food all night when I'm expediting," Telepan says. His cooks do, too: spooning sauce into their mouths, tasting vegetables and starches. The tasting began hours and days *before* service, while they made the sauces and stews and other preparations with longer lead times. Telepan was experimenting with a new salad for the menu when he took some beets from a cook's mise-en-place. Telepan put one in his mouth. He could tell they had been in the cook's mise-en-place for longer than a day. Tamping down his anger, he found the cook, handing him a piece of freshly cut beet. "Taste that," he said. And then he offered a piece of beet from the cook's mise-en-place. "Try that one. Now tell me if there's a difference." Telepan teaches how to taste, but he still prowls the line hours before service to do his own tasting.

The expediter is not just an observer, but a coach. She must not only inspect, but correct. Sometimes problems come from improper technique: an ingredient thrown in a pan that's not hot enough, a piece of raw fish that hasn't been patted dry, inconsistent cuts of vegetable or protein. But more often mishaps arise from compromising one or more of the principles of mise-en-place.

QUALITY CHECKPOINTS OF THE KITCHEN

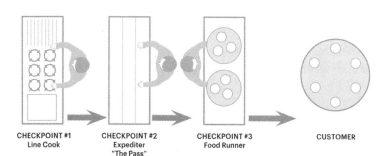

CHECKPOINT #1
Line Cook

CHECKPOINT #2
Expediter
"The Pass"

CHECKPOINT #3
Food Runner

CUSTOMER

"I tell my cooks, 'Don't try to get over,'" Telepan says. "Don't do something half-assed. Don't try to hide it. Because I'm gonna find out. I know that [dish] takes 4 minutes and it's only been 2; don't even put it up. I'd rather you take an extra minute [and] slow up service to get it right. But don't put it out, because that 1 minute you save in putting it out is going to become 6 minutes behind because you're going to have to redo the plate."

Chefs teach self-critique

Cooks must internalize what they've been taught and learn how to evaluate their work in the way their chefs do.

"I tell new cooks, 'Look at your station as if it's your restaurant and everybody is coming in to critique *your restaurant*,'" Telepan says. "'You have to keep it organized and clean in the way you want your restaurant to be when you grow up to be a chef. So how you treat your station now is how your restaurant is gonna run. Now is the time to learn those habits.'"

Cooks cut corners because of laziness, or forgetfulness, or fatigue, or sometimes embarrassment at having discovered their own mistake. "I always say to them that it's worse for them to have me find out than to say, 'Chef, I fucked up, I missed this, I gotta make it again.' I *love* that. Because it happens. In the kitchen, the machines are *human*."

Chefs fix and use mistakes

Chefs transform failure into success by incorporating mistakes into their workflow—or rather, incorporating the solutions to prevent those mistakes. Thus cooks learn that failure is always an opportunity.

Thomas Keller of The French Laundry invited a four-star former chef from New York to demonstrate some classic French preparations for the chefs of his Bouchon restaurants. But surrounded by a crowd of young chefs, this great chef grew nervous while cooking one of the most fundamental of all French preparations: the omelet.

"He totally screwed it up," Keller remembers. "I had to do something."

So Keller transformed the situation by having all the chefs make their own omelets. Now the lecture became a laboratory.

"It was extraordinary," Keller remembers. What came out of the next 30 minutes was a technique to precook omelets for his Las Vegas restaurant, where they serve 600 breakfasts every morning. "The chef tasted it, I tasted it, and all the chefs tasted it, and we go, *Wow!* It looks beautiful. It's perfect. Out of somebody's mistake and somebody's embarrassment comes a technique that none of us thought about."

Chefs calculate the cost of compromise

Chefs' standards can sometimes seem more for flourish than function. The value of a clean, white chef's jacket has little if any direct bearing on the presentation or taste of food. Yet wearing "clean whites" is a common standard. Why and when do cooks compromise? Thomas Keller explains by asking a rhetorical question.

"Are you willing to wear a T-shirt with a hole in it even when no one sees the hole?" he asks. "Yeah, maybe it's okay. Maybe it's the last day before I can wash my clothes. I've got six T-shirts and it's my sixth day and that seventh T-shirt has a hole in it. Am I going to get a new T-shirt or wash the other one? It's a compromise. We have to be available to and open to negotiating that compromise whether it's with ourselves or with each other. But the result of that compromise cannot affect in any negative way the result that we're searching for."

Because chefs know that compromise sits on a slippery slope to chaos, they're cautious and calculating about the compromises they make.

If perfectionism is the quest for quality at the expense of delivery, then settling for less is the quest for delivery at the expense of quality. Excellence itself is a compromise between the two: quality delivered.

Chefs and cooks live in this difficult dynamic from dish to dish. Every single plate must embody that balance. The greatest gem of their hard-won experience is the ability to discern that tipping point. They know when they're "phoning it in," and they can tighten things up. They know when they're being too precious and can let things go.

OUT OF THE KITCHEN

Most corporations evaluate their work on a large scale—whether on the factory assembly line or in the quality assurance process at a technology business.

The kind of evaluation we speak of here, however, is small-scale, personal inspection—not the insipid, impersonal self-evaluation questionnaires distributed by many human resources departments—but personal examination of our own individual product or service, whether as small as an e-mail or as big as a book.

Outside the kitchen we ostensibly value coaching, but we don't take its implications seriously. Most corporate or creative professionals don't have the equivalent of a chef who cares about their education or their growth. For example, it is one of the central tenets of the professional kitchen that, after an apprentice gives a chef several years of hard work, the chef himself will make calls and send that apprentice off to work for another respected chef to continue to learn and build her résumé. It's hard to imagine such a thing in the corporate world. Nor do we have the counterpart of the expediter. An assistant or secretary can act as a traffic cop for scheduling, but few in the working world have such a luxury; and, anyway, an assistant is not a mentor. Managers can function as expediters for their staff, but in the corporate world many managers perform only half of the expediter's function: They're good at critiquing work but horrible at timing the workload so that their crew doesn't get overwhelmed. In academia, teachers are sometimes observed by colleagues, administrators, and students to provide feedback; mostly, they are measured by test scores, a dubious determination of the *quality* of their instruction. Hitting a numerical target for any profession may be no better indicator of quality than an athlete who wins a point despite bad form. Those who work with words lack editors. The classic newsroom, with its layers of oversight, is disappearing. For most of us, spell-checker is as good as it's ever going to get.

We need in our world of work the means to evaluate our own work and that of others. We need the means to refine our methods and product, and to incorporate the knowledge gained from our failures. If we don't have mentors, the responsibility falls on us to create a personal culture of checks and balances, of inspection and correction, so we can *work clean* with feedback.

The best kitchens are schools, the best chefs are teachers, and the best cooks are students.

EXERCISES: SKILLS TO LEARN

SET STANDARDS

Chef Thomas Keller asks: What are your standards?

We must answer this question before evaluating our work because our inspection will only be as accurate and effective as our vision of excellence is clear. A vague vision will yield a nebulous result.

To shape your own idea of mastery, address the following questions:

1. Who is your model or mentor for the work you do? What is it about her work, process, or demeanor that compels you?

2. What is an example of an ideal product or service for the kind of work you do? What are the qualities that make it so?

3. What are the habits that help you achieve your standards?

4. What are the habits that hinder your progress toward those standards?

5. What are the environments that assist you? What are the environments that impede you?

6. What are the external rewards or consequences you desire or expect from the impact of your work?

7. In what aspects and under what circumstances are you willing to compromise your standards? What aspects are you not willing to compromise under any circumstances? What trade-offs are you willing to make?

Grappling with these questions will equip you for the next exercise.

MAKE A QUALITY CONTROL CHECKLIST

Based on what you've discovered about your standards above, use the checklist technique you learned in *The Second Ingredient:*

Arranging Spaces, Perfecting Movements on page 78 to evaluate a work product you create or a service you do. This checklist should not simply measure results. For example, if you are a salesperson, you may indeed feel that the only box that's important to check is the one beside the question "Did I make the sale?" Your checklist should reflect only the factors you can control. A checklist measures your actions, not that of others. A checklist measures *meticulous execution,* not perfection.

The items on your checklist should:

- Be actionable

- Measure quantity or quality

- Fit on one page

COUNTING MISTAKES

For 1 day, keep a tally of all the errors you make, whether great or small, whether personal or work-related. And for each of the errors, write the consequence or result beside it.

Your entries could be as mundane as "Mistake: Forgot umbrella. Result: Had to run back home to get it" or as significant as "Mistake: Misjudged distance to car in front of me. Result: Hit car."

At the end of the day, for each item, write one action you could have taken before the mistake to prevent it or make that error less likely.

The point of this log is not guilt or embarrassment! Quite the opposite, the process of logging mistakes empowers us by cultivating the following:

- An awareness of how common error is

- A habit of linking error and consequence

- An understanding of how we can reduce or prevent mistakes

KITCHEN PRACTICE: TASTE TEST

The next time you serve a meal to one or more friends or family members, ask them to write down their feedback on a piece of paper. Tell them that you are looking specifically for things to improve and that they shouldn't be afraid to be honest! Then, later that evening, read the feedback. Note how it makes you feel. Then translate that feedback into an Action list for the next time you prepare those dishes.

Encouraging and receiving feedback is difficult but crucial to becoming a better cook, a better professional, and a better person.

HABITS: BEHAVIORS TO REPEAT

MAKE FIX-IT CHECKLISTS
(OR FIX YOUR CHECKLISTS)

Chefs transform failure into success by recognizing mistakes and fixing them. Chefs do this by adjusting their recipes, whether for a dish or a process.

Outside the kitchen each of us keeps a mental, internalized recipe for the work we do. But in circumstances where we regularly make mistakes, sometimes we need a physical, external recipe to guide a course correction. We can respond most powerfully to error in our work by creating and fixing checklists.

The next time you err at work in a way that makes you cringe, write it down just as you did in the "Counting Mistakes" exercise on the opposite page. Then during your Daily Meeze determine one or several steps you could take to avoid the mistake again. If you have an existing checklist for the procedure, incorporate the change. If you don't, create a new one. Even if you only use the checklist temporarily—until you've incorporated the behavior— this tool can become a place into which you put your mistakes and also a productive channel for your emotions about those mistakes.

USE THE BUDDY SYSTEM

Wherever possible, grab a second set of eyes and ears for your important work. Cultivate relationships with people who can give you fresh perspective.

Bosses. Many managers love to teach; a few have no real investment in coaching and just expect you to do the job they're paying you to do. If you have a manager who appreciates when you ask for help, avail yourself of that opportunity.

Mentors. Even champions like you need coaches. But too many people approach mentors as "role models" or "connections." The kind of relationship we are encouraging you to cultivate is with someone who can truly evaluate your work from time to time and show you how to better evaluate your own progress.

Colleagues. From critiquing and troubleshooting projects, to meeting regularly to discuss your progress toward perfecting old skills and learning new ones, a trusted colleague can be a vital ally in the workplace.

Employees. You can train a good employee or assistant to be an extra set of eyes and ears to keep you on track and help you quality-check. Chefs are constantly teaching their skills to the people who work for them, and if you have an assistant, he will become better as you trust him more with this kind of work.

SELF-EDITING TECHNIQUES

When measuring our own product, we need to get a bit of distance from our work, in any way we can.

In *The Artful Edit,* Susan Bell recommends a series of methods any writer can use to gain perspective on her own work. These methods, slightly modified, can be used as perspective-gaining tools for many different creative pursuits, to help you take off your creator's cap and put on your editor's hat.

Change your environment. If you're looking for different perspective on your work, change the place in which you review it. For folks who write on a computer, an example of this would be printing your work out.

Bring different senses into the mix. If you create something to be read with your eyes, for example, evaluate it by listening with your ears. One example for a writer would be reading your work aloud, slowly, or in a foreign accent.

Create an inner dialogue. Assume the identity of someone else who might lend some needed perspective to your work and have an inner dialogue with him. How might he evaluate your work?

You can also avail yourself of software, apps, and services to check the quality of your work. Virtual assistants can also be helpful provided they have the right skills. For writers, Hemingway evaluates your work for clarity and brevity. Grammarly and Ginger are also powerful tools.

A chef's reprise: The review

In April 2014 the *New York Times* reviewed Telepan Local.

"Half-formed and unconvincing," critic Pete Wells called it. He couldn't get past the plates (too small), the tables (also too small), and the prices (too large). The scallops and mushrooms? Delicious, but not enough on the plate. The "wonderful little grilled cheese panini topped with a Spanish tomato-garlic-olive oil spread"? Not very shareable. Wells found the pigs in a blanket to be too much like, well, pigs in a blanket, and as for the shrimp poppers, Wells wrote that "Telepan Local seemed to be trying to imitate Red Lobster and not quite succeeding." He loved one dessert and hated another. He gave it one star.

Bill Telepan was at the uptown restaurant when the review hit the Internet. He rushed down to be with Javier and the dejected crew, and after service took them all out for drinks.

Telepan didn't think the review was unfair—he was already considering a move toward bigger plates and standard service. But he was stung by the insinuation that he was overcharging. He spent the next several months fixing the service and making the food taste as good as he thought it should. But in the summer of 2014— and summers are usually bad for restaurants in New York—Tribeca proved to be a ghost town. By November, he decided to close Telepan Local, just shy of its 1-year anniversary. The closing downtown "sucked," Telepan said, but it gave him valuable information for the future. In his next place he planned to spend much more time working on "front of house." He needed to find a neighborhood where he could build community like he had at Telepan. And he needed to stick with the food for which he had become famous.

Bill Telepan came back to the Upper West Side, to his position at the pass, and resumed his watch. Here nothing much had changed. Telepan's flagship was still thriving and had recently received its first Michelin star rating. The evening's service was punctuated again and again by Telepan's laughter.

"This is far from a clipboard job," he said.

The smoked trout, prepared by Sam, was a huge favorite. His lobster Bolognese, made by Misel, his line cook since Gotham in 1991, was as bright and fresh as Telepan's customers had come to expect. The chef didn't have to return any plates to the cooks this evening.

Bill Telepan's cooks could cook. His coaching tasted really good.

Recipe for Success

Commit to coaching yourself, to being coached, and to coaching others. Evaluate yourself.

TOTAL UTILIZATION

A chef's story: The guts guy

THE WAGON that ground its way through the streets of Providence, Rhode Island, had two doors. One side unlatched to reveal choice cuts of meat on ice—the big muscles, loins, ribs, rounds. The other side, opened in the poor neighborhoods of immigrant Italians and Portuguese, contained the organ meats of the animals—hearts, intestines, stomachs, livers, kidneys. These cuts were cheaper because the wealthier customers didn't want them. The innards didn't look or smell appetizing. To make them edible took time and technique.

Rosalie Cosentino, who came from Naples to America with her family in the early 1900s, knew how to work with these ingredients because her family wouldn't have had much to eat if she didn't. For the Cosentino family, tripe was tradition. Rosalie began with the stomach of a cow, which she soaked and boiled for hours. As the meat cooked, it mellowed, in the process releasing a stench that filled the house. Then she cooked the tripe in red wine, tomato, and herbs until it became rich and tasty.

Across the Narragansett Bay from Providence, James Thurston Easton—descended from one of the royal governors of colonial Rhode Island and from the founders of the city in which he lived, Newport—worked in the family business, the Easton Breakfast Sausage Company. The Eastons had been supplying the Eastern Seaboard with provisions made from intestines and meat scraps since before the Civil War.

The Cosentinos and Eastons, however, were in the minority among Americans who had for most of the nation's history been living "high on the hog." Limitless land, plentiful livestock, and bountiful harvests made America the land of waste. Our cooking habits, too, mirrored that laziness. The ecologically holistic example provided to the colonists by the Native Americans was swept away with the natives themselves. Subcultures of culinary thrift existed among immigrants, who brought their traditions with them from the Old Country; the poor; and the descendants of African slaves, who were traditionally given the provisions less valued by European slaveholders. From those ingredients considered inedible by many, African Americans created an entire cuisine, "soul food," a specific term now used generically by other cultures to celebrate their own humble culinary origins. But for the majority of Americans, humble was humiliating, and the squandering of our bounty was actually the real American tradition.

Only during World War II did middle-class Americans first taste real scarcity. Five months after Japan bombed Pearl Harbor, all sugar sales were halted. Thus began the first salvo of what became America's first full-scale food rationing program, which included limits on coffee, canned foods, meat, cheese, milk, and fats. Families were encouraged to grow their own vegetables in "victory gardens" to reduce demand on the supply chain. Victory cookbooks—like *The American Woman's Cook Book* compiled by Ruth Berolzheimer in 1942—offered strategies for wartime cookery, including soup making (because, Berolzheimer wrote, of "the returning necessity for using every bit of food that enters the kitchen"), saving fats and oils (desperately needed for the production of explosives), and shifting to cheaper, more plentiful foods like seafood ("There will probably be no shortage") and the more perishable, less popular meats: liver, sweetbreads, kidneys, heart, and tripe.

"This is no hardship," Berolzheimer wrote, "but a distinct advantage, for these parts contain more vitamins than those that we are more accustomed to using and since there is no waste they cost less."

In this battle, Americans like Cosentino and Easton had tradition on their side. Ironically, food rationing during World War II forced the Easton company's closure due to a wartime spice shortage. In the decades after the fighting ended—after Rosalie Cosentino's grandson John married James Easton's daughter Susan, and after John and Susan had a son named Christopher— the food economy of the United States transformed.

Developments in farming, transportation, and marketing restored and redoubled our American bounty. Food became an industry. The processed food sector grew, and along with it the expectation that raw food should have a sameness as if it were manufactured: Apples should be uniform in shape and have no blemishes. Oranges should be big and seedless and easy to peel. Corn shouldn't have different-colored kernels. Meat, too, became mass-produced, more plentiful, and cheaper than ever. It acquired packaging, antiseptic and as divorced from the animal as possible— no heads, no tails, no feet, no guts. The wagons in our cities carrying tripe and kidneys on melting ice vanished, supplanted by gleaming supermarkets with rows of choice cuts wrapped in shiny cellophane and white Styrofoam. Never mind that when the dirt came off our vegetables and the stink came off our meat, so too did much of the flavor and nutrition. Never mind that producing all this "perfect" food generated an unprecedented, obscene amount of waste. Never mind that a new generation of Americans didn't know many of the things their grandparents knew: how to cook, how to grow, how to hunt and fish. Most didn't care to know. John, Susan, and Christopher Cosentino wanted nothing to do with Rosalie's tripe, tasting of poverty and an older, forgotten America.

Growing up in Rhode Island in the 1970s, Chris Cosentino still found many things to love about his grandparents' world. On weekends at his grandfather James's home in Newport, his grandmother Helen put out pot roasts, roasted bird, or baked bluefish for dinner. Helen took Chris and his little brother fishing, clamming, and quahogging, and Chris developed a taste for raw, briny seafood. She made chowders, seafood salads, and lobster rolls. In the summer at their beach house, they hosted lobster and clam boils. And the nearby Portuguese American Club threw an annual festival where Chris tried clams and chorizo, chickpeas, and kale soup. On other weekends, Chris visited Rosalie at her three-story house on Mount Pleasant Avenue in Providence, where she grew basil in coffee cans on window ledges and San Marzano tomatoes in the back, jarring them in the basement along with her dandelion wine. Chris helped Rosalie cut and dry fresh pasta, roll pizza dough, fry soffrito, and bake tomato pie—even though the barnyard smell of her tripe during the first hours of cooking still sent Chris running for the door.

Chris Cosentino's first love was food, but the legacy, lore, and lure of lesser cuts were lost on him, as they were on the American culinary establishment. When 18-year-old Chris enrolled in the culinary program at Rhode Island's Johnson & Wales University, organ meats were absent. Butchery class brought him nowhere near a whole cow or pig. In garde-manger class, Chris learned to make classic French terrines, explained to him as a way of preserving and serving scraps and other leftover ingredients. "Cold meat loaf," he thought. But the school didn't teach the techniques at the heart of his familial legacy—charcuterie, the making of sausage.

Cosentino had to leave school for that education, finding it instead in the kitchen of Red Sage in Washington, DC. Cosentino adored Chef Mark Miller, who pioneered haute Southwestern cuisine and took teaching seriously. He showed Chris the magic of sausage making; the difference between emulsified and nonemulsified, between fine ground and coarse ground. And when Cosentino left, Miller gave him all his recipes. Cosentino, a dyslexic, taught himself to butcher by buying an illustrated veterinarian's guide. He moved to California in the late 1990s, staging at Alice Waters's revered Chez Panisse. The chef, Christopher Lee, asked his charges whether any of them had ever broken down a whole Bellwether lamb. Chris raised his hand, lying. He went downstairs and made a decent job of it.

Cosentino had worked in great restaurants across the country, but when restaurateur Mark Pastore hired him as chef of San Francisco's Incanto, he returned to his roots. Pastore opened the small restaurant to serve rustic Italian food. Peasant food. Chris knew that food. The smell of his now late great-grandmother Rosalie's tripe lingered in his nose still. But by 2003, Cosentino's palate had grown sophisticated enough to appreciate a heritage still considered unsophisticated by most Americans. He put Rosalie's *trippa Neapolitana* on Incanto's menu. He knew purveyors who could give him good tripe, cleaner than his grandmother had gotten off the meat wagon. He added spice to cut the richness. And Chris Cosentino got a lot of well-to-do but not-so-adventurous San Franciscans to try tripe and love it. Cosentino added other lesser cuts to the menu—beef heart, served as a tartare, pig trotters, blood and blood sausage—cuts that customers and purveyors previously saw as garbage, the cuts that for years could be sold only to dog food manufacturers.

Before Incanto, the only chef whom Cosentino saw serve organ meats as haute cuisine was Lydia Shire—a flamboyant cook with fire-red hair who, in her Boston restaurant Biba and in the pages of gourmet magazines, showcased dishes like sweetbread skewers, brains, and veal heart.

Halfway around the world, another chef had been making a more pointed culinary and political point. Ten years earlier, Fergus Henderson, an untrained chef, opened a restaurant in London called St. John to feature meats from every part of the animals he served, a tribute to classic but forgotten English cooking. He enshrined those recipes and techniques in a 1999 book called *Nose to Tail Eating*, served with a simple ethos and a dash of British humor. "If you kill an animal," Henderson was fond of saying, "you should eat all of it. It's only polite."

Cosentino was hipped to Henderson by Anthony Bourdain, who proselytized for the British chef during a visit to San Francisco and in his groundbreaking book and television travelogue, *A Cook's Tour*—an inspiration for Cosentino, who hadn't yet seen the world.

With the rise of Fergus Henderson's visibility, lesser cuts acquired sophistication and acclaim in the food world. Chefs exhumed and redeemed some older, exotic-sounding designations to market them: offal, or "off fall," which denoted those discarded cuts that would "fall off" the animal or cutting board when butchered; or umbles, likely from the French *nombles;* from which the English purportedly derived the phrase "to eat humble pie," equating base cuisine with humiliation. Humble no more, offal was loved by chefs in part because to cook it well was a mark of expertise. Anyone could broil a steak and roast a chicken. But to take a tough or gamey cut of an animal and make it tender and fragrant and tasty, that was the ultimate test of a cook's abilities. Offal was better food, too: more nutritious. More flavorful. And it did have the added benefit of being economically and ecologically sound. Offal became the carnivore's stake in a growing sustainability movement that had been dominated politically and philosophically by herbivores—vegetarians and vegans who had cast meat production and consumption in its entirety as the enemy. "If humans consumed all edible portions of the cow, rather than only the socially desirable cuts, we would need to raise and slaughter fewer cows to feed the same number of people," Cosentino's boss Pastore wrote in 2004. "This would unquestionably be better for the world's environment."

Suddenly Cosentino found himself the spokesman of a movement. He became known as the guts guy. Cosentino, humble about umbles, said: "All I'm doing is riding on the coattails of thousands of grandmas before me." But that wasn't, actually, all he was doing. He was reckoning with more than just his family legacy. He was grappling for the first time with the sacrificed lives on his plate. We are animals who eat other animals. Chris wanted to return to them some measure of respect. Cosentino made a decision: He wanted three spring lambs to serve for Easter. If he were going to take their lives, he vowed that the blood should be on his hands.

Cosentino drove to a friend's farm near the Bay Area. He killed three sheep. It was difficult work physically, but harder emotionally.

Now the ingredients in his kitchen took on a heightened value. Ingredients were not to be wasted. Energy was not to be wasted. Time was not to be wasted. Life was not to be wasted. Everything counted. Only a small percentage of his menu was offal, but it became important, as a principle, to show America how not to kill a living thing only to throw three-quarters of its body in the garbage can.

WHAT CHEFS DO, WHAT CHEFS KNOW

Chefs abhor waste

In French, *garde-manger* means "guard of the food."

It's a lofty title for someone who, in the modern professional kitchen, stands just above dishwasher on the hierarchy: the guy or gal in the corner with the vast array of mise-en-place plating salads and preparing other cold appetizers.

But those cold preparations speak of the garde-manger's original purpose: to make sure that the kitchen wastes nothing. For garde-mangers, that means packing meat scraps into molds and casings, sometimes with spices and congealed stock. A caviar-garnished terrine is one example of this. The humble hot dog is another. Garde-manger means, on a larger level, guarding the pantry: making sure that food doesn't go bad prematurely through improper storage; that the ingredients ordered first get served before those ordered later; that the amount of food ordered matches the amount of food used; and that the recipes themselves use ingredients in an economical way. Nowadays that responsibility is spread throughout the kitchen, with the chef herself taking the ultimate responsibility for the economy and ecology of the enterprise.

We've said from the start that the kitchen's unique circumstances—perishable product made by humans under deadline—give rise to a unique set of work behaviors. What we haven't yet articulated is that all these behaviors are innately *conservationist:* not only to conserve ingredients, but to conserve the time it takes to prepare them, the movement to make the best use of that time, the space that allows for that economy of movement, and the wits and energies of the people who have to execute these tasks.

Focus and order are *by-products* of the values and the behaviors of mise-en-place. But the behaviors themselves, the things chefs and cooks actually *do*, are all geared toward restricting waste. The goal of completely eliminating waste is impossible. And yet this thought form provides the target at which all kitchen work aims: *total utilization*, in four interrelated dimensions—*space*, *motion* (or energy), *time*, and *resources* (including ingredients, money, and people).

Chefs save space to save motion. For chefs space can be more liability than luxury if not used efficiently. Chefs conserve space to help them make motion—their effort—easier and better.

Chefs save motion to save time. Conserving motion conserves the *time* it takes to move. Conserving motion also conserves a tremendous amount of human *energy*, both physical and mental, as in refining a task by finding a better process or transforming the motion into an automatic reaction so the mind can be free to think other things.

Chefs save time to save resources. Time is the beating heart that compels both human hunger and the microbes that spoil food. Conserving time preserves the customer and the food. Conserving time also liberates human energy, both mental and physical. Being able to work in compressed time gives us more of the one thing we cannot manufacture.

Chefs save resources to save the business. Chefs conserve ingredients because every dollar they don't spend is a dollar they can keep. *Don't throw away half the carrot; find a way to use it. That's one less carrot we have to buy, and also half a carrot not wasted.* But a chef's economic interest aligns with a greater good. Buying less means moving less, both in the kitchen and in the marketplace. And while conservation slows economies—that's why Americans are urged to *buy, buy, buy!*—it also cultivates more respect for ingredients, which in turn promotes the cultivation of a better product. Saving money in this sense saves work and life.

Chefs save people

The most common ingredient in kitchens is people. Chefs spend much of their time finding, training, and retaining staff for the same reason other businesses do: It's hard to find good people, and it's tougher to lose them. And since chefs think the way chefs do, it turns out that they've developed a mise-en-place for people as well.

Years before Marc Djozlija opened his restaurant Wright & Company on Woodward Avenue in downtown Detroit—as one of several ambitious and idealistic chefs taking part in the revitalization of the city—he had learned the value of human resources. Djozlija (pronounced "Joe-zuh-*leah*") opened a Wolfgang Puck restaurant in a new casino in Atlantic City, another declining locale where it proved hard to find a staff. One recruit taught him a lesson he never forgot. Djozlija trained him for 3 days on the garde-manger station. The cook made a mess, put the wrong ingredients in dishes, and confused orders. On the 4th day, Djozlija fired him.

The cook pled for his job: "Chef, all I ever wanted to do is work for a place like this. I'll do whatever it takes. I'll try harder."

Suddenly Djozlija felt like the fault was his own. Maybe he wasn't putting the cook in a position to succeed? The casino restaurant also had another kitchen serving a casual dining room with more straightforward items—pizza, fried calamari, salads—that required less finesse and more repetition.

It was like night and day. The kid totally killed it. Six years later the cook still works there.

Djozlija thought back to the restaurants in which he worked over the years, dominated by a small but vocal minority of ambitious careerists who would have climbed over the next guy to get where they wanted to go. But all these restaurants really ran on a silent majority of cooks—good people, hard workers—who liked to come in, crush their mise-en-place, power through service, and go home. Restaurants needed those people, too. And mise-en-place not only means every *thing* in its place, but also every *person* in his or her place.

Chefs save themselves

Gilbert Le Coze and his sister Maguy had built New York's Le Bernardin into the first haute French fish restaurant in America, earning four stars from the *New York Times*. But when 49-year-old Chef Le Coze died of a heart attack in 1994, his protégé Eric Ripert was scarcely prepared to take his place.

For Ripert, the food part was easy. He just kept cooking the way he had since his arrival there. The people part was harder. Ripert had little idea how to be a leader. Like many French chefs, he had come up through tough, tense kitchens. Ripert himself had a temper—"a very powerful energy," he recalled, rising "from the belly button." Rage got the best of Ripert on occasion at Le Bernardin. Business dropped. Morale sank. He wanted to keep the restaurant's stars, but he also wanted to keep his sanity and his staff.

Perhaps by providence, Ripert picked up a book on a recent trip to Paris: *100 Elephants on a Blade of Grass,* by the Dalai Lama. Thus began Ripert's personal Buddhist practice and his reckoning with the fire in his belly. He devoted time to techniques like visualizing his anger as a dark cloud and then destroying it.

He began seeing the kitchen differently. One day Ripert gave a brusque order to one of his best young cooks. He saw the cook's hand shake. Ripert's eyes met those of his second in command, chef de cuisine Chris Muller. Now the cook was trying to sauce a plate with that same shaky hand. *It's okay,* they said. *Relax, calm down.* The hand stopped shaking. Ripert and Muller witnessed this a few more times. When they demanded something from him, his hand shook. When they encouraged him, the hand remained steady, and the plate would be better, too. To Muller, if cooks were shaking, whether externally or internally, then their focus wasn't on the plate. This excellent young chef had traveled through all the stations in the kitchen and done well. If nurturing cooks created a better product, then what Ripert and Muller needed to do was change the way they handled their people. Just as there should be no wasted words, no words should lay people to waste. Anger wastes people.

In his quest Ripert went up against culinary history. Kindness is a relatively new concept for the professional kitchen. The notion of "nurturing" cooks was so antithetical to the pressure-cooker image of a professional kitchen that it had become a cliché for the masses: *If you can't take the heat . . .*

Ripert changed his kitchen by changing himself. Muller, a mid-westerner predisposed to calm, became an excellent complement. Muller conceptualized and demonstrated the use of three voices: the normal, interpersonal one he called the "teaching voice"; the one he used to call out orders over the din of the kitchen and roar of the vents, the "service voice"; and the one he tried not to use, in the midst of crisis and trouble, his "urgent voice."

But adjusting volume and tone would only go so far. One of the reasons things got so tense at Le Bernardin was that Ripert and his cooks had a formidable number of plates to produce in very little time under exacting standards. To transform the kitchen, Ripert and Muller had to change the entire restaurant: reduce the number of tables, elongate seating periods, and double the number of cooks.

The stakes for mistakes receded, but Le Bernardin's new peace came with a price. Serving less food to fewer customers with more staff meant less profit. Someone had to pay the difference. In the end the customer did—the entitlement of a four-star restaurant serving an entitled clientele. Many other restaurants didn't have the luxury of that choice. But Ripert knew entrepreneurs who would never reduce their profit margins for their people, all the while decrying their staff's low morale. Ripert now had a holistic spirituality, which came with a holistic understanding of business. One can't pretend that goodness and kindness don't have a relationship to economics.

Ripert tried to extend his consciousness to every aspect of the business. He made a point to greet his kitchen staff every day; to know the names of all his 100-plus employees; and to counsel his cooks' careers. Like Escoffier did a century before, Ripert negotiated with a charity, City Harvest, to take as much of his leftover food as possible. And Ripert tried to preserve and purify his own time. He envisioned his life as a disk with three even slices—work, family, self—and tried to be so prepared, so practiced, and so present in each that there would be no spillover among them. Echoing the counsel of Dogen, when he cooks, he thinks of nothing else. When he is with his son or wife, he thinks of no one else.

A life of preparing, of practicing and perfecting process, and being present in everything. I wonder, how can Ripert teach those values to his staff?

"Be around me," he says.

The results: Before Le Coze and Ripert came to America, if a chef in New York wanted the best apprenticeship, he or she had to work in France. Nowadays, Ripert and Muller receive stacks of résumés from young chefs in France and everywhere else, culinarians who want to come to Le Bernardin to learn at one of the finest schools in the world for how to cook, how to work, and how to be.

Chefs let go

Chef Marcus Samuelsson commands an army of cooks in restaurants around the globe. But on weekends Samuelsson demotes himself to prep cook.

He stands next to his wife, Maya, in the kitchen of their Harlem brownstone, peeling and chopping carrots while she helms the stove. He hands her the carrots.

"The pan's got to be hot," he suggests.

"It *is* hot," she says.

"No, it's got to be *hotter* than that."

Maya dumps all the carrots in the pan. Marcus sighs. He knows that the pan wasn't hot enough when she put the carrots in. Now all those carrots have cooled the pan down so that they won't cook properly.

"Now you're not searing them, you're *roasting* them," Marcus says. "That means you're not going to get the flavor."

Samuelsson, of course, can't help himself; he knows too much about the chemistry and physics of cooking, but he knows enough about life to let it go. Maya has her own Ethiopian way of cooking; and this is *family* time, not work time. Samuelsson knows that if there is one truth in a chef's personal life, it's that you're not the chef of *everything*.

While many chefs do like everything in their lives to be ordered, a great many others reserve the rules of mise-en-place exclusively for the kitchen. One need look no further for proof than to visit a chef's spotless kitchen and then visit his shambolic office, or observe a cook during service and then hang out with her afterward. One cannot be so controlled for most of the day and not anticipate the urge to be a little out of control. For every action, there is an equal and opposite reaction.

Chefs know there must be mess in our lives, too. A riotous environment filled with books and papers and meaningful objects can stimulate us. A chaotic schedule allows for chance meetings and impromptu conversations, the kind of serendipity in which inspiration flourishes and fortunes are made. Some studies have linked mess to creativity and higher incomes.

Mess is the cure for some of order's ills, like obsessiveness and rigidity. And order is the cure for some of mess's ills, like laziness and indifference. There is a time and a place for everything: A time to work and a time to play. A time to plan and a time to abandon our plans. And yes, a time to clean and a time to let things accumulate. The world's mise-en-place encompasses all.

This balanced life is the true meaning of *working clean*. In these pages, *clean* doesn't mean neat and tidy. And what great chefs mean by working clean is not necessarily a spotless, sterile environment nor a life without spontaneity. Rather, the meaning of *clean* is conscious, ordered, prepared, persistent, honest, honorable; the opposite of unconscious, passive, unprepared, lazy, ignorant, dishonest, dishonorable. So wherever mess serves our awareness, our sense of things being right, our fullness, our alignment with reality, and our ability to honor ourselves, our family, our work, and our world—then even being messy is working clean.

Anything else is just a waste.

OUT OF THE KITCHEN

Total utilization doesn't ask us to milk *every* inch of space, trim *every* motion, use *every* moment of time and *every* resource for maximum productivity and efficiency. But working clean with resources does mean living a life where you properly value those things. *Get your most important spaces in order because space is precious. Practice and perfect the motions that make sense to refine because your energy is precious. Honor time because you're not getting any more of it. Use your resources wisely because ultimately we all must share them. And treat each other with care.*

What's the opposite of total utilization? We're living in it, at work and in the world. Societies and nations don't plan. We chew up land and leave other spaces wasted. We don't start important things and leave others unfinished. We rush. We don't see and hear things. We don't communicate. We're okay with mediocre. So much of what we do is halfway. So much of our attention is divided. We treat people as if they are worthless. In the face of our human failings, should we give up? No, the entire history of mankind is the dynamic between order and disorder. Total utilization challenges us to be alive without becoming an affliction to the world and each other. The goal of total utilization and mise-en-place is that you not waste life: yours or the planet's.

At the end of our trail we see how chefs nourish with food and with wisdom, teaching their own and teaching the world.

Chefs restore. We, their students, can, too.

EXERCISES: SKILLS TO LEARN

BETTER UTILIZATION EXERCISE

Before you attempt *total* utilization, why not try *more* utilization? Here's an exercise.

What is your most important workspace? If it's your computer, for example, organize it and leave the desk, shelves, and everything else for later.

What are your most important moves? Where do you tend to make the most mistakes? Are you not prepared for meetings? Improve those moves first.

What are your most crucial times? When do you waste the most time? Cultivate one good habit (or break a bad one) that will preserve more of that time for you.

What's your most vital resource? What resource are you wasting the most of? For example, find one household or business expense to cut.

Who matters most? Who loses out the most in your life? Maybe one of your employees isn't getting the coaching he needs from you? Maybe a spouse or child needs more of your attention? On the other hand, if you're the type to give everything to others and leave nothing for yourself, pick yourself for a change and make things right.

"TURN OFF" EXERCISE

We are addicted to our technological devices—laptops, tablets, mobile phones. We are not simply passive victims of interruption; we *seek* stimulation. While digital devices connect us to the world, the light side of digital inputs and outputs, information and creativity, comes with a dark side: intrusion and escape.

We can remedy our digital woes by working clean with our devices. The suggested regimens below, in no particular order, can help you assume control of your digital life and assist you in creating healthy boundaries among your work, family, and personal lives.

- One day per week, don't use your devices.

- For 1 week, turn off your devices from 6:00 p.m. to 6:00 a.m.

- For personal or family times when you are expecting incoming calls or e-mails, restrict your checking times to once per hour, on the hour, for 5 minutes max.

- Don't permit devices in your bedroom. That means no cell phone or tablet alarm clocks!

- If you must use a device for creative work, use software or will-power to block all communications apps for the length of your creative session. Make sure to turn off notifications or use your device's "Do Not Disturb" feature.

Remember that you are stronger than the temptations and distractions of the digital world!

KITCHEN PRACTICE: WASTE NOT

Every week, log how many food items you discard from your refrigerator and cupboards because they've gone bad. After a few weeks, note any patterns. Ask yourself the following questions:

- What can I buy less of?

- What items can I use more often and how?

- Which recipes can I learn that will help me use more of the items that usually go to waste?

- What preparations can be a regular place to use my leftovers? For example, legendary chef Jacques Pépin makes what he calls a "fridge soup" every week. Salads are another way to enliven leftovers.

In the home kitchen, lack of preparation and knowledge can lead to serious waste. If saving food is something you care about, this is a great way to get practice limiting waste in other areas of your life.

HABITS: BEHAVIORS TO REPEAT

RUN A SUITE OF ROUTINE CHECKLISTS

Here's another version of the checklist technique you learned in *The Second Ingredient: Arranging Spaces, Perfecting Movements* on page 78 to help you use the little scraps of time and space that present themselves as an approach to total utilization.

I grade papers on the train, listen to the news while I walk, and answer e-mails while I'm on hold with customer service. As long as I don't need to rest, I jump at these opportunities. But lack of preparation often prevents me from using time and space as they present themselves. There is so much to be done, and it's hard to have that "time filler" work on hand when you need it. Creating a suite of time-use plans can keep you more conscious and ready to use more of your "small time" and help you internalize those Routines as habits. These plans might include:

Downtime Routines—things to do while *waiting* for things: in line, on the phone, even while slow Web sites load. If you have to stay in place while you wait, a Downtime Routine could be something that requires very little physical movement, like straightening your desk or flagging and returning e-mails. Or if you have more freedom to move, it could be as physical as exercising, filing, or washing the dishes.

Distraction Routines—things to do when you *can't concentrate* or *need a break* from a particular project. We all have intense work to do that requires us to take plentiful breaks. But when we don't want that "break time" to devolve into unproductive time, we might want to use those scraps of time to get things done on other projects. I do a lot of organizing and communicating during the times when I need a break from writing.

Route Routines—things to do when you know you are going to *be in or passing through a particular place*. Perhaps you walk to the copier a few times a day to retrieve papers. Use that walk to deliver something on your way there, like dropping off your expense report with the finance department. If you are taking a car trip to the city for leisure, there might also be an errand you can do on the way. This habit is a great example of balanced movement.

PRESERVING PEOPLE

Dismissal is a natural reflex during and after conflict, whether that dismissal is figurative ("That person is crazy!") or literal ("You're fired!").

Here are habits that can help you transform conflict into constructive action and preserve and strengthen relationships.

- For every argument or disagreement you have with someone, channel your emotions into a private activity by listing the following: (a) one thing you could have done to prevent the conflict; (b) one thing you learned about the concerns of the other person. Regardless of whether you feel you've been wronged, your job is to think about yourself as having some power over the situation, and to think of the other person as human.

- When a colleague or employee fails or falls short in his performance, list the following: (a) what he is good at doing; (b) what he is not so good at doing; (c) what you are good at teaching him to do; (d) where your teaching has failed to provide results. Your job here is to critique your own teaching methods in equal measure to your scrutiny of his performance.

This information will consciously and subconsciously prevent or transform future conflict.

A chef's reprise: Humble pie

Chris Cosentino evangelized for offal on television shows like *Iron Chef America* and Anthony Bourdain's *No Reservations*. But TV nearly derailed his mission in 2009. He and a partner cohosted a show where they traveled to different American cities to compete against local chefs in both cooking and inane contests during which Cosentino downed obscene amounts of food as feats of endurance. A long-distance cyclist, Cosentino's natural competitiveness and code of mise-en-place (finish the action, don't quit) got the best of him. He flew home from a shoot with a distended abdomen, in excruciating pain. Pastore rushed him to a hospital, where a doctor told him that he had cancer. It was a misdiagnosis. What he did have was a lacerated, ulcerated stomach from severe alkaline burns, caused in part by ingesting a bowl of hot peppers.

His specialist put him on a restricted diet. He was the chef of an Italian restaurant and couldn't eat tomato sauce or drink red wine. It took his stomach 5 years to heal. His self-respect took a little longer. People called him a sellout. Cosentino himself felt he had been part of a project that trivialized consumption, waste, and meanness. He witnessed his son and preschool classmates, after watching his show, trying to eat their lunches as quickly as possible. This was not what he wanted. Years later, at the 2014 Mad Food Conference in Copenhagen, Cosentino choked up while speaking of the experience, swallowing a different kind of humble pie.

Television was Cosentino's crucible, but it became his redress. In 2012, Cosentino decided to compete in *Top Chef Masters* to win money for a Parkinson's disease charity—his uncle had the disease, and Fergus Henderson had it, too. He won in the final round with his beef heart tartare, puffed beef tendon, blood sausage, and Rosalie's tripe.

Back on his mission, Cosentino opened Cockscomb in San Francisco in 2014 with a menu that featured trotters, tripe, and the house special: a wood-oven-roasted pig's head—all the elements cooked in different ways and arranged artfully on a wooden platter. He founded a Web site, offalgood.com, to share recipes and techniques with the average American. Meanwhile, on the other side of the country, Chef Dan Barber opened a pop-up restaurant called WastED, where Barber—joined by like-minded guest chefs from Mario Batali and April Broomfield to Bill Telepan and Alain Ducasse—created $15 menu items made from normally discarded ingredients: a hamburger made from discarded juice pulp, "dumpster dive" salad made from bruised vegetables, and a rich beef broth made from the hard, outer layer of dry-aged beef. Pete Wells from the *New York Times* wrote that "almost every bite was delicious, with a few exceptions."

Both Barber and Cosentino marketed the revolution. "Chefs in restaurants with white tablecloths get lampooned for being precious and elitist in a growing world where a billion people are hungry," Barber later wrote. "The opposite is actually true." Great chefs see waste all the time—perfectly good but misshapen vegetables, organ meats—and it pains them that they can't sell it. Barber wanted to educate the customer. Chris Cosentino hoped to change the way people ate and lived. His motivation hearkened back to the convivial homes of his grandparents in Rhode Island, their bounty and happiness. He wanted to honor their struggle and sacrifices, to live fully in the moment while at the same time honoring the past and guarding the future. Living this way wasn't easy. It took guts.

Recipe for Success

Commit to valuing space, time, energy, resources, and people. Waste nothing.

THIRD COURSE
WORKING CLEAN
AS A WAY OF LIFE

THE COMMITMENTS OF WORKING CLEAN

MISE-EN-PLACE WORKS

Practiced successfully for decades by hundreds of thousands of people in professional kitchens across the world, the values and behaviors of mise-en-place are universal wisdom. Mise-en-place can work for us, too, providing a rock-solid foundation that will support almost anything our talent and willpower can create.

In this third course we extract the principles of mise-en-place from the kitchen and apply them to the outside world, combining them in a unified system of practical habits for everyday use. This system is called Work Clean—it's mise-en-place that works for your life, whether you have an office job, are a teacher or student, or just want to be more organized at home.

The Work Clean system shares the fundamental "work clean" philosophy of mise-en-place: commitment to three central values and the use of 10 ingredients or behaviors. But your version of mise-en-place will use different tools and demand different rituals from those of the kitchen.

In the sections that follow, we'll review the commitments of working clean and introduce the Work Clean system of organization. We'll also walk together through a typical Day of Working Clean, to see how we can integrate all of the above into our lives.

COMMITMENT PUTS US IN PLACE

The entrance requirement for mise-en-place is *commitment*.

The two terms are actually linguistic cousins. The French word *mise* and the English word *commitment* both derive from the Latin verb *mettre,* meaning "to put." When we practice mise-en-place, we "put ourselves" in place. When we commit, we literally "put ourselves" with something or someone. Mise-en-place is the commitment we put in place to put ourselves in place, to make ourselves ready for life.

Cooks with commitment build lasting careers. Cooks without it lurch through spotty, unimpressive ones. Success without commitment can only come from luck or genius. And most people don't fathom how much commitment it takes for a genius to rise from obscurity to acclaim. Watch any genius in action and you'll see a genius *in action*. Genius isn't a noun; it's a verb.

Excellence requires commitment; your commitment demands adherence to your mise-en-place, your practice, your system. Anything else and you, too, will be counting on luck or genius.

"There are two ways to succeed," says Chef Alfred Portale. "One is to be a genius, and the other is to be better prepared and work harder. And the latter is where I fall. My kitchen is *never* in the weeds. We can handle any volume. If you make sure that your mise-en-place is done perfectly, you are 90 percent of the way there."

COMMITTING TO VALUES

When we work clean we commit to the three values of mise-en-place—*preparation, process,* and *presence.* These values take on a different flavor when taken out of the kitchen, but their essence remains the same.

Value #1: Commit to preparation with a 30-minute daily planning session.

Take 30 minutes every day to clear your workstation and plan the next day, a daily personal mise-en-place called the Daily Meeze. The Daily Meeze is the central, nonnegotiable habit of working clean.

In our lives we keep all kinds of nonnegotiable habits, things we do without fail and without excuse, whether they're as mundane as bathing or as rigorous as exercise. We honor all kinds of promises to others. We show up dutifully at regular meetings. We pledge money and labor and time and abide by those agreements. We observe standard courtesies and often put others' needs above our own.

But for all the pledges that we make to ourselves and others, most of us rarely make room for a regular practice of preparation and planning. We'll spend a focused hour grooming ourselves but rush through 2 minutes of making a "to-do" list. We'll clean the kitchen even when we don't want to because we are afraid of the consequences, like insects and pests or an angry roommate, but our professional workspaces—both physical and virtual—stay chaotic even when we're fastidious about our personal ones. We don't think too much about the repercussions. Stale bread on our kitchen counter? We know what that attracts. Stale work on our desk? The ramifications aren't as visible, but perhaps more insidious and damaging in the long run.

Taking a half-hour to clear your plate and plan your day ahead imparts serenity to your life. It offloads and logs all the things your mind, your devices, your bags, and your body have been carrying, and it provides vital assurance that you'll consult that log on a daily basis without fail. In that sense, doing your 30-minute Daily Meeze can be as beneficial to your physical, mental, and spiritual health as nutrition, hygiene, exercise, or meditation.

I propose you treat your preparation routine as I treat mine: as a spiritual practice. Your Daily Meeze shares many commonalities with spiritual practices: Like yoga, tai chi, or martial arts, it involves repetitive, physical movements and mental concentration. Like that of meditation or prayer, its goal is to keep you focused on the highest good for yourself, your family, and your world. In addition to the other things I've done in my professional life, I've been a yoga teacher for 2 decades. So I say the same thing to you that I say to my yoga students: *Just add the practice to your life and see what happens.* Don't judge it, just do it. Resist the temptation to say that your practice was "bad" because you didn't get everything done. Thirty minutes a day of *any* dedicated practice—from piano to planning—is bound to transform you.

My own teacher always used to say, *Do your spiritual practice, and everything else will fall into place.* So when Thomas Keller says, in effect, *keep your station clean and everything will follow from that,* he's tapping into that same spiritual wisdom, and it's like hearing the voice of my own teacher again.

Just do your Daily Meeze, and everything will fall into place.

Value #2: Commit to a *process* that makes you better.

Now that you've prepared your plan, you must follow it. And if you want to get better at what you do, you must examine the results of your plan and your product and make corrections.

Commitment to a process that makes you better means following the schedule you've set for yourself, using checklists, and cultivating better techniques and "life hacks." It means incorporating the values and habits of working clean into your workday. It also means a commitment to the inverse: altering or abandoning processes that make you worse.

How can you tell whether a process makes you better or worse? Understand first that what we're after is *excellence,* not *productivity.* Productivity is working hard. Excellence is working clean. Plenty of well-meaning people equate working hard with a *work ethic.* But what's so ethical about working wastefully into the night while the people you love wait for you? A work ethic must include ethics or it isn't worth a damn. Any process that helps you balance your professional obligations with your personal ones is a process that makes you better.

Striving for productivity *alone* presents a danger in that a quest for productivity often crosses the line between valuing process and fetishizing it. Productivity is not the solution to all problems. Humans are beings with other commitments and considerations. We need work and we need rest. We need periods of focus and also times of aimlessness. We need time for ourselves and time for others. Without balance, the work will suffer in the long term anyway. Committing to productivity alone is like committing to only inhaling, never exhaling. That kind of commitment will kill you.

Yet productivity at any cost is the secret to the success of so many executives, chefs included. These men and women have sacrificed not only their own well-being but that of others around them: spouses, children, employees, customers. Many culinarians cop to this: They work themselves sick, and then they sicken themselves even more with drink and drugs and then keep working through it all. This severe polarity of tension and release, alas, is one of the hazards of a life dedicated to excellence in any field. But just as we see the hazard, we can envision the ideal, the commitment to process that makes us *better;* not just efficient or productive, but better in an all-around or holistic way.

Opposite the process fetishists are the *process dodgers.* To these folks, the idea of following schedules, checklists, and rules—even if they created them—connotes banality, drudgery, and boredom. Process dodgers believe they are artists, and that creativity needs complete freedom. But true creatives—the people who actually make the food, the art, the architecture, the products, and the services we enjoy—understand that excellence comes from cultivating a craft through dedicated, dogged practice. True artists have a process.

As long as we consider our betterment, we'll stay healthy. We won't be the kind of managers who make bad decisions on behalf of the people who work for us, nor tolerate such abuses from our own managers. The product of our commitment to the right process—fed by knowledge and guarded by empathy—is a *real* work ethic.

Value #3: Commit to being *present* in whatever you do.

Working clean requires your presence on a number of levels.

The first level demands that you *be* and *stay* present physically: that you show up for yourself and for your fellows, and also that you don't give up on yourself or them. Japanese cooks have a great word for this behavior: *keizo-ku.*

The second level demands that you be and stay present mentally: becoming one with the work, being "with" the work but also "with" your comrades at the same time. This manifestation of presence—to be focused *and* open—is the goal of mise-en-place: Commit to the plan and the process yet remain aware of the shifting circumstances around you.

Committing to presence means that we cultivate a practice of *listening.* When you listen, where are your eyes? Are they on your computer screen or phone, or are they on the person speaking? When you listen, where is your body? Is it pointed into the conversation, or away from it? When you listen, where is your mouth? Is it fixed to speak, or is it relaxed and open? When you listen, where is your nose? Are you breathing slowly, or is your breath held? When you listen, where is your mind? Are you hearing the words and using your mind to divine the subtext, or are you listening to your own inner narrative? Being able to listen with the coordination of your entire being, body and mind, is perhaps the most powerful human skill. It's also one of the hardest things to do, which is another way of saying you will only get better at it if you practice. The better you listen, the more control you will have to wield your powers of attention in more complex ways. The better your focus, the more you'll be able to extend that focus over a greater area.

Committing to presence means that we cultivate an ability to be *deliberate.* When you decide to do something, get it done. When you set an appointment with someone else or yourself, show up. When you say "yes," *mean* yes. When you say "no," *mean* no. When you say "11:30," *mean* 11:30. Guard against forces that distract you from the tasks at hand. The cultivation of deliberation works the same way as the cultivation of listening: Better listeners can listen to more things, and better actors can act on more things.

Committing to presence means that we cultivate *discreteness,* boundaries between our work and our personal lives. We don't lose focus and do a bunch of mindless personal stuff to disengage at work. And we don't check our work e-mail when we get bored while we're playing with our kids. We avoid scattering our energies in a way that prevents our full presence in either setting. We are "in" or "out," "on" or "off." Wherever we are, we're there. For committed, deliberate people who've been working all day, that "running list" can be hard to turn off at night. But preparation and process make presence—letting go of that inner chatter—easier. At the end of the day, the list is complete, and you can enjoy another life, a life beyond work.

COMMITTING TO BEHAVIORS

Working clean means committing to integrating the Ingredients, or behaviors, of mise-en-place into your life.

1. **Planning is prime**—*working clean with time*
   What to know. Planning is first thought, not afterthought. Right planning promotes right action, saves time, and unlocks opportunity. Planning entails the scheduling of tasks, which means being honest with time, respecting both your abilities and limitations.
   What to do. Commit to being honest with time. Plan daily.

2. **Arranging spaces, perfecting movements**—*working clean with space and motion*
   What to know. Creating ergonomic workspaces means more than making things look pretty. It means setting a place for yourself that allows economy of motion and consumes less physical and mental energy. The less you move, the more effortless your work will be and the more brainpower you can reserve for new work and new thoughts.
   What to do. Commit to setting your station and reducing impediments to your movements and activities. Remove friction.

3. **Cleaning as you go**—*working clean with systems*
   What to know. All systems are useless unless maintained. The real work of organization is not being clean,

but working clean: keeping that system no matter how fast and furious your pace is. Working clean helps you work faster and better.

What to do. Commit to maintaining your system. Always be cleaning.

4. **Making first moves**—*working clean with priorities*

What to know. The present moment is worth more than a future one because present action sets processes in motion and unlocks others' work on your behalf.

What to do. Commit to using time to your benefit. Start now.

5. **Finishing actions**—*working clean with obligations and expectations*

What to know. A project that is 90 percent complete is zero percent complete because it's not deliverable. Orphaned tasks create more work.

What to do. Commit to delivering. When a task is nearly done, finish it. Always be unblocking.

6. **Slowing down to speed up**—*working clean with emotions*

What to know. Precision precedes speed. A calm body can calm the mind.

What to do. Commit to working smoothly and steadily. Use physical order to restore mental order. Don't rush.

7. **Open eyes and ears**—*working clean with your senses*

What to know. Excellence requires both focus and awareness. Ambition, ability, and attunement can cultivate awareness.

What to do. Commit to balancing internal and external awareness. Stay alert.

8. **Call and callback**—*working clean with communication*

What to know. Efficient teams become an interconnected nervous system. Excellence requires active listening.

What to do. Commit to confirming and expecting confirmation of essential communication. Call back.

9. **Inspect and correct**—*working clean with feedback*
   What to know. Mastery is never achieved; it is a constant state of evaluation and refinement.
   What to do. Commit to coaching yourself, to being coached, and to coaching others. Evaluate yourself.

10. **Total utilization**—*working clean with resources*
    What to know. The grand ideal of working clean is no wasted space, no wasted motion, no wasted resource, no wasted moment, no wasted person.
    What to do. Commit to valuing space, time, energy, resources, and people. Waste nothing.

TOOLS FOR WORKING CLEAN

Working clean does not require a huge investment. You need only six things.

1. **A workstation.** The designated "clean space" you created in *The Second Ingredient: Arranging Spaces, Perfecting Movements*. It could be as simple as a table and chair. You must be able to work, sit, stand, and move comfortably. Mainly you'll need space to keep some of the items below handy.

2. **An inbox and outbox.** A place for incoming stuff, and another for stuff you'll be carrying out the door with you the next time you leave. The object of these boxes is to see them empty at least once per day. At the beginning of your Daily Meeze, the inbox will be full and the outbox empty. At the end, the inbox will be empty and the outbox will be full.

3 & 4. **Action list and calendar.** These are your planning tools. You can get by with paper versions of these, but I strongly recommend digital lists and calendars for the flexibility

they afford (see "Technology: software" below). If you use a printed task or "to-do" list (or as we call it, the Action list), you will need two sheets: (1) a running list to catch incoming tasks ("Action inbox"); and (2) a list of those Actions, categorized into Missions ("Action list").

5. **File box or drawer, manila folders, and markers.** If you don't have a file drawer, use a standing file or, better yet, a file box (usually square and plastic with a closing top and a handle). This is where you keep your "hot" files, the papers you refer to regularly. Do you need a big file cabinet? Maybe, but only for deep storage or occasional reference. Unless you work at an office where you need daily access to reams of client files, you don't need more space than a square file box or drawer affords.

6. **Soft towel and spray bottle.** These last tools aren't for hygiene, but for reinforcing the need for and benefits of making clean transitions between tasks.

Optional Tools

1. **Technology: hardware.** If you can afford a computer, smartphone, or tablet, by all means buy and use them. Just know that your technology becomes your virtual mise-en-place as well and must also remain clean spaces. Your technology is an extension of your nervous system, and that means you want no friction in its function.

2. **Technology: software.** Digital task lists and calendars are preferable to printed ones, but they are not magical solutions to the problem of personal organization. Without daily maintenance the digital versions tend to get just as messy as the paper ones: Calendars become littered with unaccomplished items, hidden from view as the days

progress; task lists accumulate action items but don't present them in ways that are useful for execution. The calendar and the task list should ideally be integrated as they are in the basic kitchens of the CIA. A few applications have emerged to try to bridge these shortcomings, enabling you, for example, to easily schedule tasks on your calendar, to auto-forward tasks and calendar events to the next day, or to automatically schedule new tasks in the empty spaces on your calendar. These apps, too, aren't magic bullets. What we end up with are too many overdue items (and the guilt that comes with them), unless we regularly, manually attend to them.

Here's what works: For task lists we recommend using software like OmniFocus, which has an inbox (hereinafter referred to as the "Action inbox") for easily catching and sorting incoming tasks, and also provides a way to manually sort tasks in the order that you'd like to accomplish them. For calendars, the standard options from Google, Apple, and Microsoft Outlook work just fine.

Are notebook apps like Evernote helpful? Absolutely. They're like a rolling file box that can grow as deep as you need. That also means that you must expend the effort to keep them orderly and clean.

For up-to-date links to the latest and best organization apps and technology, please visit WorkClean.com.

3. **Tools and containers.** Desks tend to fill up with tools (staplers, tape dispensers) of all kinds, or containers (for pens, paper clips, and the like). If you can keep these tools off your workstation and in a drawer, please do. If you use them quite regularly, arrange them in a way that you can have easy access. On my desk, I use a few containers to keep some items close. But I do keep objects contained; otherwise, they tend to spread. For example, on my desk I place a tray for my wallet and anything else that comes and

goes with me when I arrive and leave. Sometimes I'll gather stacks of books and papers all relating to one temporary project that I'll want to keep together and are too bulky for filing; for these I keep file boxes that I can stack by my desk or on a shelf or in a nearby cabinet.

Just do your Daily Meeze, and everything will fall into place.

THE WORK
CLEAN SYSTEM

TO WORK clean, we need a system of organization that embodies those values. The Work Clean system does this in three fundamental ways.

1. *It deals honestly with time* by eliminating the false distinction between tasks and appointments. In Work Clean, all tasks and appointments are Actions, and we include all Actions on our schedules and lists.

2. *It increases focus and reduces chaos* by tying the number of Actions directly to your number of active projects, or Missions, and by using Frontburner and Backburner designations to order those Actions.

3. *It balances immersive and process time* by creating "buckets" of time called Routines.

Actions: Your Ingredients

All the things we do in life—the thinking, the writing, the correspondence, the procedures, the errands, the conferences, the meetings, the chores—are Actions.

There is no difference between a *task* and an *appointment*. Both are Actions.

There are only two types of Actions: *scheduled* and *unscheduled*.

Missions: Your Menu

Each of these Actions we do for a *reason*.

The Mission is the reason. Your Missions are the things you want to accomplish in life and in work. Every Mission has within it a number of Actions or steps needed to accomplish that Mission. Missions give those Actions meaning, and most crucially, *order*. Missions are, in effect, top-level Actions. They are supposed to be *big* goals, with a time scope of a year or more. For example, "Finish presentation to investors" is a goal that requires within it many Actions. But it is not a Mission. That presentation is an Action that is part of a larger Mission, "Establish new company."

To create your Mission list, envision your life like Chef Eric Ripert does, by dividing it into thirds: Work, Family, Self.

For each of these three areas, list the things you want to accomplish within the next year. Each Mission should begin with a verb. Your Missions could be things like:

WORK	FAMILY/HOME	SELF
Reach target numbers for year	Refinance house	Lose 10 pounds
Set up new program	Spend more time with kids	Learn Spanish
Create side business		Get organized

For balance, pursue Missions in each area of your life. For most of us, our work Missions will be more numerous and urgent than our family and personal ones. Single people or those without children may not have many family commitments at all and thus may conceive of their lives as a simple divide between work and personal. Whatever your circumstances, all Missions— whether business or personal—take time. To be honest with time, you must consider all your Missions, not just those in your work life.

How many Missions should we have simultaneously? In my professional life, I have six right now—four writing projects, a teaching job, and one entrepreneurial endeavor. In my personal life—both for family and for myself—I have seven, ranging from "Plan fun things with wife and son" to "Renovate apartment." Overall, that's 13. That's too many. I think 10 is probably the optimum number of active Missions for most working people. And I can tell you that no matter how much I rationalize the necessity of every single one of those 13 Missions, many of them will suffer for the ambition of their author. I can't sustain that number in the long term. True, a heavy workload can encourage productivity because it compresses our time and because it forces us to plan, conserve energy and motion, and be efficient. But there comes a point of diminishing returns on that workload-to-efficiency dynamic. When we can't say "no" or "maybe later" to certain Missions in deference to our capabilities, our capabilities will say no for us when we start missing appointments and neglecting tasks. Better we decide and keep our control.

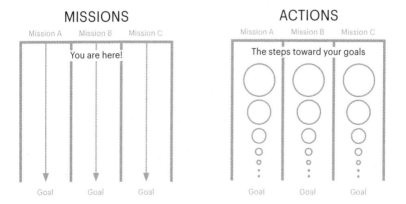

MISSIONS

Mission A   Mission B   Mission C

You are here!

Goal   Goal   Goal

ACTIONS

Mission A   Mission B   Mission C

The steps toward your goals

Goal   Goal   Goal

Frontburners and Backburners: Your Recipes

Every Mission requires a *recipe* to see it through. As in kitchens, recipes are lists of Actions that, in most cases, will happen in a particular sequence and often have sub-Actions.

The difference between chefs and the rest of us is that chefs spend a lot more time *thinking* about that sequence. They think about it in the evening when they plan their next day's service and in the morning before they head to work. They order their tasks on paper when they make lists—*first this, then that.* They reorder them in their mind while they prep and while cooking, too. You can see a representation of their mind on their stove: pans needing immediate attention in front; pots bubbling all day in the back; platters of ingredients waiting for heat off to the sides. The backlog of work can easily overcome line cooks, so they've trained their minds to do two crucial things: queue all incoming orders and then focus only on the next step for each dish currently on their burners.

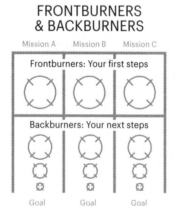

FRONTBURNERS & BACKBURNERS

Mission A   Mission B   Mission C

Frontburners: Your first steps

Backburners: Your next steps

Goal   Goal   Goal

The beauty of mise-en-place is the ability it engenders in chefs and cooks to fight chaos and tune out distraction. If a cook is responsible for 10 menu items, and each of those items has a dozen to two dozen steps in its preparation, that's anywhere from 120 to 240 individual tasks that she needs to be ready to accomplish at any given time. What this crush of work demands is not so much a sense of *importance*—which is how most systems of organization attempt to create order out of chaos—but *sequence*. It's not always about doing the so-called important thing first. It's about *ordering* our Actions within time to get the important Missions accomplished. *What's the first thing I need to do, right now, to get myself closer to the finish line and get this thing out the door?* The first move is always figuring out the first move.

Now think of each incoming order as a Mission. Each order must follow a recipe, an exact sequence and flow of Actions. And only one Action for each Mission can be executed at any given moment, even when they cascade in a flow that comes from task chaining and balanced movement, making it *seem* as if the cook is doing a million things at once. Since these Actions happen in rapid succession, a good line cook always knows what her following move will be for each order under fire.

In the Work Clean system, the Frontburner is the first Action needed to move forward on a Mission. All the following Actions are Backburners.

The Frontburners get our attention. And the number of Frontburners is itself limited by the number of Missions. If you have

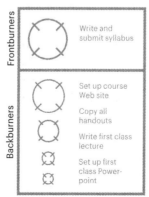

MISSION:
Teach Class

Frontburners
- Write and submit syllabus

Backburners
- Set up course Web site
- Copy all handouts
- Write first class lecture
- Set up first class Power-point

10 Missions, you will have 10 Frontburners, one for each Mission. The reward for this way of thinking is that 240 tasks become 10. If we have 10 Missions, we always have 10 tasks to accomplish, the 10 Frontburners. Ten is, of course, a more manageable number than 240, and a profound shift from the "to-do" list experience where we accumulate tasks until we have a list of hundreds. In most digital task lists, we are encouraged to give generic *rankings* of importance—priority 1, priority 2, priority 3, and so on—*not* to create a sequence. So we make little "1," "2," and "3" notations beside each of these tasks, and before long we have 50 "1s," 200 "2s," and 500 "3s," rendering those priorities meaningless and unactionable. Order, or sequence, is the only way we *really* execute: *what comes first, what comes next, and so on.* And since we can rarely do more than one thing at a time, it's not helpful to have so many tasks in our field of vision. Instead of making an ever-expanding list of hundreds of tasks (and working furiously and often futilely to check them all off), you will be keeping a list of just 10 Frontburners. Sometimes you might have five active Missions, and other times you might have 15. And in either instance your number of Frontburners will always equal your number of Missions. Simple.

The Backburners are the *following* tasks for each Mission, the ones to which you'll be pivoting after the Frontburners are finished. When you accomplish any Frontburner, the Backburner behind it slides up immediately to take its place as Frontburner, and so on, until that Mission is accomplished. The first one or two Backburners remain in your peripheral vision. Backburners get murky beyond the second or third in a Mission list. That's perfectly okay. While it's good to list out every step in a Mission before you embark, in many cases that won't be possible. We don't work so far ahead of the curve all the time. It's sufficient to make a daily habit of ordering your Backburners on the fly as your Missions progress.

In the same way that you pick your Missions with the year in mind, you select your Frontburners and arrange your Backburners with the coming week in mind.

Routines: Your Mise-en-Place

You've identified your Missions and selected your Frontburners. You have a whole bunch of stuff to do.

When do you do it? Routines are the answer to that question.

Your Routines are essentially an empty template of your ideal week. They are the planning you do before planning—like the designs that Jimi Yui does for a kitchen before he builds it and the chef and cooks move in; or the plate that Chef Masa draws and makes before creating the meal on top of it. Scheduled Routines aren't the same thing as scheduled Actions—tasks or appointments—in that they are meant to be looser, a framework *beneath* your schedule. Routines are "time buckets" in your schedule, into which you put Actions. They are like the cook's empty "nine-pans," a mise-en-place for time.

Routines are *recurring*. You may adjust them week to week, but ideally, your Routines should be just that: routine.

Routines can fall into any one of the following categories.

Personal time. These Routines are vital for health and well-being and are often nonnegotiable, so they get scheduled first. When do you have lunch? What hour would you like to be home? When

ROUTINES

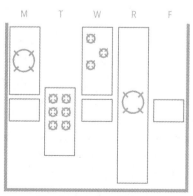

Time buckets into which you
schedule Actions

would you like to go to sleep, and when would you like to wake up? When would you like to have time with your spouse or your children or your friends? When do you do your chores? When do you commute? When would you like to exercise? All these Actions should be either blocked or shaded out on your schedule. Your Personal Routines also include making time for your 30-minute Daily Meeze.

Meeting time. Appointments, conferences, and phone calls—whether recurring or one-off—are the first form of presence required of you by your job. You are, for the most part, going to have to schedule your Frontburners around these. You may also want to block out specific times for "making the rounds" at work—not meetings per se, but a more casual time to share information with your colleagues and address issues.

Immersive time. These blocks of time you reserve for deep, focused work. For example, I take a lot of meetings between Monday and Wednesday. But Thursdays and Fridays I can usually reserve for deeper work—thinking, writing, reading, and brainstorming. Many of your Frontburners will go inside these Routines. The more you honor your immersive time, the more others will.

Process time. At work, the things that *don't* get scheduled end up absorbing much of our time: answering correspondence, impromptu conversations, emerging crises. Scheduling blocks of process time at key points in your day is just about the smartest thing you can do to be honest with time. Process Routines group similar tasks that benefit from being executed together; into these time buckets you collect individual tasks that feel too small to schedule individually but will nevertheless need time: rolling or returning calls, checking e-mails, consulting with colleagues to keep projects moving forward, processing paperwork, doing small errands. Dedicate some Process Routines to items across several different Missions; use others to clear out a group of Actions on behalf of just one Mission.

Process time Routines should be shorter and more frequent than other Routines. Remember that process time relates to the principle of *making first moves:* making sure that the people who can be doing work *for you* have everything they need *from you* in order to work while your hands are off; and it also relates to the principle of *finishing actions:* unblocking stuck projects. Process time generally encompasses smaller tasks, shorter in duration, that come in larger numbers—like answering calls and e-mails, filling out forms, giving brief instructions. Schedule process time in regular, shorter intervals throughout your day, at "stopping points" between meeting time, immersive time, and personal time. If 30 minutes of process time at the beginning of your workday will set or keep processes in motion and loosen the pressure on you, put it before ostensibly more "important" tasks. Scheduling other Process Routines around noon and in the late afternoon is a good idea. Some days I like to schedule longer Process Routines to take on tougher and longer tasks needing more attention. The frequency of your process time depends largely on the demands of your job and career. The more people and processes you manage, the more process time you need on your schedule.

Constraining Process Routines is just as important as *scheduling* them. If you let them, process tasks can easily spill over and flood the rest of your schedule. For some of us, this overflow happens daily. Schedule enough regular Process Routines so that the pressure of these tasks is kept low, and honor their beginnings and endings. Those good habits will then make it easier to "clear the decks" for yourself when a real crisis emerges and you absolutely must push off other appointments. The more quickly and efficiently you work within your Process Routines—grouping together alike Actions such as e-mails, calls, forms, and errands—the less spillover you will have.

Scheduling Routines

In plotting out your Routines, pay particular attention to transition times between home and office, and between appointments. Leave some of these transitions open as times to breathe and relax. Keep others for Routines. The time between home and office on certain days, for example, can be reserved for errands. If you have a long commute by public transportation, you can reserve those times for reading or other Immersive Routines. Remember, a Routine is not an Action, but a time bucket for Actions, in the same way that a plate is not a meal. But the way you arrange your table determines what you can fit on it.

Conceiving, scheduling, and keeping your Routines helps you maintain a workable life and a sane mind. It means that your weekly schedule becomes a mise-en-place for time, wherein everything you do—major or minor, urgent or optional—has its right place.

Advanced Concept: When Actions Are Routine, They Become Routines!

Some Missions don't need lists of Actions, but rather one simple Action, repeated. For example, if your Mission is to "Get healthy" and one of your intentions is to run three times per week, an Action item like "Run 3x per week" is not something that could ever be checked off your list because it is supposed to happen regularly and indefinitely. The Action item you'd want to schedule in this case is "Schedule Personal Routine: run 3x per week." The result is a Routine that stays on your calendar.

How Missions, Actions, and Routines Fit Together

Missions require Actions to be completed. Those Actions require order, so you can know what to do and when to do it—hence the idea of Frontburners and Backburners, what comes first, what comes next. And those Frontburners must actually happen in time; they need scheduling.

There are two ways to schedule an Action: (1) as a stand-alone appointment on your calendar; or (2) grouped into a scheduled Routine containing smaller tasks.

For example, when you have a Mission requiring an Action like spending 2 hours writing a presentation, you would make an appointment with yourself, ideally within one of your Immersive Routines. But when you have a bunch of smaller, similar Actions— returning a bunch of calls, dissecting e-mail threads, reading small articles, etc.—instead of scheduling them all separately, put them into their own Process Routine. In this way you will handle lots of incoming requests and tasks that feel too small to list as Actions within your Mission lists: Just throw them into a Process Routine on your schedule.

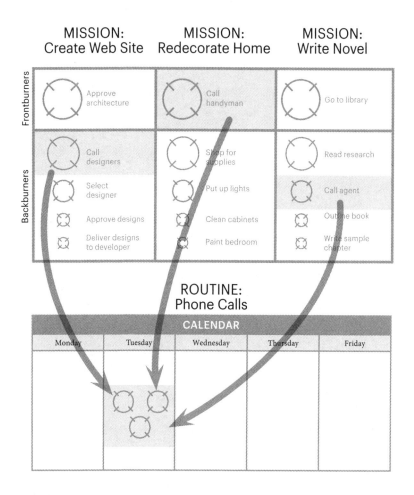

We now share a common Work Clean vocabulary.

- *Missions,* your menu of big goals

- *Actions,* the steps to achieving your Missions, ordered into *Frontburners* and *Backburners*

- *Routines,* your mise-en-place for time, into which those Actions are scheduled

In the next section, we use this vocabulary as we walk through an ideal day in the life of working clean. While the following scenario is geared toward office work, you will find much here that's applicable to academia, field work, professions and trades, and more.

The first move is always figuring out the first move.

A DAY OF WORKING CLEAN

The world is a giant gerbil wheel right now. I think if we just became a little bit more organized, used a little bit more mise-en-place, understood what we really need, and only do what we really need, I think we'll have more time. You'll be able to sit down at the table with your kids and actually cook a meal. Get up a little bit earlier so you can breathe. You want to greet the day.

—Chef Dwayne LiPuma, Chef Instructor, Culinary Institute of America

EVENING: PREPARATION

Tomorrow begins today. So in the evening—as some of us prepare to leave work or others are at home after the kids are put to bed—we embark on *the* core practice of mise-en-place in our lives, our 30-minute Daily Meeze.

THE DAILY MEEZE *has four parts, each with a specific function and each taking a certain balance of the time.*

1. Clean your station (approximately 15 minutes).

2. Sharpen your tools (approximately 5 minutes).

3. Plan your day (approximately 10 minutes).

4. Gather your resources.

What tools do we need? Our planning tools, Action list, calendar, and a timer.

Below, we'll walk through the Daily Meeze together, step-by-step.

STEP ONE: CLEAN YOUR STATION
(approximately 15 minutes)

Before you can organize, you need to gather the items that must be organized, wherever they may be hiding. *Clean your station* means *clearing and logging all your inputs, both physical and digital—* any place where you collect the "stuff" you must do. And since we have so many inputs, this part of our Daily Meeze, cleaning your station, takes the most time.

First: Empty and Log Physical Inputs

1. *Wallet.* The receipts and business cards that we pick up throughout the day accumulate here. Dump them into your desk inbox.

2. *Bag or purse.* Our "containers" are not only filled with papers, but books, stray cords, pieces of clothing, even food. Empty these containers. Put the stuff that needs to be logged into your desk inbox. Return the accessories and larger items to their right places. Replace what needs to go back in your bag. Trash everything else.

3. *Desktop.* Because our desktop usually ends up becoming a de facto inbox, sweep it for sticky notes, scraps of paper, and larger items. Dump these items into your desk inbox.

4. *Desk inbox.* Now that we've put our loggable items into our inbox along with what's already in there, process all these, logging the Action items onto your Action list or calendar. File or trash anything not actionable.

5. *Notebook.* If you have a notebook in which you write prompts for action, log those items onto your Action list or calendar.

What are "inputs"? Inputs are channels for incoming tasks. Those channels can be physical containers or surfaces, like a desk or inbox or a notebook in which you've written a reminder for yourself, or they can be digital containers or surfaces, like your e-mail browser, task app, or notetaking software.

What is "clearing"? For your physical inputs, clearing means literally emptying or sweeping them for loose items that we've collected to prompt our own action: business cards, sticky notes, mail, etc. For your digital inputs, clearing means scanning your applications and virtual desktop for action items.

What is "logging"? All those action items will need to be collected, sorted, and processed in one of three ways.

1. Trash (like a receipt or note you don't need to keep)

2. File (like a book you've been carrying that needs to go back on your shelf)

3. Log (like an Action item written into either your Action list or calendar)

Log any Action that you *can* schedule immediately ("Call doctor tomorrow") on your calendar at either the appropriate time or as an "all-day event" if you are not sure of the time.

Log any Action that you *can't* schedule immediately (and many Actions should indeed be sorted into Missions before scheduling) in your Action inbox.

You may, if you wish, log an item *simultaneously* onto your Action list and calendar, so that you always have a record of it.

Second: Clear and Log Digital Inputs

The proliferation of digital inputs is why it's so important to consolidate your streams of communication as much as possible, as we detailed in *Call and Callback*. If you work with a digital Action list and calendar, much of the logging here can be done by "cutting-and-pasting" text from your inputs into your planning tools. Scan the following applications and virtual "surfaces" on your mobile devices and/or computer for action items, logging each one.

1. *E-mail.* For many of us e-mail is the most vital channel, so it goes first.

   a. Scan your inbox and flag all the e-mails that need action.

   b. Archive both flagged and unflagged e-mails, clearing your inbox.

   c. Open the Flagged folder and log these into your Action inbox either by cut-and-paste or by forwarding the flagged e-mails to your digital task lists (many task lists make this possible).

   d. Unflag all logged e-mails.

2. *Voice mail.* Check your voice mail messages for Action items and log them. Delete your voice mails.

3. *Text or instant messages.* Texting and IM are channels for quick and easy communication. But they are inconvenient for collecting Action items. Review the day's texts for any requests you've been sent or promises you've made. Log them.

4. *Corporate communication software.* Many companies use third-party or proprietary software to keep employees in touch. Many of these applications have their own calendars and task lists. Some of us may use them as our default planning tools for work. What we don't want are two separate calendars and Action lists, one for work and one for personal use, unless we can view them in one consolidated way.

5. *Notetaking software.* Cut-and-paste action items into your tools, or forward them via e-mail to your Action list.

6. *Social media.* Cut-and-paste or transcribe any action items into your Action list.

7. *Digital "stickies" and desktop notes.* Review and log these.

8. *Web browsers (on all devices).* We sometimes accumulate "open" browser windows to prompt us to action. Log and close these by cutting-and-pasting or forwarding the Web addresses to your planning tools.

EMPTY PHYSICAL INPUTS

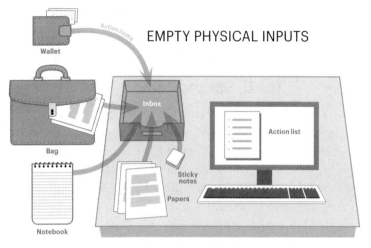

LOG PHYSICAL INPUTS

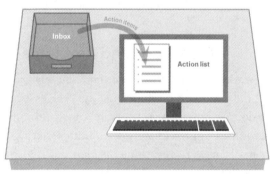

CLEAR AND LOG DIGITAL INPUTS

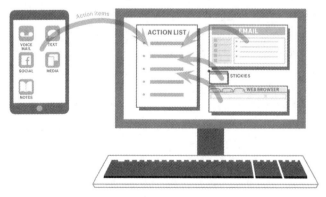

9. *Digital photos.* We sometimes take photos on our mobile devices to prompt action or collect ideas. Log these as well.

Third: Set the Table

Now that we've cleared our physical and digital inputs, it's time to do what chefs and cooks do: clean and tidy our workspace.

For our physical workspace, we take a few seconds to do *kichiri*, or straightening, moving our tools and other objects on our desk so that we can see them all and they're arranged in an orderly fashion. We can even wipe our space with a damp paper towel or cloth, a simple act that has a profound effect for many people.

For our digital workspace, this means filing or trashing stray documents and closing background apps and windows.

Everything before your eyes should look clear and open.

Questions and Problems

Can I work on some Action items immediately instead of logging them? If the tasks can be done quickly, yes. As long as executing Actions doesn't prevent you from creating a rhythm and cleaning your station in approximately 15 minutes, acting on items like quick e-mail answers and things of that nature is perfectly fine. One example from my own Daily Meeze is bills: When I get one, I pay it right away. Remember: Whether moving on an action item or marking it for later action, you are still *making first moves.*

What if I haven't logged all my flagged e-mails? Don't worry, they're still flagged, still in your folder, and you can get to the rest of them tomorrow. But try to clear all your flags every day, or else the Actions in them may get buried over time. If you find it difficult to clear your flagged e-mails every day, consider scheduling a weekly or daily Routine to handle your e-mail backlog.

How can I possibly clean my station in 15 minutes? Work quickly. Cleaning your station is not a time to carefully consider things, but to move your fingers and hands and arms and legs to get your stuff where it needs to be. If you receive 100 e-mails or more every day, clearing your inbox *will* be challenging. Half of those e-mails may need to be flagged for action. But those actions should have no immediate bearing on your ability to scan, flag, and sort the e-mails themselves. You have to actively and ruthlessly compress your time. Your Daily Meeze should be a *hustle*. Clearing your station is intense work, and it may become the most focused part of your day. A few mise-en-place ingredients help in this effort.

■ *Perfect your movements.* Stand up. You'll be less inclined to file and replace large items if you remain seated.

■ *Slow down to speed up.* Working quickly comes from first working slowly. If you wish, give yourself a few days for an extended 60-minute Daily Meeze to get used to the motions and the decisions you have to make. But once you've gone through the motions several times, speed them up.

■ *Finish the action.* Slowing down also helps when you hit a particularly dense bit of input, like a long document of notes from a meeting that you must methodically pick over for action items. As you find yourself getting impatient or ornery, slow down. Breathe. Finish the action. Move through the work deliberately until it's done. There: You don't ever have to see that document again.

■ *Clean as you go.* Avoid bad habits like dumping loose items on random surfaces during the course of your day. Try to get everything to your desk inbox.

When cleaning our station, we must ensure that our inputs are cleared and that the Actions we've received are logged. This is the "wave" we must surmount and stay on top of every day.

STEP TWO: SHARPEN YOUR TOOLS
(approximately 5 minutes)

The next step in your Daily Meeze, a quicker one, is to make sure your planning tools are in perfect order, adjusting and sorting all the Action items in your calendar and Action list.

First: Adjust Your Calendar

Part of creating today is redeeming yesterday. Look at your schedule's past 24 hours. Now:

1. Reschedule the appointments that didn't happen or tasks that didn't get done.

2. Unschedule the items that you can't or don't want to reschedule immediately, putting them back on your Action list if they are not already on it.

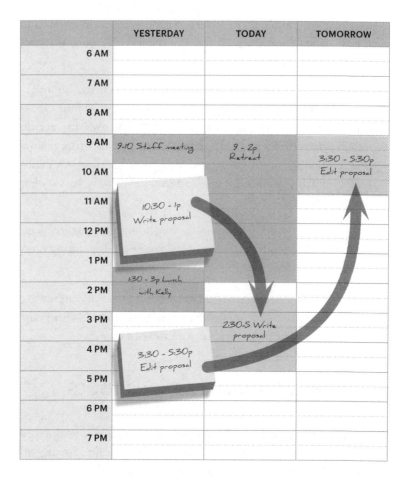

3. Review and adjust your scheduled Routines. Make sure these time buckets square with what you have in store for the day ahead.

Tip: I "check off" Action items that I have accomplished by switching their color, so I can easily see what's been done during the course of my day and week.

Second: Adjust Your Action List

After clearing your station, your Action inbox will be filled with uncategorized items. Here's what you do next:

1. Assign each incoming Action item to a Mission. After that's done . . .

2. Adjust the order of each Mission to display the proper Frontburner at the top. Order the next several Backburners. Often a new Action will become the Frontburner, bumping the former Frontburner down a notch; or else a new Action will become a Backburner itself.

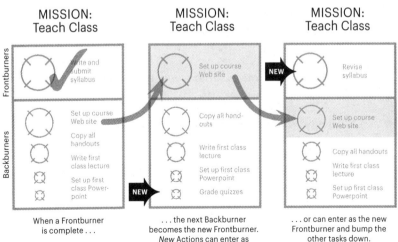

MISSION: Teach Class

MISSION: Teach Class

MISSION: Teach Class

When a Frontburner is complete . . .

. . . the next Backburner becomes the new Frontburner. *New* Actions can enter as Backburners . . .

. . . or can enter as the new Frontburner and bump the other tasks down.

Tip: Sometimes incoming Actions can be best executed by grouping them into Routines (i.e., calls to return, errands to run). If you have a digital Action list, you can use tags to create task lists for your Routines. For example, you might have three Actions from different Missions that are all things you want to read during one Routine you've set aside for reading. You can tag each of these Actions as "Reading" and refer to that bucket of Actions the next time you're ready to run that Routine.

You should now have a fully ordered Action list and no incomplete Actions from days past on your schedule.

STEP THREE: PLAN YOUR DAY
(approximately 10 minutes)

You face tomorrow knowing the Actions and Routines that are already scheduled for tomorrow on our calendar. With that information, you:

1. Make a list of the Actions and Routines already scheduled for tomorrow along with the other Actions and Routines you *want* to add to tomorrow.

2. Identify which Actions are immersive (longer, requiring 30 minutes to several hours) and which are process (quicker, can be grouped together).

3. Ballpark how many hours you have available for new Actions and Routines.

4. Schedule new Actions and Routines on your calendar, aiming to

   a. *Maximize* the number of Frontburners

   b. *Balance* immersive and process time

   c. *Stay under* your Meeze Point

Optional: Create a daily timeline, your schedule in list form. Every day, I create an analogue of my schedule on a sticky note. It

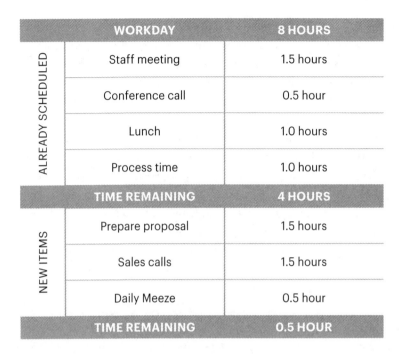

WORKDAY	8 HOURS
ALREADY SCHEDULED	
Staff meeting	1.5 hours
Conference call	0.5 hour
Lunch	1.0 hours
Process time	1.0 hours
TIME REMAINING	**4 HOURS**
NEW ITEMS	
Prepare proposal	1.5 hours
Sales calls	1.5 hours
Daily Meeze	0.5 hour
TIME REMAINING	**0.5 HOUR**

contains exactly the same thing that my schedule does, but in list form. It's not necessary, but it encourages me to always view my appointments as tasks—rather than as impediments to accomplishment. Plus, the size of a sticky note and the size of my handwriting work together to keep me under my Meeze Point. If I can't fit all my tasks on a sticky note, I know I'm doing too many.

Don't overschedule. You may be tempted to throw a bunch of things on your calendar and fill up every available block of time in the name of efficiency. *Don't do that.* Leave spaces in your schedule, especially before and after meetings, not only to account for travel time, but to allow for the kinds of interactions and processing of Actions that inevitably precede and follow them. Leave space, even to do nothing, or to call a friend, or to take a quick walk.

Pushing yourself a little here and there is good. But you don't want to create task lists and calendars that are so impossible to execute and disconnected from reality that you end up not trusting them, not trusting yourself, and not using them. If you *know* you don't have enough time to accomplish all the things you've set out for yourself but schedule them anyway, that's not ambition, that's denial. *Run your calendar or your calendar will run you,* it's that simple. You are going to have to say "no" to many things. You are going to have to be the executive, which necessitates being an executioner, the decider, the one who kills one option to save another.

Instead of overscheduling, try underscheduling. Couture entrepreneur Coco Chanel once famously advised, "Before you leave the house, look in the mirror and take one thing off." It's also great advice for creating your daily schedule. Give yourself one less thing to do. Your day will be full and complete anyway. And if you end up being able to do more than you've planned, then you get to experience the joy of exceeding your own expectations.

STEP FOUR: GATHER YOUR RESOURCES

As part of wrapping up your Daily Meeze, gather the resources you need for the next day. If you do your Daily Meeze at home, load up the bag you'll be taking with you tomorrow. I check the next day's weather the previous night so that I don't spend precious moments the next day on my wardrobe. Some people lay their next day's clothes out the night before. Do whatever you can do to give yourself as little as possible to plan or do the next morning.

Track Your Progress

Tracking your Daily Meeze helps you work your way to the 40-day mark, an important psychological and physiological milestone for creating a new habit, increasing your chances of success.

Time's Up!

Now we put our planning tools in their proper places, turn off our devices, and leave our workstation. We enjoy the rest of our evening.

Questions and Problems

That's the ideal. But what if, on some days, we have so many new items in our inputs that we can't get through them all?

Should we extend our Daily Meeze if we can't get everything done? I think that 30 minutes of planning per day on average is enough to handle a working person's busy life. Less than 30 minutes of planning wouldn't be a serious enough commitment. Beyond 30 minutes begins to feel out of balance with our other needs and duties and causes a lot of stress. It's vital that we constrain the Daily Meeze. Limits promote discipline and efficiency. We're not going for a lazy, lopping, sprawling, distracted planning session. As we've said, your Daily Meeze should be a *hustle*. Keep it tight, move smoothly and quickly, make choices. But when all the demands of our Daily Meeze are difficult to squeeze into 30 minutes, here are some suggestions.

Do part of your Meeze one day, and the other part the next. If one day you have an excess of stuff to organize, it may be fine to do the second part of that incomplete Meeze on the next day. For example, you might not get to clear all your inputs in 15 minutes. So you leave the rest of it until tomorrow. Usually we can miss a day of *full* planning and still remain ahead of the game. The important thing is to do your daily 30 minutes, whatever you happen to accomplish within it. If you keep a good planning practice, you will catch the excess the next day.

Schedule an "overflow" appointment with yourself. If you've spent most of your Daily Meeze cleaning up incoming mail and absolutely need to make time to move things around on your Action list and calendar, schedule another 15 or 30 minutes with yourself for later or for the next day.

Schedule different Meezes for different days. You may have to check your e-mail every day, but do you really need to check Facebook and Twitter and LinkedIn that frequently? Or maybe you've found that you can schedule your Actions several *days* at a time, or that you don't need to reorder your Mission lists *every* day, or even that organizing your task list is something you need only do once per week. If so, do those tasks only on certain days, freeing time to concentrate on other elements of your Daily Meeze.

Make moves after *your Meeze.* Don't execute any Action items during your Meeze. Just flag and log, and handle your Action items afterward.

Even after trying these alternatives, you may find that 30 minutes is just not enough for the kind of workload you have. If you have the energy and willpower for a regular 45-minute or hour-long planning session, then you might be able to do that. In my experience, however, planning for more than 30 minutes per day gets you into an area where you might be accommodating bad habits rather than confronting them.

Does my Daily Meeze need to be daily? To form a habit, yes. My teacher always said that it takes 40 days of unbroken practice to break an old habit, 90 days to confirm a new habit, and 120 days for you to *become* the habit. One study published in 2009 found that turning a conscious action into a nonconscious, automatic one took an average of 66 days. I think a 40-day commitment to your Meeze is sufficient to start. If you skip a day in that initial 40-day period, start the 40 days over. It's hard to form a habit and so easy to stop, so we want to treat our Daily Meeze as inviolate, the way a chef or cook would treat her mise-en-place.

Can't I skip the Daily Meeze on some days? Not until you make the Daily Meeze a habit. Thereafter you can skip weekends, vacations, and other days off. For me, the Daily Meeze is a spiritual practice that serves all parts of my life, so on weekends I focus more on organizing personal things. I rarely skip a day unless I am on vacation or immersed in a project that requires me to go on a personal retreat.

What if I've stopped doing my Daily Meeze for a while? You will likely see the results in your work life. Start again today!

If I work both at home and in an office, should I do two Daily Meezes? No. You will keep your good habits and behaviors at both workstations, but only one of them will be primary. If you feel you need to give them equal attention, consider doing your Daily Meeze at home on weekends, or alternate between your two workstations every other day.

The ingredients in action

The Daily Meeze embodies every ingredient of mise-en-place. It's a *planning* ritual. It requires *arranged spaces* and *perfected movements*. It is *cleaning as you go* exemplified. While we execute our session, we must *make first moves, finish actions,* and *slow down to speed up*. The object of the Daily Meeze is organization, and what we are organizing mainly is our communication: keeping *open eyes* for the important things, *calling back* vital correspondence, and *inspecting and correcting* our calendar and Action list, toward the ultimate ideal of *total utilization* of our time and energy.

MORNING: PROCESS

Our evening was about preparation, and our Daily Meeze was intentional and intense. But that tension of planning now gives way to the release and relaxation of *having planned*, enabling us to wake this morning with a light heart and clear head.

GREET THE DAY

A big part of having a successful day is leaving enough time in the morning to nurture yourself with Personal Routines. Meditate, exercise, make a healthy breakfast, talk with your spouse, play with your child. If your job or career doesn't afford you the luxury of those Routines, then at the very least you can wake 5 minutes earlier to center yourself for the day ahead. Once that day begins, honor your plans by following *process*.

MORNING CHECK-IN

You've planned for the probable, but anything is possible. In the moments before we leave home in the morning, we often make mistakes that affect our entire day by forgetting, overlooking, or ignoring things.

Before you embark on your day, do the following:

1. *Check your schedule.* Make sure you know your Actions, your *moves* for the day. Make sure you've gathered the resources you need.

2. *Check your vital inputs* (like e-mail or your workplace's messaging software). Has anything come up overnight that might necessitate a change in plans? Some days you may find that you need to rearrange your schedule. That's fine! Your careful planning has not gone to waste. Quite the contrary, your planning should lessen the anxiety of change and give you the confidence to say "no" or "later" to the things that you must push off your schedule. The people to whom you've made commitments will appreciate your forewarning, rather than bear you ill will for not making good on promises to them.

3. *Run checklists.* To minimize error, use checklists. Some of these lists will be mental or mnemonic. For example, I have a word I say before I leave the house—"BUCK," for Bags, Umbrella, Cap, Keys—because too often I forget those things. On days that I teach class, I run an extended checklist on my computer because I have in the past forgotten too many items on that list *not* to do so. I resist running the list sometimes because it feels too obsessive; but as stupid as I may feel when I do it, I always feel and look good when I come to class prepared.

GETTING THERE

Part of our planning and our execution is thinking about when and how we want to arrive: hurried, harried, flustered, and late? Or early, calm, prepared, and happy?

We really *do* have control over these feelings. The two biggest levers of control are:

1. *Giving ourselves enough time on our schedules to travel.* Whether flying 3,000 miles or simply walking across the

street, we know how much time to allow ourselves. We just have to *account for it* in our planning.

2. *Honoring the start and end times we've set.* If we know it takes 45 minutes to get where we're going and we leave only 30 minutes to get there, or if we fail to end a previous engagement in time to make our next appointment, we dishonor our plan and the time of those who await us— especially if that next appointment is one we've made with ourselves for, say, an immersive work session.

Is it okay to be late occasionally? Absolutely. Are there good reasons to be late? For sure, just so long as our reasons aren't on balance due to lack of preparation or poor process. The point isn't to *never* be late or spontaneous. The point is to stop the wasted time, energy, and resources that come from *our* carelessness. Life produces enough chaos without us manufacturing more of it.

PROCESS TIME

The first thing you do when you get to your workplace is spend a short block of time—perhaps 30 minutes—on process work. For an office worker, this Process Routine might mean catching up on e-mails, voice mails, and paperwork. For an artist or freelancer who works from home, this might entail starting the dishwasher to make sure that process happens *while* she focuses on her next immersive task; or calling the plumber for a visit because once her work starts, she'll forget to do this. For the plumber, that might mean checking in with dispatch between house calls.

For *any* professional, process time is about *making first moves*—setting processes in motion that can happen while the hands and mind are otherwise engaged.

TRANSITION MEEZE

When process time is done, before moving into the next appointment or task, do a 1- to 5-minute Transition Meeze.

The goal with the Transition Meeze is the deskbound equivalent of *cleaning as you go*. It enforces and reinforces *arranged spaces* and keeps things in their right places. Here's how to do it.

1. *Reset the table*. Put the previous project away. Close and replace open files. Close open applications. Close browser windows. Wipe any debris off your desk. Do *kichiri*, or straighten your desktop, setting all objects in their right places.

2. *Check your schedule*. Before you jump into your next project, relax and check your schedule and Action list. What's coming up? Who's added you to a meeting? Does anything need to be moved around?

3. *Check your e-mails*. Quickly flag all the e-mails that need action. Archive them all. Then go into your Flagged folder and decide which e-mails you can address quickly, in a few seconds or minutes, and execute those.

If you have time left over, do something to release the tension of work. Stand up and stretch. Talk to a friend. Check social media or your favorite Web site. Drink some water. Take some time for this Transition Meeze, but no more than 5 minutes.

A good Transition Meeze will make your Daily Meeze a breeze. For example, if you tend to leave things in clumps and piles for the end of the day, you may find yourself unconsciously dreading or avoiding your daily planning session. But if you work clean in the transitions between your big actions and appointments, your daily planning will feel lighter and be more productive.

IMMERSIVE TIME: USING INTENTIONAL BREAKS

We've set aside 2 hours for writing an important report. We've arrived at our workstation on time. We have our resources at the ready. We begin.

Yet just 2 minutes later we find ourselves goofing off online.

We go into our tool kit and begin an intentional break (see *The Fifth Ingredient: Finishing Actions*), logging each break we take in our session. For the first hour, we're having a hard time focusing, so we log "mental" breaks frequently. Occasionally we are interrupted by colleagues, so we log a couple of "work" breaks. But gradually we settle in. We took five breaks in the first hour and only two breaks in the second. As we near the finish, we get antsy to take another break. But we look at the progress we've made on the memo. We make a choice to push through and *finish the action*. We get the work done. We feel good.

AFTERNOON: PRESENCE

After noon our best-laid plans and carefully followed processes often crumble under the stresses and surprises of the day. But with proper mise-en-place and the awareness that comes from it, even sudden changes in direction are easier and cause less upheaval because we stay present.

THE SURPRISE: REACTING TO TRIGGERS

In the middle of an immersive project, we've muted our phones and quit our e-mail program to keep ourselves focused. But because we also know that we work in a company where crises often emerge, we've made sure to check e-mail regularly—triggered by an hourly chime we've set for ourselves on our phone—so that we keep *open eyes and ears* for what's happening in our work environment.

At 1:30 p.m., we open our e-mail program to find that an urgent meeting has been called for 3:00 p.m.: The president of the company is asking all department heads to revise their budgets for a 10 percent cut. The meeting not only requires our attendance but our preparation. We know that we'll need at least an hour to prepare and an hour for the meeting, and that means our plans for finishing this project by 4:00 p.m. are in jeopardy. This calls for some quick thinking and action.

THE TIE-UP: FINISHING WHEN YOU CAN'T FINISH

We had about 90 minutes of work left on our immersive project, and we have only 30 minutes until we need to start prepping for the meeting. Since we can't finish our current project in 30 minutes, our next best alternative is to try to find a way to tie our work up so that we can finish it later.

The first step is to find a stopping point. *Do we stop now or try to get as much done as possible?* We can still work on it for 30 minutes. But we decide that it's probably better to start our meeting prep earlier, to *make first moves* now because we can have a cushion of time in case complications arise. So instead we decide to work for only 15 more minutes, just to outline the part of our project we haven't done, so that when we resume, we'll have a quicker ramp-up time to *finish the action.*

The second step is to set expectations, to call the person who gave us the deadline. We ask for a 2-hour extension (another cushion) and figure maybe we can stay at work a little later tonight. It turns out, however, that our colleague has been called into the same meeting as we have. *Everyone* is behind. We don't have to stay late. We just have to find some time tomorrow to finish. But instead of immediately resuming our immersive work—that's our instinct, to rush now that the pressure is on—we take 30 seconds to find the time on tomorrow's schedule and block off 90 minutes for our current project.

THE TRIAGE: CLEARING THE DECKS

This new meeting has pushed two *other* Actions off our schedule. And since we know that they are less crucial than the meeting, we can clear our calendar without fear. We will make sure that tonight, during our Daily Meeze, we reschedule those items.

But because of our new budget meeting, a new opportunity arises to execute an Action, "Get approval on new program." We can actually take care of that in the new budget we're making. In this way, we practice *balanced movement*, using one motion for multiple moves.

THE RUSH: SLOWING DOWN AND INSPECTING

We and our colleagues work furiously to prepare our budgets in time for the meeting. But we're making mistakes—leaving out information, paying less attention to details. We decide to take a breath, literally. We stand up, stretch, and think: What's the most important thing we can be doing to deliver this assignment? Getting the *numbers* right. So we work slower this time, even though the clock is ticking. As we work, we notice something odd: The budget is missing some line items that we saw on a colleague's spreadsheet. We take a few moments to consult with our colleague and realize, to our dismay, we've been working on an *earlier* version of the budget, the wrong version. We'll have to redo our work, quickly. But if we hadn't allowed ourselves extra time for prep, and if we hadn't *slowed down* and used the buddy system to *inspect and correct* our work, we might have missed the mistake altogether and put forth budget numbers that would have shortchanged us.

THE MEETING: PRACTICING PRESENCE

While we're in the meeting, we are obsessing about the mistake we made: *How did we miss that new budget?*

Suddenly we realize that we're spacing out in the meeting. So we jot down a quick note—"Explore budget mistake"—in our notebook and make an effort to be more present: We put our pen down, we turn our body to face the colleague who's speaking, we keep eye contact, we breathe, we listen.

THE MISTAKE: RUNNING ROUTINES

Part of our commitment to excellence is using process to remedy and redeem mistakes. We view error as a chance to get better. In this case we decide to take a few minutes to figure out how we spent nearly an hour working on the wrong budget form. We realize that we *had* that new budget all along. We listed it as an Action in one of our Mission lists, but as a Backburner item that kept getting pushed back. We mention this to a colleague, and he commiserates: "They send too many e-mails. No way we can read them all."

Years ago we would have agreed. But we have a different view of responsibility now. Other people are reading these things and taking them seriously. We can't say we don't have time. Time to step up. Since Routines are the way we make time for things that we "don't have time" for, we make a commitment to establishing a new one: 30 minutes of reading every Friday before we leave for the weekend, for all the reports and articles and meeting minutes we get sent throughout the week. The new Routine will squeeze even more time from our ability to do immersive work, but because we are managing more people and a bigger budget now, we know that this kind of process work comes with the territory.

The other reason we missed the new budget is that we didn't remember to check to make sure we had the latest version when we were editing. There is, now, simply too much to remember to keep it all in our head. So we decide to *perfect our moves:* We make a note to create a new checklist to run when submitting budgets, because financial documents are too important to our well-being to miss details like this.

EVENING: PREPARATION

It's 4:30 p.m. and our meeting is done. We actually *do* have the time, exactly 90 minutes, to finish the report that we had to push until tomorrow. We can finish it now and still get home on time.

But because we've already *rescheduled* that obligation for tomorrow, pushed it safely off our plate, we decide to do to our 30-minute Daily Meeze a little earlier today. Setting a timer, we go through our 15 minutes of cleaning our station. Because we've been assiduously flagging e-mails and clearing our inbox all day, we get through everything quickly. And because we've also been tinkering with tomorrow's schedule, we don't have much to add to it (nor can we, our tomorrow being pretty much filled with the work we pushed off today). We use the extra time in our Daily Meeze session to do some deeper cleaning at our desk—purging some old files and making space.

We can actually be spontaneous, leave now, and get home at least an hour earlier than usual. It would be nice to surprise our family in some way.

Maybe we'll cook.

Without even thinking about what we're doing, our left hand reaches for our notebook and our right for a pen.

We begin by making a list. . . .

CONCLUSION

The Miracle of Mise-en-Place

IN MODERN LIFE, there are few things we dread more than cleaning up a pile of work.

Yet cleaning itself is relatively easy—we can do it with the sweep of a hand or the flick of a cursor.

Establishing a system is also easy—lots of lists, color-coded schedules, empty manila folders, markers, and good intentions.

The hardest thing to do is maintain that system, to actually *work* clean: with space, with time, with resources, with people.

With our Daily Meeze we can maintain any system, because our Daily Meeze is *a system of organization designed to maintain systems of organization.*

And the idea that underlies our Daily Meeze is the same one that underlies mise-en-place as a whole: *Excellence requires human presence.*

Excellence is why, in this age of fast food, people still visit high-end restaurants. It's why, even in the age of technology and robotics, the most sought-after products are often crafted by hand and the most expensive services are personal. It's why, even though corporations are born, grow, and become hugely profitable, these same companies teeter and fall as their customers leave and their managers and employees flee.

You can't automate excellence, though we will likely keep trying. It's futile. Why? Because people are actually *worth* something. Thus *Work Clean* is a manifesto for people who see a future for people.

People like *you* who cultivate a personal mise-en-place know that no teacher, no system, no software, no algorithm, no company, and even no amount of money or resources can do the job for you. You are the one who has to push the button. You are the one who must decide. You are the one who must make the moves and take the steps. But you understand the sacrifice and choices and work involved.

The miracle is you.

EPILOGUE

The Dishwasher

THE TEENAGER standing at the pot sink beheld the job before him. Perhaps tens of thousands of adolescents in restaurants across the country at that same moment faced a similar sight, wanting nothing more than to leave work, play ball, listen to music, hang with friends, or engage in other youthful diversions. The dishwasher at the Palm Beach Yacht Club in Florida desired those things, too. But rather than carelessly dash through the work, Thomas Keller decided the quickest route to the outside world would be to wash the dishes with as much care as he could muster.

The first thing Thomas realized was that to get the work done quickly, his movements had to be small and *efficient*. To be efficient, his movements had to repeat. Thomas grew to respect and love *repetition*, doing one thing, over and over. For his movements to be repetitive meant that the dishes themselves had to be *organized*, stacked in a predictable pattern—bread plates here, service plates here, dessert plates there. He began demanding that the servers return those plates to him in a predictable manner.

The point of washing dishes, Thomas decided, was to actually get them clean. Why leave crud on plates if it meant he had to redo them, doubling his work? The thing he liked about his job was that he didn't have to guess whether he was doing it right. He got instant critical *feedback*. If he didn't stack, scrape, scrub, spray, and then inspect the dishes correctly, he saw the results seconds later when the dish machine door opened. Washing dishes in this way became a sport. Thomas didn't like losing. He made corrections.

Every sport has its *rituals,* and those of the dishwasher became indispensable for Thomas. The first thing he did every morning was clean the bathrooms. Every 2 hours, he changed the water in the dish machine. He changed the soap at specific times. He took the garbage out at specific times. He swept the floor at specific times. The exactitude was critical. If he didn't start or finish tasks at certain times, that might cause a cascade of events that would keep him working longer and less effectively. If he didn't change the water in the dish machine regularly, the strainer baskets would fill with pieces of food, and soon the dishes would be covered in sediment, and he'd have to run them through again. If he didn't take the garbage out, the garbage can would overflow, causing more mess. He learned that if he started messing with ritual, suddenly it wasn't a ritual anymore. Even if the garbage wasn't *completely* full, he emptied it. He didn't mess with time. You could see the results of not doing so.

Thomas finally saw that he was a crucial member of a *team* whose sole purpose was to feed the guests. The guests needed food and drink. Thus the cooks needed dishes, the bartenders needed glasses, and the servers needed silverware. And one person, Thomas, gave them all those things. Without him nothing worked.

The behaviors Thomas Keller learned as a dishwasher— organization, efficiency, feedback, rituals, repetition, and teamwork—stayed with him when he was promoted to cook. He kept them when he moved up to Rhode Island and met his first mentor, Chef Roland Henin. The disciplines supported him as he worked his way through fine kitchens in New York, where he became a chef of a renowned restaurant. They sustained him after he left that restaurant rather than compromise those disciplines. They steered him to California, where he found a small restaurant in the Napa Valley called The French Laundry, and they helped him round up the money to buy the place. They powered him as he cooked through the lean years, through his first good review, and his first Michelin stars. They kept him humble even when he was named the best chef in America by the James Beard Foundation. And they grounded him when he opened restaurants around the country and became the chief executive of his own corporation. For Thomas Keller, the six disciplines of the dishwasher, as he calls them, have guided his trajectory from the start and lead him still.

It starts with organization. The French Laundry makes sense. When something offends Keller's eye or feels just slightly off, the chef starts asking how he can make it better, and he doesn't stop asking until he finds an answer and good sense is restored. He'll question anything, even the sacrosanct. The tools of chefs and cooks are sacred. Cooks guard their knives. Keller cherishes his spoons; he's had some for decades. "God forbid if I should lose one," he says. Those holy items travel with the cook in a vessel, the knife roll, the daily opening of which looks just like a sacrament. But Keller always found these knife bags unsightly and inefficient, stowed on top of shelves at cooks' stations with their straps hanging down. So he decided to get rid of them. He built knife drawers at every station and asked his cooks to keep their tools in the kitchen.

The idea of leaving their precious knives in an unlocked drawer overnight felt alien to his cooks, but for Keller the exercise was about building a team as much as it was about organization. "These are your colleagues," he says. "Why shouldn't you trust them? If you need to borrow one of my knives for whatever reason, I'm going to trust that you're going to not only use it properly, but you're going to clean it, you're going to return it to my drawer."

Keller asks his cooks to abide by rituals like "shaking in and shaking out." When cooks arrive, they walk around, shake everybody's hand, and say hello. *This is our house,* Keller says. *This is how we respect one another.* Departure works the same way. If cooks don't shake out, the other cooks notice.

Even Keller's take on efficiency is geared more toward personal growth than productivity. That plaque beneath the wall clock that reads "Sense of Urgency" isn't about the customer's meal; it's about the cook's career. "The sense of urgency is defined in our kitchen as an opportunity for you to finish your job before you have to finish your job," Keller says. "If you have aspirations and ambitions to become the *poissonier*, for example, then you can actually have time to go over to the fish station and work with the poissonier for 15 or 20 minutes and learn something. . . . You're going to get to the next level by being ready for the next level before that opportunity arises. Because when I look around the kitchen, I'm going to choose the person who's already prepared to be that person. That's a mise-en-place that is an individual mise-en-place," Keller says. A *career* mise-en-place.

Because Keller values repetition, he's floored when young apprentices declare that they're bored. *You're a cook*, he says. *Get used to it. You're going to be doing this the rest of your life.* Keller puts his new cooks in the back room by themselves at night: skimming stocks, making shells for truffle egg custard, cutting vegetables. But the night shift isn't relaxed; it's 5 hours of compressed work, punctuated by unpredictable requests from the kitchen during dinner service. This, says Keller, is the life of a chef: balancing work that a cook knows must be done against constant interruptions and new requests. Through these challenges, he sees his apprentices craning their necks toward the kitchen. They want in on the action. But Keller says: *Pay attention to what you're doing here. You can learn. It's repetition. It's responsibility. It's self-motivation. It's interruption. Being ready for all the unknowns.*

But of all the disciplines, Keller knows that taking and giving feedback is the hardest to learn and teach. Keller warns his young cooks: *You're going to get feedback all day long. You have to take it as just pure information. There's nothing personal here. You can't be crippled by critical feedback. You have to grow through it.* At the same time, Keller encourages his chefs and managers to be, literally, soft spoken. "When I whisper, they're leaning in," he says. "They're getting close to hear me. You yell at somebody, they're pulling away from you. When you're giving really critical feedback, you want them coming in to you. *I'm really disappointed in you doing that.* Then they go, *Oh my God.* It becomes so much louder to them."

Thomas Keller still envisions his job as a sport, where he is no longer a player but the coach of a franchise charged with cultivating, training, and promoting a deep bench of talent. He coaches with the disciplines of the dishwasher, the disciplines of mise-en-place. "I think they pretty much can be translated to almost any profession," Keller says.

The dividend of these values is excellence. The price is constant attention. "You can never stop asking the question: 'How can I do something better?'" Keller says. "Once you stop asking the question, you'll never do it."

Outside Keller's kitchens, that attention to planning, process, and presence is often too high a price to pay.

"Mediocrity has become something that's acceptable," Keller says, "and in many cases, something that is aspirational."

To get by and get over, to work less and get paid, to be, essentially, *above* work. Many people pursue this American dream.

Keller, America's greatest chef, pursues another. He works toward it as he always has: He beholds his kitchen. If there are dishes to be done, he washes them. If the floor is dirty, he picks up a broom and he cleans.

INTERVIEWS

MANY THANKS to these chefs, cooks, bakers, chef-instructors, culinary faculty, culinary students, managers, waitstaff, entrepreneurs, and restaurateurs for sharing their observations, experiences, and behaviors in interviews and discussion either in person or by phone. Though the narrative of this book focuses primarily on a select few of these people, all were helpful in creating the philosophical bedrock for this project.

Ilan Ades
Chris Albert
Carlos Arciniega
Candy Argondizza
Greg Barr
Denise Bauer
Riccardo Bertolino
Rachel Black
Ari Bokovza
Caitlyn Borgfeld
Jimmy Bradley
Elizabeth Briggs
Eric Bromberg
Matt Campion
Hailey Catalano
Dominick Cerrone
Richard Coppedge
Juanito Cordero
Chris Cosentino
Jessica Crochet

Lucian Davis
Marc Djozlija
Sarah Donnegan
Zoe Dries
Wylie Dufresne
Josh Eden
Mark Erickson
Gerard Fischetti
Michael Gibney
Gary Giudice
Marcus Gleadow-
   Ware
Melissa Gray
Michael Guerriero
Jawed Halepota
Rob Halpern
Dorothy Cann
   Hamilton
Ronald Hayes
Sam Henderson

Avi Hoffer
Ryan Hunter
Joel Javier
Charlene Johnson-
   Hadley
Liam Kamp
Thomas Keller
Ryan Kemp
Andrew Kochan
Shuichi Kotani
Keith Krajewski
Tim Lanza
Matthew Lightner
Toni Linen
Dwayne LiPuma
Malcolm Livingston
Arbil Lopez
Elise Macur
Noah Marion
David McCue

Randy McNamara   Brian Plant   William Telepan
Sam Mendes   Alfred Portale   Alexandra Tibbats
Misel Mendoza   Larissa Raphael   Amy Trubek
Kathleen Merget   Eric Ripert   Alyston Upshaw
Rossi Morillo   Katie Ritter   Tom Vaccaro
Sara Moulton   Michael Ruhlman   Patrice Vassell
Chris Muller   Scott Samuel   Howie Velie
Rahmie Munther   Marcus Samuelsson   Natasha Veloso
Ayanna-Tamar Mutaz Yukihiro Sato   Mark Viloria
Francois Nadon   Ralph Scamardella   David Vinjamuri
Kaitlyn Ngo   Andi Sciacca   Jean-Georges
Kelly O'Connor   Jason Sheehan   Vongerichten
Ronald Ohler   Reggie Soang   Melissa Walnock
Charlie Palmer   Andres Soltner   Ian Whalley
Michael Pardus   Fritz Sonnenschmidt Jarobi White
Ryan Pascullo   Angelo Sosa   Jordan Williams
David Pasternack   Rudy Speckamp   Sang Yoon
Jacques Pépin   Masa Takayama   Jimi Yui
Alexander Phillips Erica Tatham

The above list does not include the kitchen staff and students, too
numerous to mention here, with whom I had dozens of more casual
conversations.

The following nonculinarians helped me with their observations
about workplace organization: Andrea Duncan Mao, Tori Horowitz,
Jozen Cummings, Mary Pryor, Mark Brodie, and Rachel Sullivan.

Special thanks to Dr. Joseph LeDoux for his generous clarification
of many neurological issues related to human learning.

Full endnotes and sourcing for *Work Clean* are available online at
workclean.com/endnotes.

GRATITUDE

TO THE PEOPLE who helped me conceive and build this book before the first words were written: Larry Lieberman, Sara Moulton, David Dunton, Harvey Klinger. To Jen Levesque, Mollie Thomas, Mary Ann Naples, Yelena Gitlin Nesbit, Hope Clarke, Chris Gaugler, Gail Gonzales, Bob Niegowski, Jean Lee, and the entire team at Rodale. To Jeff Levine at the CIA, who was with me every step of the way; and to Tim Ryan, Michael Sperling, and the faculty, staff and students of the CIA. To Dorothy Cann Hamilton and the ICC. To Michael Ruhlman for his example and encouragement. To the folks who opened doors: Chloe Mata Crane, Jeannette Park, Margarita Sullivan, Nancy Aranson, Kimberly Blanchot, Jaime Caldwell, Jetty-Jane Connor, Lynne Estes, Irene Hamburger, Jacqueline Hensel, Stacy Himes, Benjamin Kemper, Michelle Lipa, Ron Longe, Dana Meeks, Griffin Parker, Liz Pierson, Jessica Rosen, Meghan Sherrill, Lina Varriale, Christa Weaving, Richard Kashida, and Steven Charron. To Dr. Ruth Beitler and Major Erin Hadlock at West Point. To Tom Cole, Nina Gregory, April Fulton, Maanvi Singh, and Frannie Kelley at NPR. To those who provided help and feedback: Marshall Malin, David Tischman, Christian Moerk, Milind Shah, John Mietus, Jon Smith, Phonte Coleman, Marc Gerald, T-Love, Tamara Palmer, Gabriel Tolliver, Charlie Stettler, Jarobi White and Kamilah Rouse. To my NYU colleagues at the Clive Davis Institute: Jeff Rabhan, Nick Sansano, Jason King, Jeff Peretz, Jim Anderson, Bob Christgau, Bob Power, Errol Kolosine, Lauren Davis, Michael McCoy, Nora York, Matthew Morrison, Brianne Powell Hayes, Nikki Mirasola, Alan Watson, Chelsea Falato, Marat Berenstein, Ashley Kahn, Vivien Goldman, Harry Weinger and our incredible students. Thanks to Allyson

Green, Sheril Antonio, and Dan O'Sullivan. To my colleagues on VH1's *The Breaks*: Maggie Malina, Bill Flanagan, Seith Mann, Darren Goldberg, Gary Guidice; to Jason Goldberg; to Doug Herzog, Chris McCarthy and Amy Doyle; and to our incredible cast. To Laurie Pozmantier and John Buzzetti, Jake Stein and Scott Prisand. To my crew of creatives who strengthened me with their support for this book, and the last: Joe Schloss, Jay Smooth, Jeff Chang, Adam Mansbach, Sophia Chang, Joan Morgan, Miri Park, Oliver Wang, Elizabeth Mendez Berry, Shawn Setaro, Brian Coleman, Adisa Banjoko, Aliya S. King, Erik Parker, Elliot Wilson, Jerry Barrow, Michael Berrin, Dvora Myers, Chris Faraone, Stephen Henderson, Michaelangelo Matos. To my chefs: Sylvester Burke, Ophelia Barnes, Phillips Peters, Bill Stephney, Bill Adler, Cory Robbins, Tom Silverman, Manny Bella, Rick Rubin, Russell Simmons, Forest Whitaker, Jim Biederman, Jesse Collins, Ryan Dadd, Stephen Murray, Michelle Kerrigan, Nat Robinson, Mel Klein, Kim Nauer, Sam Freedman, June Cross, David Blum, Julie Hartenstein, Rich Lieby, Josh du Lac, Jonathan Shecter, Joe Boskin, Floyd Barbour, Hubert Walters, Adelaide Gulliver, Murray Levin, Howard Zinn, Jim Curtan, Santokh and Suraj Khalsa, Gurmukh and Gurushabd Khalsa, Shakti Parwha Kaur Khalsa, Kartar Khalsa, Siri Ved and Gurujodha Khalsa, and Harbhajan Singh Khalsa Yogiji. To the friends who have kept me and my wife afloat and happy, and to our parents and our wonderful, loving extended family. To Wendy S. Walters: best wife, best editor, best confidante and best friend. And to our son Isaac, who brings both a healthy mess and a divine order to our lives.

INDEX

Underscored references indicate boxed text. **Boldface** references indicate graphics.

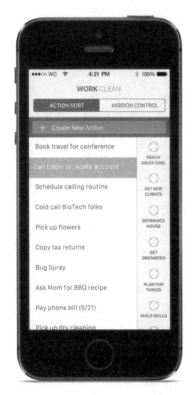

BW May/16